Marsden Hartley

Marsden Hartley, 1915. Photograph by Alfred Stieglitz. Philadelphia Museum of Art; The Alfred Stieglitz Collection

Marsden Hartley

Barbara Haskell

Whitney Museum of American Art • New York
in association with
New York University Press • New York • London

Exhibition Schedule

Whitney Museum of American Art
New York, New York
March 4 – May 25, 1980

The Art Institute of Chicago
Chicago, Illinois
June 10 – August 3, 1980

Amon Carter Museum of Western Art
Fort Worth, Texas
September 5 – October 26, 1980

University Art Museum
University of California
Berkeley, California
November 12, 1980 – January 4, 1981

Library of Congress Cataloging in Publication Data

Haskell, Barbara.
  Marsden Hartley.

  Catalogue of an exhibition held at the Whitney
Museum of American Art, New York, Mar. 4 – May 25,
1980, and at other museums.
  "Complete bibliography and list of exhibitions
by Peter Freeman": p. 194
  "Marsden Hartley: published writings by
Peter Freeman": p. 209
  1. Hartley, Marsden, 1877-1943 – Exhibitions.
I. Hartley, Marsden, 1877-1943. II. Whitney
Museum of American Art, New York.
ND237.H343A4   1980   759.13   79-25117
ISBN 0-87427-027-8 (WMAA soft cover)
ISBN 0-8147-3405-7 (NYU case bound)

Designer: Nathan Garland
Typesetter: Trufont Typographers, Inc.
Printer: William J. Mack Company

Contents

6   Forewords by Tom Armstrong
and A. James Speyer

8   Marsden Hartley

71   The Middle Years

111   Return to Maine

145   Color Plates

185   Chronology of Hartley's Life and Work

194   Complete Bibliography and List of Exhibitions

209   Marsden Hartley: Published Writings

212   Catalogue of the Exhibition

Forewords

The retrospective exhibition of Marsden Hartley's painting, and the accompanying catalogue, continues the tradition at the Whitney Museum of American Art of supporting primary research in American art history. It is therefore fitting that the show opens in 1980, the 50th Anniversary of the founding of the Museum by Gertrude Vanderbilt Whitney. As the most important patron of American art in her time, Gertrude Vanderbilt Whitney always encouraged scholarship as part of her activities in behalf of American art and artists. She assisted many organizations and publications, including *The Arts*, the most influential American art magazine of the 1920s. Edited by Forbes Watson, this magazine provided a public forum for the critical recognition of American art. Mrs. Whitney believed that the acquisition and exhibition of art objects should be associated with scholarship, a policy she followed throughout her life.

It was thirty-eight years ago that the event largely responsible for the initial research on Hartley took place. In April 1942, representatives from museums throughout the United States were invited by the Whitney Museum to meet at the Museum and establish the American Art Research Council. Juliana Force, Director of the Museum, was appointed Chairman of the Council, and the Museum's Research Curator, Lloyd Goodrich, and Curator, Hermon More, were appointed Director and Associate Director respectively. The purposes of the Council were to research and, for the first time, to systematically document the works of American artists. Among the artists selected for study was Marsden Hartley. The task was undertaken by Elizabeth McCausland. McCausland's unpublished material has been invaluable to Barbara Haskell in her intensive study of Hartley's life and work.

When we originally considered this exhibition and catalogue, we were very anxious to work with The Art Institute of Chicago. Our association with the Institute goes back many years: at the founding of the American Art Research Council, the Advisory Committee included a representative from The Art Institute of Chicago. Moreover, the Institute's staff has had an abiding interest in Hartley from 1949, when Georgia O'Keeffe presented the museum with the Alfred Stieglitz Collection, which includes large holdings of Hartley's work.

The collaboration on this project has been especially rewarding and gratifying. With the increase in biographical and critical writing on American artists, their ongoing relationship with the culture of Europe has become a dominant theme. It seems particularly appropriate, therefore, that Hartley's work, which developed from an association with European art, will now be seen in depth in Chicago alongside masterworks of this art in a great international museum.

The restlessness of American artists, who alternately identified with American realism and European modernism, is evidenced by Hartley's life and reflected in his work. Barbara Haskell has wisely decided that the first detailed biography of Hartley should serve as the framework for the study of his art.

We are grateful to all who have joined in this effort to bring suitable recognition to Hartley. A special debt is owed to the lenders to the exhibition. This first presentation of the evolution of Marsden Hartley's work is possible because of their cooperation.

Tom Armstrong
Director
Whitney Museum of American Art

The Art Institute of Chicago has a deep interest in the work of Marsden Hartley because of the fine group of his paintings in our permanent collection. In 1975, deciding to organize a retrospective exhibition, we naturally discussed the matter with the Whitney Museum of American Art, hoping they might cooperate in the venture. Subsequently the roles reversed, and The Art Institute of Chicago was happy that the larger staff capacities of the Whitney could be devoted to the joint project. This Marsden Hartley exhibition will be an important event at participating museums throughout America, and it will certainly constitute a special occasion in Chicago. Interestingly, the earliest exhibition of the artist's work in this city was held concurrently with an exhibition of drawings by Pablo Picasso at The Arts Club of Chicago in 1928. The first permanent representation of paintings by Hartley was secured by this museum more than twenty years later, in 1949, as part of the Alfred Stieglitz Collection, which Georgia O'Keeffe gave in memory of her late husband. This brilliant gift included ten paintings by Hartley which illustrate his progress from 1909 through 1935. The Stieglitz Collection as a whole is certainly one of the most important enclaves of early 20th-century art in the museum, especially as it permits comparison among the works of Marsden Hartley, Arthur Dove, and Georgia O'Keeffe. The development of these three artists fixes in large part the progress of the earliest abstract art in the United States. While Dove and O'Keeffe have both been extensively presented in recent retrospectives, this is the first major exhibition for Hartley.

In this exhibition there are over one hundred paintings illustrating the clearly articulated stylistic periods throughout Hartley's career. These are differentiated both formally and subjectively. But except for the brief period in 1916-17 when he was preoccupied with simplified geometric abstraction in near monochrome, his work was consistently infused with strong emotional content and color. At the same time, the varieties of Hartley's style should not detract from an awareness of his tenacious focus in expression from the beginning to the end of his life. Perhaps Hartley's most remarkable sensibility was toward nature: human, landscape, still life. He interpreted his subject material with a bold directness, the more powerful because of his innate refinement and cultivation. It is interesting that his literary statements about himself reveal discrepancies between his rational and his intuitive responses—deploring imagination and its indulgence, analyzing his own painting on the basis of intellectual decision. Hartley thought seriously of himself as a writer—whether poet, philosopher, or critic—but while his literary accomplishments embellish his reputation and provide insight into his character, fundamentally they serve to emphasize his position as primarily a visual artist. His paintings reflect exposure to radical advances in art abroad, filtered through awareness of American folk art and of the earthiness of folk mores. At his best, he delivered paintings in the great Expressionist tradition, passionate and primitive.

A. James Speyer
Curator, 20th Century Painting and Sculpture
The Art Institute of Chicago

Marsden Hartley

Fig. 1   Marsden Hartley, ca. 1908–9

Marsden Hartley occupies a singular position in the history of American art. Considered one of the leading American practitioners of an abstract style in the first half of the twentieth century, he is treated as a key figure in every history book on American art and his work hangs on museum walls throughout the country. Yet no major monograph—no full-scale and scholarly study of his life and work—has ever been published. For this reason, even basic information about his career is often unknown or erroneous.

The history of Hartley scholarship began in 1944, one year after his death, with the American Art Research Council. Under the auspices of the Whitney Museum of American Art, the Council began compiling a catalogue raisonné of Hartley's work. Their assembled material on Hartley was subsequently turned over to Elizabeth McCausland who, until her death in 1965, was preparing a book on Hartley's life and art. Working initially with the Council, McCausland amassed a large body of notes and primary documents on Hartley, who was a voluminous correspondent. Simultaneously, a collection of his unpublished manuscripts and letters—including those written to Stieglitz, Hartley's niece Norma Berger, and Gertrude Stein—was being assembled, through the efforts of Donald Gallup, for the Collection of American Literature at Yale University. Unfortunately, because of interpersonal problems with the executor of Hartley's estate, McCausland was refused permission to quote from any of Hartley's letters and unpublished manuscripts and was, perhaps even more regrettably, denied knowledge of and access to a great deal of important primary source material. To compound the problem, McCausland died before ever fully organizing her own notes or completing her research. Nevertheless, her herculean effort at assembling material became the foundation for all subsequent Hartley scholarship.

Because McCausland's research was incomplete, however, many of her facts and observations—hitherto accepted and repeated—were inaccurate. Moreover, after McCausland's death scholars were restricted from the full use of her material. Several gained access to various parts, and their findings greatly relieved the dearth of information about Hartley. Restrictions on access to the McCausland papers were lifted over three years ago, when the Whitney Museum of American Art announced its decision to mount a major exhibition of Hartley's work. It quickly became obvious that the accompanying study would involve more than simply reviewing the primary documents at Yale and those assembled by McCausland (now preserved at the Archives of American Art, Washington D.C.). It would, in addition, entail a search for previously unknown material in order to redress past errors concerning the basic facts about Hartley's life and the evolution and dating of his paintings. This then is what the Hartley research project has involved.

From the beginning of the research, it was apparent that Hartley's most dominant characteristic was his itinerancy. Constantly moving to avoid crises and escape his insecurities, Hartley as an adult never occupied the same rooms for more than ten months. Early in his life, he developed a penchant for solitude and a simultaneous desire for crowds—mutually exclusive needs which created a rootless personality. His restless nature can be seen in his art as well; it led to frequent style changes, often the result of seeing others' work, often a reaction to new geographic stimulations, and just as often an attempt to find personal approval and affection — needs which are demonstrably products of his childhood experiences. Because the events of Hartley's life and his constantly changing styles were so interdependent, I have chosen to discuss his paintings within the context of his biography, a relatively unfashionable approach among contemporary art historians.

Within its fluctuating styles, Hartley's career falls into three main divisions. As did most modern American artists, he went abroad in the years before World War I to absorb the lessons of European modernism. But unlike the rest of the American art community, he was as influenced by the German Expressionists as by the Fauves and the Cubists. In his work of this period, which drew images from the German military environment, he united the expressive intensity of the Blaue Reiter artists, the compositional structure of the Cubists, and a mystical symbolism generated by his own spiritualist inclinations. These paintings were equal in achievement and sophistication to any work being done by the key figures of the European avant-garde.

Forced by the war to return to the anti-German environment of the United States, however, Hartley lost his direction. He abandoned abstraction and spent the next two decades wandering through Europe and America, experimenting with various French-based styles. Not surprisingly, given his models, he renounced the expressionist-imaginative approach of his early years in favor of representational objectivity. His expatriation separated him from the other core members of the Stieglitz group — Arthur Dove, John Marin, Georgia O'Keeffe — who remained in America after their initial introduction to modernist theory, and drew on their intuitive responses to natural landscape forms to express a distinctly American vision. It took Hartley nearly two decades of hesitancy to return to these roots. In his later years, he went back to his native Maine and produced a group of richly toned, expressive landscapes whose spiritual grandeur equals, if not surpasses, the intensity and achievement of his German military paintings. Like the paintings of the other American modernists, Hartley's work neither influenced nor provided a foundation for the succeeding generation of artists. Fully a quarter century later, it is the early modernists' honest, direct attitude toward subject matter, and their intense commitment to the idea that art in itself represents a spiritual reality, that makes their work so relevant to our present generation.

Fig. 2   Eliza Jane Hartley, date unknown

Early Years: 1877 – 1908

Hartley's lifelong search for support and affection was the product of a lonely, insecure childhood.[1] Hartley grew up in a lower working-class home in Lewiston, Maine, a factory town to which his father, Thomas Hartley, had immigrated in 1860 from Stalybridge, England.[2] Although he found employment as a cotton spinner and sent for his bride-to-be, Eliza Jane Horbury, the American dream proved elusive, and the family remained perennially on the edge of poverty. Of the nine children born to Eliza and Thomas Hartley, only five survived childhood. Edmund, as Marsden Hartley was christened, was the youngest, born on January 4, 1877.

Edmund was not particularly close to either of his parents. He later described his father as a reserved, weak man who never found the ambition or opportunity to make a financial success of his life.[3] His mother died when he was eight and he could only remember her as a woman whose face was lined with illness.[4] But her death threw the family into chaos. Unable to maintain a household with three small children, Thomas Hartley sent his two youngest daughters to live with their older sister in Cleveland, keeping only Edmund with him. "From the moment of my mother's death," he later wrote, "I became in psychology an orphan, in consciousness a lone left thing to make its way out for all time after that by itself."[5]

The trauma of abandonment was soon aggravated. In 1889 Hartley's father married Martha Marsden, a warm and vivacious childhood friend from Stalybridge. But when they decided to join the rest of the family in Cleveland, Edmund was left behind with another married sister in Auburn, Maine.[6] Years later, Hartley was still haunted by the tragedy of this period: "I had a childhood vast with terror and surprise. If it is true that one forgets what one wishes to forget, then I have reason for not remembering the major part of those days. . . ."[7]

Compelled to contribute to his sister's family income, Hartley left school at fifteen and went to work for three dollars a week in a shoe factory, checking the shoe lots as they passed from one department to another. The following year he joined the family in Cleveland, where he found work, again for three dollars a week, as a messenger and office boy in a marble quarry on the Cuyahoga River.

Shy and insecure, Hartley lived an imaginative, private life during adolescence, pursuing solitary activities. He developed an interest in collecting beautiful natural objects, a pastime which stimulated his awareness of color-texture relationships. Hartley's growing aesthetic sensibility led him to John Semon, a local adherent of the French Barbizon School of landscape painting. In 1896, he arranged to take weekly painting lessons in Semon's studio on the top floor of the City Hall building. Semon was a formative influence on Hartley's decision to become an artist. According to Hartley, it was Semon who planted the "art virus in my soul."[8]

In the summer of 1898, Hartley went with Semon on a two-week vacation to Semon's country place in southern Ohio, and upon his return found that he had been fired from his job at the quarry. Having progressed satisfactorily under Semon's tutelage, he enrolled in an outdoor painting class conducted by Cullen Yates, a local, Paris-trained artist Hartley described as a "half-hearted" Impressionist. At the end of the summer, Yates held an exhibition of the students' work, which brought Hartley's paintings to the attention of a trustee of the Cleveland School of Art.[9] As a result, Hartley received a scholarship to the school, and thus began his first professional training.[10]

Hartley's recollections of the Cleveland School focused on Nina Waldeck, a drawing teacher who became his first spiritual mentor. She gave Hartley a copy of Ralph Waldo Emerson's *Essays,* which he carried with him for five years and later called the "greatest book" of his life.[11] Emerson's endorsement of inspiration over reason, as well as his intuitional orientation, had a profound effect on Hartley's thinking, providing the artist with the foundation for his subsequent spiritual-mystical attitudes.

At the end of Hartley's first semester at the Cleveland School, Anne Walworth, a trustee of the school and member of its instruction committee, offered him a five-year stipend to study in New York: four hundred and fifty dollars a year, with three hundred for winter schooling and the rest for summer expenses. Although his father considered him a failure for entering the art profession and predicted that he would end up indigent and unhappy, the solitary nature born of a lonely childhood allowed Hartley to turn his back on the family and move to New York.

In the fall of 1899, Hartley enrolled in the New York School of Art (known as the Chase School), where he received instruction from Luis Mora and Frank Vincent Dumond, and attended the Saturday morning critiques given by William

Merritt Chase.[12] Chase passed on to Hartley his belief in the importance of being an artist, and a fiery enthusiasm for the physical act of painting, as well as his technique of handling pigment with rapid painterly flourishes. According to Hartley, Chase instilled in him the idea that the brushstroke was the basis for expression in painting, although he disliked what he considered Chase's emphasis on technical virtuosity over content.[13] Chase's bravura handling of paint was not yet evident in Hartley's realistic, delicate pencil drawings, but it became one of the salient characteristics of his later style. In one of his late works, *White Cod* (pl. 66), the influence of Chase's loose, painterly style is readily apparent.

At the close of the school year, Hartley returned to Lewiston, where he began a correspondence with fellow art student Richard Tweedy. The letters reveal Hartley's growing preoccupation with the Emersonian notion that nature embodies a divine spirit. Encouraged by the example of Emerson and Henry David Thoreau to seek knowledge in the natural world, Hartley spent his time studying flowers and butterflies, much as he had done as an adolescent. "There is nothing," he wrote to Tweedy, "that sets all things at peace with me as a communion with Nature. She seems to have a balm for every pain and a cheerful song for every sorrowing heart."[14] Spurred on by the transcendental idea that divinity can be perceived in nature, he began to produce delicate botanical drawings. Although not extant, they indicate a willingness to turn to nature for subject matter.

Hartley was an intense, serious young man at this time, searching for a system of spiritual values, and he felt that art could enrich the spirit: "One can enjoy life so much more," he wrote to Tweedy, "because of the knowledge that comes with art. One learns to look for art in everything and one aspires or should aspire to be art in everything. Beauty is my one aim in life, beauty in character, in thought, in work, in deed, and in expression on canvas of Nature divine, and the glorification of the God of all, who provided us with these beauties."[15] Hartley's search led him to the church. He had sung in the local Episcopalian church as a boy, and he now became a devout and zealous churchgoer, who spoke with dismay of missing a single service. When he returned to New York at the end of the summer, he volunteered for work at the church mission. That winter he even considered entering the priesthood, feeling it might be a more altruistic occupation than that of an artist.[16]

His commitment to art prevailed, however. That same fall of 1900 he transferred to the National Academy of Design, feeling that he could no longer afford the fifteen-dollar monthly fee at the Chase School. He was attracted by the Academy's ten-dollar annual fee as much as by the more structured classes and greater discipline that he felt prevailed there. For the next four years he attended the Academy during the school season and returned to Maine in the summer. None of his instructors seem to have had a lasting influence on him, either through their work or their teaching, although Hartley later credited Francis C. Jones with having taught him to use white.[17]

Hartley corresponded during the school year 1900-1901 with two wealthy artist-socialists, Charles Fox and Curtis Perry, whom he had met in Lewiston the previous summer through a local artist, Alice Farrar.[18] Fox and Perry ran a Utopian school in Portland, Maine, and a summer art commune in North Bridgton, Maine, which they encouraged Hartley to attend. He accepted their invitation and went to the colony in July 1901. Organized around communal principles, the colony strove to develop a new social consciousness through the study of art and nature. Hartley apparently never saw either artist paint and their influence lay primarily in strengthening his view of the interrelationship between art and spiritual pursuits. Their aim, he wrote approvingly, was "to live the higher life and to apply it to their art."[19]

Fig. 3 *Walt Whitman's House, 328 Mickle Street, Camden, New Jersey,* ca. 1905. Oil on board, 24.1 × 14 cm (9½ × 5½″). Mrs. Hudson D. Walker, Forest Hills, New York

Fig. 4 *Shady Brook,* 1907. Oil on canvas, 71.1 × 61 cm (28 × 24″). Lewiston Public Library, Maine

While in North Bridgton, Hartley became intrigued with the vista of Maine's Center Lovell Mountains. When Academy classes recessed for the summer of 1902, he took up residence outside the town of Center Lovell in a cobbler shop. He felt a strong affinity for the local landscape and spent the next two summers here and in North Lovell, living in a converted schoolhouse.

Hartley's grant from Anne Walworth ran out in November 1904. For the first time since he had begun painting, he was dependent on his own resources. To support himself, he worked for the next two years as an extra at Proctor's Theater Company in New York for four dollars a week. While on tour with the company in Philadelphia he met Horace Traubel, editor of the political-spiritual newspaper, the *Conservator,* and the companion and biographer of Walt Whitman. Despite Hartley's shyness and reticence, he projected an intensity and earnestness which attracted the older, more established man. Hartley spoke later of the "love" letters he received in this period from Traubel, who remained a good friend until his death in 1919.   (On the whole, Hartley did not often write about his homosexuality; most references to it come from others' descriptions.)[20] Through Traubel, Hartley became immersed in Whitman's writings and philosophy. He was also introduced to a predominantly homosexual community of intellectuals and radical thinkers with intuitive-mystical orientations akin to those he had already evolved through his reading of Emerson and Thoreau.[21] Whitman's spirited celebration of the individual and his exaltation of nature and common experience further stimulated Hartley's transcendental inclinations.

Despite Hartley's emotional involvement with spiritualist philosophies, his painting style remained conventional. The one extant painting from this period, *Walt Whitman's House* (fig. 3), indicates that he continued to imitate academic realism. He himself recognized the discrepancy. In a letter to the Irish-American poet Seumas O'Sheel, he said: "I feel something in the chasms and the voids of life that are far more powerful and enthralling and I may sometime find expression for it." [22]

At the end of the East Coast summer tour in 1906, Hartley returned to Lewiston, hoping to teach painting and make contact with his father and stepmother, who were once again living there. He now adopted his stepmother's maiden name, Marsden, perhaps wanting to reconcile himself with his father and to draw closer to his stepmother.[23]

His paintings this season show that he had progressed from academic realism to an evocative kind of landscape painting similar in composition to that of John Twachtman and George Inness, both of whose work he had admired while a student.[24] These paintings, which may be designated as Impressionist landscapes, came closer than his earlier work to evoking a moody, otherworldly quality (fig. 4). In them, Hartley adopted the muted, restrained palette of the American Impressionists; although most extant paintings are rendered in dark colors his color scheme was described as light, or "opal," in a 1906 Lewiston article.[25] Hartley's attitude was equally consistent with that of the American Impressionist tradition. Feeling that nature was never the same in two consecutive moments, Hartley worked by getting an impression of the subject he wished to paint in one glance, and then retaining that impression until a sketch of it was drawn on the canvas. He felt the details of the painting could be developed later, but that the particular mood of nature must be grasped quickly. From the example of American Impressionists like Twachtman (fig. 5), whose work developed considerably later than their French counterparts and was consequently influenced by Post-Impressionism, Hartley had assimilated an overall decorative treatment of the picture surface. Using his muted palette, he wove together irregularly shaped areas of color with a delicate tracery of lines to create a decorative picture surface. His

Fig. 5　John Twachtman. *Ice Bound*, 1888–89. Oil on canvas, 64.8 × 76.5 cm (25¼ × 30⅛″). The Art Institute of Chicago; Friends of American Art Collection

Fig. 6　*Storm Clouds, Maine*, 1906–7 (see Plate 70)

commitment to the decorative quality of all-over surface pattern was also influenced by the Japanese prints he had been interested in while a student, several examples of which hung in his Lewiston studio.

However, in his painting technique, Hartley differed radically from these antecedents. His inspiration for dispensing with the Impressionists' traditional method of applying scumbled paint had come from a color reproduction of *Ploughing in the Engadine* (fig. 7) by the Italian Divisionist painter Giovanni Segantini, which he had seen in the January 1903 issue of the magazine *Jugend*. The magazine had devoted the entire issue to Segantini: two of his paintings had been reproduced in color, four in black and white. In Segantini's distinctive "stitch" stroke — a method of building up an image out of small, interlocking lines of color — Hartley saw a technique for rendering the heavily wooded mountainsides of Maine. Although not incorporated into his work until the fall of 1906, this stitch technique was an important device, and Hartley credited Segantini with showing him "how to begin painting my own Maine mountains." [26] This Divisionist paintstroke had become the dominant characteristic of Hartley's work by the winter of 1906-7 (fig. 6), as his style shifted from an Impressionist approach to a Neo-Impressionist one.

The aesthetic achievements of these paintings notwithstanding, this period proved difficult for Hartley. Unable to reconcile with his father, or to generate sufficient income from his teachings, Hartley wrote in desperation to Thomas Mosher, a well-known publisher and Whitman admirer, to whom Traubel had introduced him the previous summer, and pleaded for a job. Mosher invited him to summer at Green Acre, a retreat that Mosher and Traubel visited in Eliot, Maine, where Hartley would get room and board in exchange for erecting tents. Hartley consented, and at Green Acre during the summer of 1907 he was introduced to formalized Eastern religion.

Green Acre, founded by Sarah Farmer, the daughter of New England Transcendentalists and social activists, was conceived as an institute where artists, theologians, and mystics could exchange spiritual and philosophical views in a pastoral setting. Farmer became increasingly involved with Eastern religion, and by 1901 had converted the colony into a school of Bahá'í faith. At the time of Hartley's visit, Green Acre was still a meeting place for yogis, swamis, and various other Eastern mystics. Farmer had also been a patroness of Arthur Wesley Dow, the influential art teacher who is said to have painted at Pont Aven with Gauguin,

Fig. 7　Giovanni Segantini. *L'aratura in Engadina* ("Plowing in the Engadine"), 1886. Oil on canvas, 116 × 227 cm (45⅔ × 89⅓″). Bayerische Staatsgemäldesammlungen, Munich

and who based his teaching on Oriental and Synthetist principles of art. Although Dow had stopped attending Green Acre by 1907, Hartley may have been exposed to his theories through Dow's paintings, which hung in the guest lodge, or through Sarah Farmer herself.

During this period, Hartley's growth as a painter began to be recognized. That fall, Mrs. Ole Bull, a wealthy patroness of the arts and frequent visitor to the colony, arranged for an exhibition of Hartley's work at her house in Eliot, Maine, thereby giving him his first public exposure as a painter. The paintings, all of which had been executed the previous winter in Lewiston, were sufficiently well received to net ninety dollars.

With the onset of winter, Hartley moved to Boston. Here, in paintings such as *Landscape, Lewiston* (fig. 8), his dark Impressionist palette lightened and he began emphasizing the physical properties of paint by dragging heavily loaded brushstrokes across isolated areas of the canvas. Although not distinctly mystical, the airy color tones in these paintings begin to suggest a transcendental vision similar to that found in Inness' work. Hartley exhibited one of these paintings at the Rowlands Gallery, where it was seen by Desmond Fitzgerald, a prominent Boston collector of Impressionist art. Fitzgerald invited Hartley to his house and, according to Hartley, bought one of his paintings for four hundred dollars.[27]

Fig. 8 *Landscape, Lewiston,* 1908. Oil on canvas, 64.1 × 77.5 cm (25¼ × 30½"). Private collection

Hartley and 291: 1908–1912

With the money he received from Fitzgerald, Hartley returned to Maine in the autumn of 1908 and set up house in abandoned quarters on a farm in the Stoneham Valley near North Lovell. Here he painted what he considered his first mature pictures. Preliminary work on the paintings was begun outdoors, and they were finished inside when the weather and color had changed. It was dismally cold that winter, but the confidence acquired from his exhibitions in Eliot and Boston, and from the sale of a painting to Fitzgerald, spurred him on. That winter he made his first major break from convention, developing what is best called his Neo-Impressionist style.

Perhaps the most remarkable aspect of Hartley's new approach to painting is that it began in virtual isolation, with no *direct* exposure to the developments which had taken place in Europe. Through reproductions, Hartley evolved a painting style based on discrete strokes of intense color that set him apart as the only Neo-Impressionist painter in America, with the exception of Maurice Prendergast, whose work he possibly saw in Boston. The dominant characteristic of these paintings is their overriding emphasis on color and the physicality of paint. As early as 1900 Hartley had written, "I see color in nature so brilliant and it is impossible for me to 'bring it up' to the right key."[28] Until this time, however, he had not approached color with confidence. He now employed it vibrantly, amplifying the Segantini stitch by interweaving brilliant daubs of discrete color across the plane of the canvas in an overall decorative pattern. The material quality of these paint daubs was accentuated by heavily applied pigments, which enliven the surface with a uniform impasto, sometimes an eighth of an inch thick. Discarding conventional perspective, Hartley united foreground and background in a single continuous plane. In works such as *Cosmos* (pl. 71), he reduced forms to decorative, curvilinear shapes defined only by the direction and pattern of the strokes and by distinct areas of color.[29] This mode suggests the influence of the European Neo-Impressionists, particularly Richard Pietzsch, whose work had been reproduced in *Jugend* in 1906 (fig. 9). In Hartley's paintings of the

Fig. 9 Richard Pietzsch. *Vorfrühling im Harthale* ("Early Spring in Harthale"), n.d. Reproduced in *Jugend,* no. 14 (1906), p. 281.

Plate 1   *Carnival of Autumn*, 1908–9 (cat. no. 2)
Museum of Fine Arts, Boston; Charles Henry Hayden Fund

Plate 2   *The Summer Camp*, 1908–9 (cat. no. 4)
The Fine Arts Museums of San Francisco;
gift of Mr. and Mrs. John D. Rockefeller 3rd

snowstorms around Center and North Lovell, turbulent, graphic brushstrokes take on an expressiveness reminiscent of the undulating brushstrokes of Van Gogh (fig. 10). This is especially true of the crayon and pencil drawings Hartley made at this time, which derive both form and power from agitated strokes (fig. 11). In the concurrent series *Songs of Winter*, his divisionist stroke gives way to a loose, gestural fluidity which anticipates his abstract landscapes of 1910.

Hartley introduced into these Neo-Impressionist works the cloud and mountain motifs which were to remain central to his imagery throughout his career. His clouds are not atmospheric mists, but distinct forms, hovering like weighty, sculptural masses over mountains which, in these 1908-9 paintings, fill the entire canvas with an almost claustrophobic closeness. "I am happy to say," Hartley wrote, "I've always been noted for the living element in my skies. . . . [I] make them live as much as the rest of the scene—for it is in reality the sky that makes a scene vivid."[30] His mountains were equally weighty presences whose monumentality he seemed to identify with, perhaps feeling that they embodied the strength and constancy he lacked in his own life. As Hartley described the mountain, it differed from other elements "in that little or nothing can be done to it by the ravages of silent agencies. . . . It is this element of hypnosis in nature itself which makes us cling to it as a relief from the vacuities of human experience. Mountains are things, entities of a grandiose character, and the one who understands them best is the one who can suffer them best and respect their profound loneliness."[31]

In foregoing realism to express the ecstasy and dynamic spirit he perceived in nature, Hartley finally achieved a painting style that reflected the intuitive mysticism which now dominated his thinking. He reinforced the mystical overtones of these paintings by ascribing to them such titles as *Cosmos* and *Hall of the Mountain King*. His own descriptions are equally visionary. He wrote ebulliently of having "come back to the original child within, the romanticist," noting that his new work embodied "little visions of the great intangible. . . . Some will say he's gone mad—others will look and say he's looked in at the lattices of Heaven and come back with the madness of splendor on him."[32]

In March of 1909, Hartley took the paintings to Boston.[33] There they were very well received by Maurice and Charles Prendergast, who wrote letters of introduction on Hartley's behalf to Robert Henri and William Glackens in New York. Glackens arranged to show the Neo-Impressionist work in his studio in Washington Square to members of the progressive art group known as The Eight. Their response was mixed. Arthur B. Davies reacted enthusiastically to the paintings, feeling that they embodied the essence of American mysticism, but Everett Shinn and John Sloan expressed reservations, Sloan noting later in his diary that Hartley's mysticism was "a little too much for me."[34]

Hartley was desperately anxious to have his paintings seen in a gallery. When his friend O'Sheel suggested that Alfred Stieglitz might be interested, Hartley eagerly requested a visit. Stieglitz agreed to look at Hartley's work and told him to leave his paintings at the 291 Fifth Avenue gallery for a few days. Although Stieglitz had planned to close the gallery for the summer (for which reason he had already refused Max Weber an exhibition), he felt there was something in these paintings, and in Hartley's earnestness and commitment, that merited attention. Always responsive to new ideas and willing to act on impulse, Stieglitz agreed to hold an exhibition several weeks later. Hartley had told Stieglitz that 291 was the only gallery of interest to him and that he wanted to show nowhere else. Stieglitz later recalled that he had been moved by these remarks and by Hartley's comment that he could live on only four dollars a week.[35] Hartley's first one-man exhibition in New York opened at 291 on May 8, 1909, establishing him as a member of the

Fig. 10 *The Blast of Winter*, 1908. Oil on canvas, 76.2 × 76.2 cm (30 × 30"). Mr. and Mrs. Everett Birch, St. Thomas

Fig. 11 *Self-Portrait*, 1908. Crayon on paper, 30.2 × 22.5 cm (11⅞ × 8⅞"). Hirschl & Adler Galleries, New York

most progressive art circle in America.

The exhibition failed financially, but it thrust Hartley for the first time into a cosmopolitan society and exposed his pictorial innovations to public scrutiny. The exposure intensified Hartley's inherent insecurity, particularly because he was still searching for a personal vision. At this moment, Hartley found a role model in Albert Pinkham Ryder, whose works he saw in the gallery of N.E. Montross, a contemporary dealer. In Ryder's paintings, Hartley perceived an aesthetic vision which was not only accepted by those whose opinions he valued, but also reaffirmed his own pictorial and emotional background; encountering Ryder was like returning to a world he had already experienced. "I was a convert to the field of imagination into which I was born. . . . I had been thrown back into the body and being of my own country." [36] Profoundly affected by Ryder's art, Hartley sought out the older artist in his studio on 15th Street and saw additional works (fig. 12).[37] The small group of landscapes Hartley painted in the remaining months of 1909 were strongly influenced by Ryder. These paintings—the Dark Landscapes—were done "solely from memory and the imagination" and were "as close to Ryder as possible" (pl. 3).[38] This acknowledgment of Ryder's influence indicated Hartley's readiness to openly link himself with other artists, a practice he continued throughout his life.

What Ryder provided Hartley with was a model for uniting mystical and romantic qualities with an expressive realism which employed the rhythmic patterning and dark palette Hartley had evolved in his 1906–7 Impressionist landscapes. The austere mood of Ryder's work was equally appealing, for it corresponded to Hartley's feelings of loneliness and isolation. His description of Ryder aptly characterizes his own despair at the time: "[Ryder] saw with an all too pitiless and pitiful eye the element of hopelessness in things, the complete succumbing of things in nature to those elements greater than they that wield a fatal power." [39] This period was one of despondency for Hartley, who, Stieglitz suggested, was on the verge of suicide. He was still extremely poor; he had to work in a friend's studio because he lived in a cold, hall bedroom.[40] The Dark Landscapes are somber expressionistic canvases, depicting deserted farms overshadowed by mountains and dominated by broken, anthropomorphic trees. Probably referring to Hartley's farmhouse in North Lovell, they convey a mood of gloom and despair that reflects his anguished memories of Maine. Stylistically, these paintings draw heavily on the somber palette and moody, rhythmic shapes in Ryder's work, as well as on Ryder's preoccupation with heavy, irreducible forms. They represent a distinct break with Hartley's previous style, the first of many such abrupt transformations his work would undergo.

Hartley's life improved during the next two years (1910-12). Montross was touched by his financial plight and offered him a stipend of four dollars a week. His Dark Landscapes were relatively well received and Stieglitz included several of them in the "Younger American Painters" exhibition he organized in 1910. Hartley became an active member of the Stieglitz circle, frequenting the 291 exhibitions and attending the luncheons given by Stieglitz at the Holland House Restaurant, where he was exposed to the group's ongoing discussions about art and aesthetics. In these years, Stieglitz became his first real mentor; not surprisingly, the course of his work paralleled Stieglitz's own increasingly advanced convictions and enthusiasms.

It was at 291 that Hartley discovered the artists who would next constitute the great influences on him: Matisse, Picasso, and Cézanne, whose works were shown in three major exhibitions at the gallery.[41] Through these French artists, Hartley moved from a concern with spiritual-religious issues and personal expression to an involvement with formal, abstract problems.

Fig. 12   Albert Pinkham Ryder. *The Tempest,* n.d. Oil on canvas, 70.5 × 88.9 cm (27¾ × 35″). The Detroit Institute of Arts; Dexter M. Ferry, Jr. Fund

Plate 3   *The Dark Mountain*, 1909 (cat. no. 5)
The Art Institute of Chicago; The Alfred Stieglitz Collection

Plate 4   *Deserted Farm*, 1909 (cat. no. 6)
University Gallery, University of Minnesota, Minneapolis;
gift of Ione and Hudson Walker

Fig. 13 *Kezar Lake, Autumn Morning*, 1910. Oil on cardboard, 30.2 × 30.2 cm (11⅞ × 11⅞"). Fogg Art Museum, Harvard University; Cambridge, Massachusetts; bequest of Lee Simonson

Fig. 14 *Composition*, 1910. Oil on board, 29.2 × 29.2 cm (11½ × 11½"). Fogg Art Museum, Harvard University; Cambridge, Massachusetts; gift of James N. Rosenberg

Matisse was the first influence. Hartley learned about the French painter from the 291 exhibition in February 1910, and from discussions at the gallery, particularly with Max Weber, who had studied in the Matisse class organized in Paris by Sarah Stein. The landscapes Hartley produced in the summer of 1910 — for example, *Kezar Lake, Autumn Morning* (fig. 13) — were predominantly small studies, measuring only twelve by twelve inches. Hartley described his approach in these paintings to his niece: "I do not sketch much these days for I work almost wholly from the imagination — making pictures entirely from this point of view using the mountains only as backgrounds for ideas. . . . this is difficult art — almost anybody can paint from nature — it calls for real expert power to create an idea and produce it as one sees it in the mind."[42] The results combined high key, Fauve color with thickly impastoed, distinct brushstrokes which, as in Hartley's 1908-9 paintings, create a flattened, artificial space. In several works, such as *Composition* (fig. 14), the entire expression is conveyed through the brushstroke itself, creating a degree of gestural abstraction that would not be surpassed in America until Abstract Expressionism.[43]

The second decisive influence on Hartley was the Picasso show in late March-April 1911 which, according to Stieglitz, Hartley studied for hours at a time.[44] Picasso's Analytic Cubism proved too radical, however, for Hartley to incorporate immediately in any but a few isolated pictures. These experiments were probably undertaken that spring, for Stieglitz's notation on the back of one of them, *Landscape No. 32* (fig. 15), indicates that it was the first painting Hartley did after the 291 Picasso show.

Picasso was the impetus, but Max Weber's Cubist work provided the foundation on which Hartley's understanding of Cubism was built. From the autumn of 1909 until his expulsion from the gallery in 1911, Weber was extremely close to Stieglitz. He knew more about avant-garde French art and aesthetics than anyone in America and was a great source of information for those who came to 291. Hartley's brief Cubist experiments resemble the two-dimensional geometrized leaf forms in Weber's 1911 paintings — *Forest Scene*, for example — as much as they do Picasso's Analytic Cubism (figs. 16, 17).

Cézanne's influence on Hartley proved more significant than either Matisse's or Picasso's.[45] Hartley's letters make it clear, however, that he missed the 291 Cézanne exhibition in March 1911, and did not see any of Cézanne's paintings firsthand until Davies took him to the Havemeyer Collection in late 1911 or early

Fig. 15 *Landscape No. 32*, 1911. Watercolor on paper, 35.9 × 25.4 cm (14⅛ × 10″). University Gallery, University of Minnesota, Minneapolis; bequest of Hudson Walker from the Ione and Hudson Walker Collection

Fig. 16 Max Weber. *Forest Scene*, 1911. Gouache, 32.4 × 20.3 cm (12¾ × 8″). Present whereabouts unknown

Fig. 17 *Abstraction*, 1911. Oil on cardboard, 41.3 × 33.7 cm (16¼ × 13¼″). University Gallery, University of Minnesota, Minneapolis; bequest of Hudson Walker from the Ione and Hudson Walker Collection

Fig. 18 Max Weber. *Still Life with Bananas*, 1909. Oil on canvas. 81.3 × 66 cm (32 × 26″). Forum Gallery, New York

Fig. 19 *Still Life No. 11*, 1911. Oil on canvas, 24.1 × 19.1 cm (9½ × 7½″). University Gallery, University of Minnesota, Minneapolis; bequest of Hudson Walker from the Ione and Hudson Walker Collection

1912. When Hartley began his Cézanne-inspired paintings in 1911, he knew the master's work only in reproduction. In Maine that summer, Hartley created a series of Cézannesque still lifes based on black-and-white illustrations in Meier-Graefe's Cézanne monograph, and on ideas about Cézanne he had picked up from Weber, an ardent champion of Cézanne's work, whose own exhibition at 291 in January 1911 included Cézannesque still lifes (fig. 18).[46]

Hartley's Cézannesque still lifes of that summer, such as *Still Life No. 11* (fig. 19), rendered in a color scheme of deep greens, tans, and browns, show a respect for geometric simplicity and the solidity of objects, but lack the delicacy of Cézanne's compositions and the shimmering texture of his brushstrokes. In this series, Hartley completely abandoned his earlier interest in visualizing mysticism and the moods of nature to focus on the formal, abstract issues of color and form. He had "but one ambition — to put down with a sense of authority and artistic conviction an object — some days for form only — then for color — and so it is good to get at this problem of expressing the impersonal — things without mood — things existing for themselves only as shapes + forms with color. . . ."[47] In August he mentioned that he tacked to his wall Cézanne's statement "Where color reaches richness form attains fullness";[48] and a month later that he was "setting aside entirely the mood of nature and interesting myself wholly in the problem and its rendering. . . . Picasso taught me much on this point. . . . I do not find him as edifying however in his viewpoint as Cézanne."[49] Stieglitz approved of Hartley's new direction: in February 1912, he gave him his second 291 show, made up primarily of these recent still lifes.

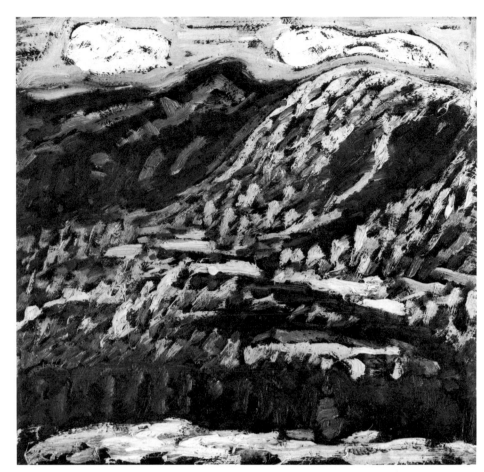

Plate 5 *Birch Grove, Autumn*, 1910
(cat. no. 7)
The Museum of Modern Art,
New York;
The Lee Simonson Bequest

Plate 6 *Maine Mountains, Autumn*,
1910 (cat. no. 9)
The Museum of Modern Art,
New York;
The Lee Simonson Bequest

Plate 7   *Red Tree*, 1910 (cat. no. 10)
National Collection of Fine Arts, Smithsonian Institution,
Washington, D.C.; gift of Flora E.H. Shawan

Plate 8 *Still Life*, 1912 (cat. no. 12)
University Gallery, University of Minnesota, Minneapolis;
bequest of Hudson Walker from the Ione and Hudson Walker Collection

Hartley in Paris: April 1912– May 1913

That spring Stieglitz arranged to send Hartley to Paris for a year, the trip financed through a sale of one of Hartley's paintings to Agnes Meyer and through funds procured by Arthur B. Davies from Lillie Bliss. Hartley arrived in Paris on April 11, 1912 and immediately threw himself into the Parisian art world, making the rounds of galleries and museums and searching out the art he had deified from a distance. He quickly sought out the American contingent in Paris—Lee Simonson, an artist he had known in Center Lovell, Elie Nadelman, Edward Steichen, Alfred Maurer, Arthur B. Carles, and Jo Davidson—and began to frequent the popular artists' cafes: the Dôme, the Rotonde, and the Restaurant Thomas.

Like other American artists in Paris, Hartley gravitated to the salon conducted by Leo and Gertrude Stein at 27 rue de Fleurus, where, amidst an impressive array of the period's most advanced paintings, he met the celebrities of Parisian bohemia. In the decade before World War I, the Saturday evening gatherings at the Steins' served as an international meeting place and forum for modern art, attracting not only vanguard Parisian artists, but a mixture of students, wealthy collectors, and curious foreigners. For the Americans, the soirées provided a cultural oasis and a center for the study of radical developments in Parisian modernism. Hartley, who had gone to the Steins' apartment that spring on Simonson's introduction, was overwhelmed by his first view: "I had to get used to so much of everything all at once of course . . . a room full of staggering pictures . . . all burning with life and new ideas—and as strange as the ideas seemed to be—all of them terrifically stimulating—a new kind of words for an old theme . . . I felt indeed like a severed head living of itself by mystical excitation."[50] Gertrude Stein developed an interest in Hartley and he became a regular guest at the salon later that winter.[51]

Despite the lure of Parisian society, Hartley formed his closest friendships with the German coterie that gathered at the Restaurant Thomas on the Boulevard Raspail. The group included Arnold Rönnebeck, a sculptor and officer in the German army, Rönnebeck's cousin Karl von Freyburg, whose handsome features and gentle demeanor Hartley lauded, and the American artist Charles Demuth. These German connections were to be an important influence, for they eventually led Hartley back to the rendering of spiritual values in painting, which he had abandoned when he became involved with formal problems.

That first summer, however, Hartley's work followed the French models that held sway in Stein's circle. When Simonson went south in June to work with Stanton Macdonald-Wright, Hartley sublet his studio at 18 rue Moulin de Beurre. His work evolved rapidly from the Cézannesque style of the previous year into paintings such as *Still Life No. 1* (fig. 20), which fused Cézanne's composition and structural approach with the palette and decorative emphasis of Matisse. As the summer ended, he moved to a more abstract Cubist style, typified by *Still Life with Fan* (fig. 21), which employed the compressed space and angular, faceted lines of Analytic Cubism.

Although Hartley had adopted a Cubist vocabulary, the mystical leanings of the German group eventually began to dominate the intellectualism of the French. "Personally," he wrote to Rockwell Kent, "while I do not altogether dislike the French I turn to the Germans with more alacrity for they are more sturdy like ourselves."[52] In July 1912, he was introduced to Wassily Kandinsky's work while studying a treatise on Paul Gauguin in the magazine *Rhythm*: Kandinsky, a Russian working in Germany, had been presented as one of Gauguin's followers. Intrigued, Hartley sought out *Der Blaue Reiter*, the new magazine which Kandinsky had recently published.[53] By the first of September Hartley had apparently

Fig. 20 *Still Life No. 1*, 1912 (see Plate 9)

Fig. 21 *Still Life with Fan*, 1912. Oil on canvas, 92.7 × 72.4 cm (36½ × 28½"). Nebraska Art Association, Thomas C. Woods Fund; courtesy of the Sheldon Memorial Gallery, Lincoln researched the matter thoroughly: in a postcard to Stieglitz he recommended Kandinsky's book *On the Spiritual in Art*, arranged for mutual friend, Katherine Rhoades, to take a copy of *Der Blaue Reiter* back to New York, and expressed his affinity for primitive art, which *Der Blaue Reiter* had linked with the expression of inner feelings.[54]

Hartley's introduction to primitive art, however, had occurred earlier. Its aesthetic value was stressed repeatedly by the Cubists and by Max Weber, who especially admired Mexican and Pre-Columbian art and contributed an essay on the subject to the July 1910 issue of *Camera Work*.[55] Weber also incorporated Mexican pottery into a number of his 1910 still lifes, which Hartley had seen (fig. 22). And Hartley, in the early summer of 1912, had depicted American Indian artifacts in works such as *Indian Pottery, Paris* (fig. 23).[56] Stimulated further by *Der Blaue Reiter*, he visited the Trocadero Museum, the Paris museum of primitive culture, in September and attributed the shift in his work to the art he saw there.[57] His letters of September and October confirm his belief in the spiritual expression of primitive culture: "Modern art is now taking a plunge inward and men are revolting against superficial ideas. Each man is trying to look to himself and see what he finds there";[58] "The more elemental and primitive the people, the more inwardly intense have been the modes of expression";[59] "These [primitive] people had no mean ambition. They created out of spiritual necessity"[60] — the latter phrase borrowed from Kandinsky's book, *On the Spiritual in Art*.

Fig. 22 Max Weber. *Mexican Statuette*, 1910. Gouache on cardboard, 73.7 × 61 cm (29 × 24"). Forum Gallery, New York

The mystical ideas presented in the German almanac, along with the primitive art at the Trocadero Museum, encouraged Hartley to reject the French masters whose formal approach he had been emulating. It was as if his imitation of Picasso, Matisse, and Cézanne had been a brief fling that, upon renewed contact with a mystically oriented group, he abandoned in favor of the spiritual approach which had always been his own. By October, he could write to Stieglitz that he was experiencing "a recurrence of former religious aspirations" which were taking "a fine form in personal expression."[61]

This period in Hartley's development is marked by what at first glance appears to be a paradox: he continued to employ the structural vocabulary of Analytic Cubism which he had begun to use earlier in the summer (fig. 21), but he regarded his paintings as spiritual expressions. He dismissed the theoretical intellectualism of Picasso's Cubist abstractions, while simultaneously using Cubism's angular, faceted forms. He did this without apparent contradiction because he attributed to Picasso's work an intuitive revelation of the inner essence of objects. "I like Picasso," Hartley wrote, "because he remains true to the intuitive processes which are the most creative naturally — I know now that what I see in his work is a pure rendering of thought forms."[62] In describing his evolution, Hartley makes it clear that he was led into abstraction by way of Picasso; indeed, from the late fall of 1912 on, Hartley's letters speak not of the influence of *Der Blaue Reiter* or of primitive art, but of Picasso. He told Stieglitz that Picasso "is still the only force of the moment,"[63] and that his new, mystically inspired work had been generated by examining "an issue out of Picasso."[64]

Fig. 23 *Indian Pottery, Paris*, 1912. Oil on canvas, 50.2 × 50.2 cm (19¾ × 19¾"). La Jolla Museum of Contemporary Art, La Jolla, California; gift of Mr. and Mrs. Hudson D. Walker in memory of Izetta Dwinnell

Arthur B. Davies and Walt Kuhn were among the first to see Hartley's new work, when they visited him in November 1912 to select paintings for the forthcoming Armory Show. However, they chose for the show two Cézanne/Matisse-style paintings from the summer. "I would not have chosen them myself," Hartley wrote of the still lifes, "chiefly because I am so interested at this time in the directly abstract thing but Davies says no American has done this kind of thing — and they would serve me and the exhibition best at this time. I am to send six drawings and these will be the abstract thing of the present."[65] These six drawings, known only through the thumbnail sketches which Carl Zigrosser made at the time of the Armory Show,[66] represent Hartley's first exploration of his new idiom. They illustrate his assimilation of the angular drawing and fragmented contours of Analytic Cubism. Although in the furor that surrounded the European entries to the Armory Show little attention seems to have been paid to Hartley's drawings, they presented him as one of the earliest American abstractionists.

By the middle of November, Hartley had finished six paintings which he referred to variously as Intuitive Abstractions, Cosmic Cubism, and Subliminal Cubism.[67] Using the flat, interlocking planes and rectilinear outlines of Analytic Cubism (fig. 24) as his basic structure, Hartley applied thin washes of pale color to his canvases to give them an inspirational, transcendent effect (fig. 25). In addition to the influence of Picasso, Hartley credited the diaphanous quality of Cézanne's watercolors with revealing to him a method for achieving "a pure spiritual rendering of forms in space."[68] He wrote to Stieglitz about his new paintings: "I am rapidly gaining ground in this variety of expression and find it to be closest to my own temperament and ideals. It is not like anything here — It is not like Picasso — it is not like Kandinsky not like any 'Cubism' — It is what I call for want of a better name subliminal or cosmic cubism. . . . I did these things before I went to London [in November 1912] as a result of spiritual illuminations and I am convinced that it is my true and real utterance — It combines a varied sense of form with my own sense of color which I believe has never needed stimulation — I am convinced of the Bergson argument in philosophy, that the intuition is the only vehicle for art expression and it is on this basis that I am proceeding — My first impulses came from the mere suggestion in Kandinsky's book *The Spiritual in Art*. Naturally I cannot tell what his theories are completely but the mere title opened up the sensation for me — + — from this I proceeded — In Kandinsky's own work I do not find the same convincing beauty as his theories hold — He seems to be a fine theorist first and a good painter after. . . ."[69]

In this letter, Hartley not only clarifies the extent of Kandinsky's influence upon his increasingly mystical outlook, but also suggests another important source of inspiration: Henri Bergson. It was Bergson's philosophy that impelled Hartley to eliminate recognizable images from his paintings. Bergson's theory of intuition stated that not analytic thinking, but intuition alone was capable of perceiving the fundamental core of life. Bergson's views had been widely disseminated among the artists of the 291 circle. Since these artists equated intuition with abstraction, Bergson's theories had a liberating effect on those attempting to break away from representational painting. Hartley referred frequently to Bergson in his letters to Stieglitz, and excerpts from Bergson's essays were printed in *Camera Work* in October 1911 and January 1912.

In addition to Bergson, the Christian mystical literature then in vogue in Europe, which Hartley read voraciously, also stimulated him. He later reported to Stieglitz that it was "out of the heat of the reading" that he had started to work.[70] Hartley identified these influences as being "without geography — It is a universal essence — I came to it by way of James' pragmatism — slight touches of Bergson — and directly through the fragments of mysticism that I have found out of Boehme — Eckhardt, Tauler — Suso — + Ruysbroeck + the Bhagavad Gita. . . ."[71]

Hartley attempted to inject into his paintings an analogous mystical quality by lightly coloring his canvases with dematerialized washes inspired by Cézanne, and by inserting into his basically Cubist structure a calligraphic network of lines and floating eight-pointed stars, as well as various Christian and Oriental mystical symbols such as a Buddha in a lotus position, crosses, and three upraised hands crowned by an arch (fig. 27). Hartley wanted the paintings to be immediate expressions of his inner state. He later wrote that in making these works he had

Fig. 24 Pablo Picasso. *The Poet*, 1911. Oil on canvas, 130 × 89 cm (51½ × 35¼"). Peggy Guggenheim Museum, Venice

Fig. 25 *Musical Theme No. 2 (Bach Preludes et Fugues)*, 1912. Oil on canvas mounted on masonite, 60.9 × 50.8 cm (24 × 20"). Private collection; courtesy Andrew Crispo Gallery, New York

proceeded "more or less in the style of automatic writing" and had let his hand be guided by his unconscious.[72] His intent was to suggest spiritual, cosmic attitudes rather than to convey specific meanings. He "had no intention or hope of being profound"; it upset him when an American journalist and his occultist wife visited him and said, "You have no idea what you are doing—these pictures are full of Kabbalistic signs and symbols. . . ."[73]

In attempting to replace all references to the external world with a purely spiritual content, Hartley embraced the idea of painting visual equivalents to musical experiences. In the fall of 1912, he began incorporating such references into his paintings, many of which include musical notes; *Musical Theme No. 2 (Bach: Preludes et Fugues)*, one of the first, even adds the parenthetical words of the title to the bottom of the composition (fig. 25). Hartley implied in a letter to his niece that his attempts to use color to paint music were unique.[74] In fact, the relationship between music and painting was a common concern of the period. In the years before Hartley went to Paris, the comparison between the two disciplines was central to the American critics and writers who were coming to terms with abstract art. Writing for *Camera Work*, Charles Caffin and Sadakichi Hartmann proposed an art based on the arrangement of visual elements in accordance with musical principles. As early as 1904, Hartley had encountered Whistler's theories of the synaesthetic correspondence between music and art. The concept of "analogies" had played a key role among literary and visual Symbolists, particularly Maurice Maeterlinck, a great favorite of Hartley's. The first non-photographic artist to exhibit at 291, Pamela Coleman Smith, explored the mystical realationships between painting and music, and Hartley was aware that Gauguin and Odilon Redon had claimed a similar affinity in their work, as had František Kupka and Robert Delaunay. All of this was reinforced by Kandinsky's vehement espousal of musical analogy in *On the Spiritual in Art*.

As the series progressed through the beginning of January 1913, the paintings became brighter and more lyrical. Hartley continued to use a basically Cubist format of darkly outlined forms within a densely packed, shallow space, but his incorporation of circular, calligraphic images and effervescent colors differentiated his work from traditional Cubist compositions. Hartley was eclectic at this time, absorbing and recombining other artists' styles. The structural vocabulary of Picasso's Analytic Cubism and the dematerialized washes of Cézanne's watercolors were his points of departure. To these Hartley added Kandinsky's lyrical forms and bright palette—despite his claim that Kandinsky was a better theorist than painter. Moreover, Hartley's goal of depicting interior, metaphysical states, which had been stimulated by ideas in *Der Blaue Reiter*, had been reinforced by the symbolist art of Redon.[75] Hartley valued Redon's use of psychologically charged dream images, and approvingly quoted to Stieglitz Redon's statement, "I have made an art after myself."[76] The thin oil washes Redon used in his late paintings served as additional models for Hartley's evanescent paint quality.

Hartley left for a three-week trip to Berlin on January 13, 1913. The city immediately enchanted him. He was overwhelmed by its speed, brilliance, and cleanliness, and vowed to return there eventually to live. On the way back to Paris he stopped in Munich, where he discovered that his artistic reputation had preceded him, apparently by way of a German woman who had recently visited 291. The highpoint of his visit was a one-hour meeting on January 24 with Kandinsky and Gabriele Münter at Kandinsky's home. With Rönnebeck and Münter serving as translators, Hartley described his new paintings. Kandinsky seemed interested and suggested exchanging photographs of their work.[77] Hartley was awed by the older artist: "I have never been in the presence of an artist like

Fig. 26   *Painting No. 6*, 1912–13. Oil on canvas, 111 × 81.3 cm (39¾ × 32"). Weyhe Gallery, New York

Fig. 27   *Musical Theme (Oriental Symphony)*, 1912–13 (see Plate 73)

him—so free of convention with a hatred of all the traditions that cling to art—bohemianism—uncleanness—lack of mental order—this chaos which makes Paris so charming to those who love looseness—For myself I am weary of it—."[78]

Personal contact with Germany and with the art community there strengthened Hartley's confidence in himself as an artist and in the importance of mystical content in his paintings. He identified with the mysticism of the German movement and felt that in Munich he had "found his place in the art circles of Europe."[79] But Hartley did not want to appear derivative, and he took care to emphasize that he had independently evolved his own style of mystical expression before traveling to Germany. He carefully differentiated his mysticism as singularly American and as representing a return to his earlier work. "So far as I can learn no one has presented just this aspect [Hartley's mysticism] in modern tendency—Kandinsky is theosophic—Marc is extremely psychic in his rendering of the soul life of animals—It is this which constitutes the most modern tendency without knowing until I had been to Munich—I find myself directly associated. . . . The new German tendency is a force to be reckoned with—to my own taste far more earnest and effective than the French intellectual movements. . . . I could never be French. I could never become German—I shall always remain the American—the essence which is in me is American mysticism just as Davies declared it when he saw those first [1908-9] landscapes. . . . [They] were so expressive of my nature—and it is the same element that I am returning to now with a tremendous increase of power through experience."[80]

After his return to Paris, Hartley arranged to send three or four of his Intuitive Abstractions to the Galerie Goltz in Munich in hopes of obtaining an exhibition there. He wrote self-confidently to Stieglitz that he knew he would hear from the artists in Munich as soon as his pictures arrived: "Kandinsky especially as I know that what I have to express coincides perfectly with his notion of das Geistige in der Kunst."[81] Kandinsky represented for Hartley—as had Ryder in 1909—an established figure who reinforced ideas he had already developed. Indeed, the new group of paintings Hartley started in late January 1913, are more strongly influenced by Kandinsky than those executed earlier. *Painting No. 1* (fig. 28), with its organic shapes and emotional lyricism, directly recalls Kandinsky's compositions (fig. 29). Of the approximately twenty paintings in his Intuitive Abstraction series, however, most were executed in 1912, prior to his meeting with Kandinsky, and do not show such direct influence. Hartley reported having completed nearly fifteen canvases by February 1, but since he had not returned to Paris until the last week in January, it is probable that most of these were completed before his trip to Berlin.

Hartley's growing sense of artistic importance was reinforced by the acknowledgment his work began receiving. From Paris, he wrote to Kandinsky and Münter, and his letters show that he fully expected their assistance in his endeavor to procure an exhibition in Germany. He had also written to Franz Marc, whose exhibition he had seen at the Thannhauser Galleries in Munich. Marc eventually invited Hartley to exhibit with the Blaue Reiter artists at the forthcoming Herbstsalon, apparently because he liked the way Hartley wrote.[82] In Paris, Gertrude Stein provided equally strong support. His visits to the Stein salon had grown more frequent in late 1912 or early 1913, and it had begun to function for him as a counterpart to Stieglitz's 291 circle.[83] Stein visited Hartley's studio twice during March 1913 and requested that four paintings, among which was *Painting No. 1*, be sent to her home, where they hung alongside works by Cézanne, Picasso, Matisse, and Renoir. Stein was outspoken in praise of the strength and uniqueness in Hartley's work; at Hartley's request she wrote to Stieglitz about him. She

Fig. 28 *Painting No. 1*, 1913 (see Plate 74)

Fig. 29 Wassily Kandinsky. *Study for Painting with White Border, Variant No. 1*, 1913. Watercolor, ink, and pencil on paper, 30.3 × 24.1 cm (11-15/16 × 9½"). Städtische Galerie im Lenbachhaus, Munich

pronounced Hartley the only artist using pure color to create pictures and stated that his paintings achieved what was only a direction in Kandinsky's work.[84]

Thus, after less than a year's exposure to the European art world, Hartley had begun to make a significant place for himself. His work not only exhibited the most avant-garde styles of painting and aesthetic theory, but it was at the same time both independent and personal. Hartley's unique amalgamation of Cubist structure, bright color, and mystical references created an original statement. When Simonson's return to Paris in April 1913 forced Hartley out of the sublet atelier, he packed his things for Berlin, confident of his reception by the German art world.

First Berlin Period: May–November 1913

En route to Germany, Hartley stayed with Franz Marc in Sindelsdorf for a few days before going on to Munich, where he wrote to Stieglitz that he had made arrangements to show his paintings in June at the Galerie Goltz. Soon after Hartley's arrival in the city, Marc, Kandinsky, Münter, and the American artist Albert Bloch visited the Galerie Goltz to see the paintings he had sent from Paris. Apart from four works, which Stein had retained, this group probably represented the majority of Hartley's Intuitive Abstraction series. To have the major artists of the German art movement gathering to examine one's paintings was an honor, but Hartley's self-esteem had grown to the point where he not only took this for granted, but fully expected their enthusiastic response. When Kandinsky offered criticism instead of praise, Hartley reacted with reservations about Kandinsky's work, suggesting, as he had earlier, that the older artist was a theoretician rather than a creator.[85] In contrast, he posited himself as the true artist, along with Picasso and Cézanne, with faith in intuitive rather than intellectual solutions and an inability to explain his work. The Germans did not entirely share this view, but they encouraged Hartley, saying that they admired the "sense of truth" and "intensity of personality" in his paintings.[86] Marc later wrote to Hartley, praising the sincerity in Hartley's work but noting that with more experience he would be able to do more with color and form.[87]

Hartley arrived in Berlin on May 17. As on his previous visit, the strength and power of the Imperial German culture immediately enthralled him. For Hartley, whose childhood and youth had been so uncertain and frightening, Berlin gave him a brief but intense period of security and happiness. He was deeply impressed by Berlin's orderliness and intensity, which he perceived as the pervading influence of the military. With its daily parades of foot soldiers and horsemen, all outfitted in elegant costumes and bristling with barely contained force, Berlin was an ideal environment — all his life Hartley was attracted to the feeling of anonymity which pageantry and crowds provided.[88] He wrote to Rönnebeck over twenty years later that no one understood better than the Germans that in cities one could go out and "be common" without attracting attention.[89]

That Berlin was also a distinctly male-oriented city was equally appealing. The presence of the military coupled with a large homosexual subculture created a brazenly decadent atmosphere. As Hartley said of himself, he "lived rather gayly in the Berlin fashion — with all that implies. . . ."[90] His friendship with Rönnebeck and Lieutenant von Freyburg, which he described as a "beautiful triangle," entered a romantic and idyllic phase. Von Freyburg had left Paris for Germany in July 1912 and Hartley had not spent much time with him until Berlin. At thirty-six, Hartley was deeply attracted to the handsome, twenty-four-year-old von Freyburg, later calling him "the one idol of my imaginative life."[91]

Despite, or perhaps because of, his excitement with Berlin, Hartley did not paint for the first nine weeks after his arrival. In late June, he wrote a despondent letter to Stieglitz in which he intimated that his relationship with von Freyburg was not progressing as he wished. Confiding personal doubts was out of character for him at this stage of his life, however, and he apologized several days later in a more characteristically ebullient tone. By the middle of July he managed to resume work, although he was not as prolific in this first Berlin period as his enthusiastic progress reports to Stieglitz would suggest.

The paintings stimulated by the Berlin environment differ in both form and content from his Intuitive Abstractions, for they are infused with the spirit of Hartley's Germany. His intention was "to express a fresh consciousness of what I see and feel around me — taken directly out of life and from no theories and formulas as prevails so much today."[92] He perceived German life as "essentially mural . . . big lines and large masses — always a sense of the pageantry of living."[93] In attempting to invest his paintings with this same force and sense of power, he solidified the floating, linear arabesques of his Intuitive Abstractions into massive, densely packed forms delineated by heavy outlines.

Fig. 30   *The Warriors*, 1913 (see Plate 12)

Hartley's desire to paint "vivid sensations of finite and tangible things,"[94] was manifested by a return to images based on observed reality. Although these were often combined with abstract shapes, their primary stimulus — unlike that of the Intuitive Abstractions — was external. The eight-pointed star, which had appeared in his Paris compositions, but occurred even more frequently in works of this period, derived from an actual, perceivable element in the environment. "I am seeing eight-pointed stars here by the thousands —," Hartley wrote to Stieglitz. "A symbolist friend says it is a fine star for me — on the Kaiser's breast it is always — on the helmets of the thousands of soldiers — on the pavements on the table cloths. . . ."[95] Similarly, *The Warriors* and *Portrait of Berlin* were inspired by the military review that Hartley witnessed on May 27, 1913, and described in his autobiography (figs. 30 and 31). These works were among the first in the Berlin series, judging from their diaphanous washes of paint and centralized focus, two properties Hartley gradually abandoned as the series progressed.

The subject matter of these pictures is marked by military imagery derived from direct observation, and by an increasingly mystic symbolism. It thus differed from his Paris work, since it no longer relied on the expression of internal, spiritual states. Some of the symbols Hartley introduced, such as the eight-pointed star, were drawn from what he saw around him, but more often the mystical imagery was based on the symbolic associations of numbers, colors, and shapes.[96] As with his Intuitive Abstractions, Hartley never attached precise symbolic meanings to forms, so that these Berlin pictures remain personal and intuitive. This approach permeated *Painting No. 48, Berlin* (fig. 32), a work he described to Stieglitz as a large, mystical presentation of the number eight.[97] Although Hartley noted that he saw the number eight everywhere in Berlin and disavowed any specific occult content, he insisted on its mystical implications. "There is a real reason for all these signs but it remains mystical — + explanations are not necessary."[98] For numerologists, however, the number eight signifies cosmic transcendence over the material realm and into the spiritual one; it represents the "resurrection into higher consciousness and a new manner of living."[99] The inclusion of the number eight in Hartley's later German officer portraits commemorating the death of a friend indicates that, on some level, he was aware of its associations.

Fig. 31   *Portrait of Berlin*, 1913 (see Plate 13)

Hartley's investigation of the mysticism of colors was more superficial. He acknowledged their symbolic properties but never held a consistent attitude about them, and refrained from theoretical formulations, perhaps to avoid comparison with Kandinsky's elaborate color and image theories.[100]

As the Berlin series evolved, Hartley began to work more abstractly (pl. 15). He gradually replaced linear structure and diaphanous washes with juxtaposed areas of modulated, monochromatic color, an approach which may have been stimulated by collage techniques and by Synthetic Cubism, then in its infancy in Paris. *Movements* (fig. 33), probably one of the last paintings in the series, is a completely abstract work whose flat patterning prophesies Hartley's subsequent paintings. Although the coarse brushwork, hot palette and dynamism of these works link them with the expressive idiom of the Blaue Reiter artists, Hartley's entire Berlin group represents an accomplished and genuinely personal artistic statement. By combining the pictorial energy of the Blaue Reiter Expressionists with the tightly knit, collage format of the Cubists, he achieved a remarkable synthesis of the expressive with the structured.

These paintings made a considerable impression in Berlin art circles. Hartley was invited to exhibit in the prestigious Herbstsalon of 1913, the last great art exhibition held in Germany before the war. Organized by Herwath Walden, this group show included the most progressive and esteemed artists of the time. Such was the Germans' respect for Hartley that the selection committee hung five of his paintings in the same room with works by Kandinsky and Henri Rousseau.

Despite critical success, Bernhard Koehler, the Blaue Reiter's principal patron, did not purchase any of Hartley's work, and his financial situation grew desperate. In late June he had asked Stieglitz to send him the funds remaining from those accumulated for his trip abroad; by October he had not received a check and was destitute. Once again he found himself struggling to survive and maintain his spirits.[101] Hartley was forced to write to Gertrude Stein, asking for the one hundred francs she had offered to pay for a drawing he had given her.[102] He also cabled Stieglitz for emergency funds to pay his back rent and to repay his loans from Rönnebeck's father.

Hartley managed to continue to paint without seeking employment. On October 18 Stein sent him two hundred francs — double the amount he had asked for. Stieglitz, however, responded with irritation, for he was growing impatient with Hartley, wanting him to return to the United States with his new paintings to exhibit and sell them at 291. On October 20 Hartley finally received a check from Stieglitz along with a severe reprimand: "Your European trip was made possible through American cash, cash which was forthcoming because a few people felt you were entitled to a chance. Now I personally don't see any reason why an American should be called upon to give you additional cash without seeing what you have done. . . . But people who give money without seeing are very rare. . . . I am not opening the little gallery until I know definitely whether you are coming or not. Everything is held in abeyance for you. You are to have the first chance. A certain responsibility toward the others rests on your shoulders."[103] Two days later Hartley acknowledged the receipt of Stieglitz's check and informed him of his intention to sail for New York in November. Moreover, perhaps trying to mollify Stieglitz, he recounted the following accolade from Gertrude Stein: "I have already told you that Gertrude Stein has said to [Rönnebeck] that she considers me the most important man of the moment in art — this in itself is good — but there is more. . . . she thinks I have gone miles beyond them all — Picasso included because I have succeeded in leaving out the physical element and giving for the first time the pure spiritual. . . ."[104]

Hartley left Europe on November 15 on the S.S. *George Washington*, bringing with him his Intuitive Abstractions and his Berlin paintings. He had considered withdrawing the five paintings scheduled to tour with the Herbstsalon exhibition, but decided against it. He did, however, arrange with Stein to ship the four she

Fig. 32 *Painting No. 48, Berlin,* 1913 (see Plate 14)

Fig. 33 *Movements,* 1913 (see Plate 75)

held in Paris, making a total of at least seventeen large pictures for his 291 exhibition. Perhaps feeling uneasy about the relatively small number of Berlin paintings, he suggested that Stieglitz include in the exhibition the Bavarian glass paintings Hartley had purchased in Munich.[105]

Although Hartley had acknowledged the necessity of returning to New York in order to ensure the financial success he so desperately needed, he felt homeless in America and considered it a deadly place.[106] In an effort to retain a vestige of European memories, he gravitated to the cosmopolitan circle surrounding Mabel Dodge, whom he had met at Gertrude Stein's in Paris. After years of living in Europe, Dodge had relocated in New York, and by the spring of 1913 had established a salon that rivaled 291. Enthusiastic and intuitive, she was sympathetic to naive mysticism and spiritual inclinations, and well known for her unique ability to attract and stimulate fascinating people in lively evenings which brought together figures from the world of arts, criticism, literature, and social reform. Although the 291 circle was equally illustrious, Dodge, unlike Stieglitz, did not always take center stage. Hartley found he preferred associating with the Dodge group. In addition to the radical writer John Reed, who lived with Dodge, her frequent guests included the writers Carl Van Vechten, Lincoln Steffens, Hutchins Hapgood, and Max Eastman (editor of the radical journal *The Masses*), and the artists Jo Davidson, Andrew Dasburg, and Maurice Sterne. The fact that Hartley was just as comfortable with Dodge's left-leaning group as he had been with Berlin's strict military society reveals his total disregard of politics as a factor in his social life.

The exhibition of Hartley's Paris and Berlin work opened at 291 on January 12, 1914. The accompanying brochure included forewords by Mabel Dodge, three of Hartley's speeches from Gertrude Stein's play, *IIIIIIIII,* in which Hartley appeared as the character *M_____N H_____,* and a statement by Hartley. All were reprinted in the January 1914 issue of *Camera Work*. Hartley's essay stressed the inadequacy of verbal explanations of art. He denied any dependence on existing styles, claiming that his art represented a personal expression of the "inner content in all things." Apart from minimizing the influence of his stylistic sources, this statement is a fair approximation of his goals as a painter. The exhibition was well received critically and generated enough income to cover Hartley's expenses for another year abroad. "The artists are elated and enthusiastic and the people say queer and interesting things — It all seems to start up new phases of emotion in people."[107] Despite the economic and emotional support he had received, Hartley was glad to leave for Europe in March. Although he could not know it, his departure marked the end of a brief period of financial and emotional well-being.

Plate 9   *Still Life No. 1*, 1912 (cat. no. 13)
Columbus Museum of Art; gift of Ferdinand Howald

Plate 10   *Musical Theme No. 1 (Bach Preludes)*, 1912 (cat. no. 11)
Mr. and Mrs. Paul C. Schorr, III, Lincoln, Nebraska

Plate 11 *Abstraction with Flowers*, 1913 (cat. no. 15)
University Gallery, University of Minnesota, Minneapolis;
bequest of Hudson Walker from the Ione and Hudson Walker Collection

Plate 12 *The Warriors*, 1913 (cat. no. 21)
Max Zurier, Palm Springs, California

Plate 13   *Portrait of Berlin*, 1913 (cat. no. 20)
Collection of American Literature, Beinecke Rare Book and Manuscript Library,
Yale University, New Haven; gift of Mable Dodge Luhan

Plate 14 *Painting No. 48, Berlin*, 1913 (cat. no. 19)
The Brooklyn Museum; The Dick S. Ramsay Fund

Plate 15   *Military*, 1913 (cat. no. 16)
Wadsworth Atheneum, Hartford, Connecticut;
The Ella Gallup Sumner and Mary Catlin Sumner Collection

Fig. 34   Robert Delaunay. *Homage to Blériot,* 1914. Oil on canvas, 251 × 251.7 cm (98⅝ × 99″). Kunstmuseum, Basel

Fig. 35   *Pre-War Pageant,* 1914. Oil on canvas, 100.2 × 81 cm (39½ × 31⅛″). Columbus Museum of Art, Ohio; gift of Ferdinand How-ald

Second Berlin Period:
March 1914–December 1915

Hartley stopped in London on his way back to Germany in order to see the retrospective exhibition of William Blake, whose paintings and writings he ad-mired, but his plan was thwarted when the exhibition was moved to Manchester. He then went briefly to Paris. He visited the Salon des Indépendants, noting his preference for Delaunay's work over that of the American Synchromist Morgan Russell.[108] By April 30, he was back in Berlin, waiting for the shipment of his paintings from New York. His spirits and finances seemed stable. Stieglitz had arranged in March for the dealer Charles Daniel to buy several paintings. The total price of six hundred dollars Daniel was to amortize in seventy-five-dollar-a-month installments after the money generated from Hartley's exhibition sales was exhausted.[109] Two weeks after his return to Berlin, Hartley was at work, noting that it seemed "good and quite novel to be actually wielding pigment."[110]

The paintings Hartley executed in this period break stylistically with those of his first Berlin group. Brightly colored and emblematic, they are characterized by radiating disk forms stimulated by Delaunay's *Homage to Blériot,* which Hartley had seen at the Indépendants exhibition (fig. 34). In these paintings, Hartley eschews the loose modulated brushwork of his first German series for flat areas of intense color, contained within discrete boundaries and laid against solid tonal fields (fig. 35). These features became the distinguishing characteristics of his second German series.

Hartley's initial ebullience at being back in Europe lessened as the prospect of war increased. By the end of July his letters alluded to the psychic pressure building up in Germany as Russian troops mobilized on the border. When the Emperor and Empress returned to Berlin at the end of July after failing to prevent Austria's declaration of war on Serbia, thousands of Germans gathered in the streets and at the castle. Tension throughout the city became intolerable. Combat, Hartley conceded, "is now not a romantic but a real reality."[111] On August 1 and 3, Germany declared war on Russia and France, respectively.

Hartley had by then completed four pictures on the theme of "Amerika." These paintings were visually derived from American Indian culture, which was highly popular in Europe. Indian road shows had toured the continent as late as 1914 and large collections of American Indian art had been assembled by Berlin's Ethno-graphical Museum and by the Trocadero Museum in Paris. European artists as diverse as August Macke and Giorgio de Chirico had used Indian motifs in their compositions; Hartley himself had depicted Indian artifacts in several of his 1912 still lifes (fig. 23). While in the United States, he had observed the interest surrounding the American Indian collection at New York's Museum of Natural History. The experience further stimulated him to adopt American Indian subject matter, perhaps seeing in it a means of emphasizing his American background. As with the literary expatriates of the twenties who wrote in colloquial prose about American themes, this paradox of Hartley's wanting to be in Europe, yet wanting to retain his American identity endured throughout his career. With the prospect of war in Europe, Hartley may also have turned to Indian themes as an antidote to the impending catastrophe: by painting symbols of what he perceived as a gentle race, he could affirm the idea of human nobility. Several months after the war broke out, he wrote to Stieglitz that he wanted to be an Indian, that the true expression of human dignity would be to paint his face with the symbols of the race he adored, go to the West, and face the sun forever.[112]

The paintings these sentiments inspired were, in stylistic terms, logical exten-

Fig. 36   *American Indian Symbols,* 1914. Oil on canvas, 94 × 94 cm (37 × 37″). John J. Brady, Jr., Des Moines, Iowa

Fig. 37 *Painting No. 2 (Arrangement, Hiero-glyphics)*, 1914. Oil on canvas with painted frame, 108 × 88.3 cm (42½ × 34¾") overall. William H. Lane Foundation, Leominster, Massachusetts

Fig. 38 *Berlin Ante-War*, 1914 (see Plate 17)

Fig. 39 *Bavarian Votive Painting*, 1763. Reproduced in *Der Blaue Reiter* (Munich 1912); reprinted, *The Blaue Reiter Almanac*, The Documents of 20th-Century Art (New York: Viking Press, 1974)

sions of his previous work (fig. 36). He continued the practice evolved earlier that spring of juxtaposing discrete, uniform color areas whose boundaries were delineated with pencil. However, by replacing solid tonal areas with patterns, equally distributed around the canvas, Hartley achieved a more overall, decorative effect. Recognizable objects such as horses, bows, teepees, and Indians in headdresses were treated as patterns which he combined with the abstract, sweeping curves, zig-zag lines, and inverted v's of *Movements* (fig. 33), a painting of his first German period. In the Amerika series, areas of the canvas were left raw, for Hartley executed the paintings rapidly, as if his work pace were an analogue to the frenzy preceding the outbreak of war.

After war was declared, Hartley's focus shifted from American Indian themes to symbolic still lifes depicting unicorns, mounted horsemen and idyllic landscape scenes (fig. 38). In structure, these still lifes evolved from the American Indian paintings, as is apparent by comparing *Painting No. 2 (Arrangement, Hiero-glyphics)* with *Berlin Ante-War* (figs. 37 and 38). Unlike his Amerika series, the figurations in these new paintings do not function solely as patterns, but rather retain their identity as independent objects. Hartley reserves abstract decoration for the painted frames, a distinguishing characteristic of this group of paintings. Although the red, yellow, and blue color scheme is, as before, applied thinly in flat, bounded areas, these paintings are structured more as symmetrical tableaux than as collages of decorative elements. The resultant stasis of representational images visually relates the paintings to folk art and to the Bavarian glass paintings championed by the German artists, of which Hartley owned several examples.

Although these still lifes function symbolically, for the most part, the symbolism remains relatively personal and impenetrable. All that can be clearly read is the general mood of transcendence and idyllic serenity. *Berlin Ante-War,* for instance, utilizes the symbolism of the enveloping cloud motif from the Bavarian votive paintings Hartley had seen in *Der Blaue Reiter* (fig. 39). In the votive paintings this motif signified a heavenly spirit. In Hartley's painting, the spiritual, deified object is a Prussian horseman, possibly von Freyburg. Above him, clouds envelop a heraldic image of a kneeling white horse with a figure eight on its flanks, the symbol of cosmic transcendence. Cross-inscribed roundels are scattered throughout the upper portion of the paintings, further suggesting a religious-transcendental reading. The tiers of landscape elements in the lower part of the painting suggest rural peacefulness.

The onset of war was accompanied by personal tragedy for Hartley. In late September, he learned that his father had died on August 4. This, however, seems to have affected him less profoundly than the death of his cherished friend von Freyburg, who was killed in action on October 7. Hartley was stunned by his friend's passing and was unable to paint for almost a month.[113] Obsessed by masculine beauty throughout his life, the young officer had come to represent, in Hartley's mind, the classical embodiment of handsome youth. In his death, von Freyburg's image became an icon for Hartley.[114] Hartley considered their relationship a spiritual marriage, worthy of worship.[115] Whether his love for his friend was ever consummated, however, remains a question. Von Freyburg, in his letters, had been polite and reserved, using the formal pronoun and addressing the artist as "Mr. Hartley." In Hartley's "Letters Never Sent," written much later, he "wrote" to von Freyburg about a dream which he viewed as a consummation of their "intended relation."[116] In the dream a snake, coiling and writhing at Hartley's feet, was suddenly struck by lightning. Hartley described being able to "still see its mouth spraying open in agony—showing its flame illuminated fangs—can still hear the sizzling of its flesh in the conflagration of its coils." A white light rose from the coils and enveloped Hartley, and he saw von Freyburg's face before him.

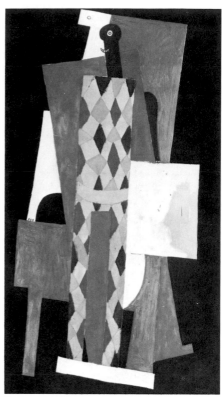

Fig. 40 Pablo Picasso. *Harlequin*, 1915. Oil on canvas, 182.9 × 105.1 cm (72¼ × 41⅜″). The Museum of Modern Art, New York; acquired through the Lillie P. Bliss Bequest

Fig. 41 *Portrait of a German Officer*, 1914 (see Plate 82)

Added to Hartley's despair over von Freyburg's death was the everpresent threat of financial destitution. The increasingly erratic mails delayed Stieglitz's letters and remittances for weeks; Hartley was forced to write to Mabel Dodge and Lee Simonson, begging them for the sums they still owed on paintings purchased from his 291 exhibition. Alone and scarcely able to buy materials, Hartley struggled to paint in the midst of a growing holocaust. By early November, he had found a beginning. After that the new work came quickly. These German military paintings, or War Motifs as Hartley called them, reflect his simultaneous repulsion and fascination with the war. Haunted by the tragedy of von Freyburg's death, he was nevertheless magnetized by the pageantry and energy of war. Out of this duality emerged a series of paintings based on German military emblems in which Hartley's power as an expressionist and his fully developed skills as a painter joined with a profound commitment to a personal vision. The War Motif series is a group of unique, intensely powerful canvases whose achievement equals that of the key artists of the European avant-garde. Hartley was swept up in the frenzy of their emotional strength. He wrote to Stieglitz that he was now "expressing myself truly — I have perfected what I believe to be pure vision and that is sufficient. Then too I am on the verge of real insight into the imaginative life. . . . I am no longer that terror stricken thing with a surfeit of imaginative experience undigested. . . . I am well on the verge of understanding which is beyond knowledge." [117]

Despite their expressive breakthrough, the style of these War Motif paintings owed much to the body of work which preceded them. Especially in the early stages, as Hartley experimented with various approaches before finally adopting what became his new style, he drew on images and structural arrangements he had used previously. Elements such as the left-sweeping wavy lines, and shields enclosing crosses, which would characterize the War Motif series, were culled from his American Indian paintings (fig. 36); similarly, works such as *Himmel* (pl. 19) and *Abstraction (Military Symbols)* (pl. 20) display structural and imagistic characteristics of earlier paintings. Hartley quickly arrived at a technique derived from Cubist collage, juxtaposing visual fragments of the German military environment in a tightly knit, hieratic format. He painted arrangements of badges, German imperial flags, and military emblems like the Iron Cross and regimental insignia (fig. 41). Flattened out and locked together, these various images form an overall design of overlapping and interlocking planes similar to Picasso's Synthetic Cubist compositions. The stripes and designs of flags evolve into abstract motifs of lines and patterns, and helmet cockades appear as concentric circles and repeated arcs. With these paintings, Hartley became the first American artist to wholeheartedly and consistently adopt the vocabulary of Synthetic Cubism, a style which differed from Analytic Cubism in its reliance on combinations of flat, colored geometric shapes (as in Picasso's *Harlequin*, fig. 40), rather than on the prismatic fragmentation of three-dimensional forms. Yet the looser forms, coarse brushwork, and dramatic color of Hartley's military paintings create a visual excitement and intensity that affiliates them with the Expressionist tradition.

Moreover, Hartley's German military series was unique in introducing symbolism into a Synthetic Cubist structure. He began the series with a group of symbolic paintings which refer specifically to a German officer. *Painting No. 49, Berlin* (pl. 81) was probably one of the first. Its silver ground and predominant yellow and red colors link it to his prior series, the symbolic still lifes. In subsequent officer paintings, Hartley set a color scheme of red, yellow, blue and green against a black background, creating a more somber tone of death and war. Against the decorative military patterns he placed the white, feathered helmet of the Kaiser's Royal Guards, the spurs and tassels of the Guards' dress uniform, and

Fig. 42 *Painting No. 5*, 1914–15 (see cover)

Fig. 43 *Military*, 1915. Oil on canvas, 60.6 × 50.2 cm (28⅞ × 19¾"). Professor and Mrs. Nelson Goodman

the Iron Cross. Certain elements of these German officer paintings referred specifically to von Freyburg (fig. 41): 24 was his age when he died; K.v.F., his initials; and 4, his regiment number. Hartley's inclusion of the number eight, signifying cosmic transcendence, and of the number nine, signifying constant regeneration, further suggests that these paintings were iconic representations of von Freyburg. Rönnebeck, however, claimed that the officer portraits also alluded to him, that the "E" referred to his regimental emblem and the Iron Cross to the one he had received.[118] This suggests that most of these portraits portray not only von Freyburg, but the broader notion of a German officer.

Using symbolic objects to illustrate a subject's psychic and physical characteristics was a radical approach to portraiture, although precedents for it did exist. Marius de Zayas, the Mexican caricaturist associated with 291, created complex diagrams of algebraic formulas and geometric shapes which represented his subject's inner nature and external features. These had been reproduced in the April 1914 issue of *Camera Work*, published in October of that year. Similarly, Gertrude Stein had eschewed literal description in her word-portraits of Matisse and Picasso in favor of symbolic word associations. Hartley was a great admirer of Stein's work and had acknowledged earlier that his search for new forms of expression was reinforced by her writings.[119]

As the series of officer portraits progressed, the elements of portraiture and symbolic iconography were replaced by more purely decorative combinations of abstract patterns. Although still military in mood, the specificity of the earlier officer paintings disappeared. In place of the centralized format and iconic presence evoked earlier, Hartley loosened his images and spread them over the entire picture surface. Whereas the officer portraits had existed in a shallow picture space created by overlapping and interlocking planes, these later paintings became completely flat, with little suggestion of spatial recession. Areas of the canvas—for example, the upper right portion of *Painting No. 5* (fig. 42)— became the models for the totally flat approach which Hartley seems to have begun pursuing toward the end of the series (fig. 43).

Hartley's German military pictures generated an increasingly enthusiastic response in Germany. Four paintings were sold in April 1915, and in September an exhibition of his 1908 drawings was held in Frankfurt. This was followed by a large exhibition in Berlin in October 1915, which included forty-five of the German paintings, some late drawings and, as in Frankfurt, a large number of his 1908 drawings. Though the exhibition generated no sales, major reviews appeared in the newspapers. Despite these successes, Hartley eventually found it impossible to remain in Germany because of the food shortages, and on December 11, 1915, he sailed for New York on the S.S. *Rotterdam*.

Plate 16   *Indian Fantasy*, 1914 (cat. no. 28)
North Carolina Museum of Art; Museum Purchase Fund

46

Plate 17   *Berlin Ante-War*, 1914 (cat. no. 23)
Columbus Museum of Art; gift of Ferdinand Howald

Plate 18   *Forms Abstracted, Berlin*, 1914 (cat. no. 25)
Whitney Museum of American Art, New York;
gift of Mr. and Mrs. Hudson Walker (and exchange), 1952

Plate 19   *Himmel*, 1914 (cat. no. 26)
William Rockhill Nelson Gallery and Atkins Museum of Fine Arts;
Friends of Art Collection

Plate 20 *Abstraction (Military Symbols)*, 1914–15 (cat. no. 33) Washburn Gallery, New York City

Plate 21 *Painting No. 46, Berlin*, 1914–15 (cat. no. 36) Albright-Knox Art Gallery, Buffalo, New York; Philip Kirwen Fund

Plate 22 *Painting No. 47, Berlin, 1914–15* (cat. no. 37)
Hirshhorn Museum and Sculpture Garden, Smithsonian Institution

New York and Provincetown: 1916

Hartley remained in New York throughout the winter and spring of 1916, except for a February trip to Croton-on-Hudson to visit Mabel Dodge and her current paramour, Maurice Sterne, Hartley's former classmate at the National Academy. The entire winter was a difficult one for Hartley. For all the suffering he had witnessed in Berlin, the city had given him the home and security he had always lacked. His forced withdrawal from this congenial atmosphere left him feeling psychologically orphaned; he struggled with a sense of abandonment not unlike that he had experienced at his mother's death. Not only was he separated from his closest friends, but he now found himself in an environment where these very friends were regarded as the enemy. Anti-German sentiment had reached such a feverish pitch that in New York City the music of Beethoven and Mozart was banned from performance. Psychologically depleted, Hartley was unable to re-establish the emotional connection with America that he had had before he went abroad. He was so depressed and withdrawn during his stay with Dodge that he even had pieces of chiffon hung on the walls of her guest house to soften what he considered the "repellent" light. His moods, which had always fluctuated between amiability and introspection, entered a severely neurasthenic period. Dodge finally asked him to leave, writing later that his "solitary and unassimilable" nature made it more painful for her to have him there than to demand that he depart.[120] His odd reply to her reveals his self-image as a perennial outsider, never able to establish lasting connections with his wealthy patrons: "I belong really to a less specialized species, to commoner elements. I must never do more, at most, than walk in as graciously as possible, sit a little, and pass out again for there is always the quality of wonder in being really not quite anywhere at all times. That is my kind of activity I am thinking."[121]

Hartley painted a small number of works in the winter and spring of 1916, but the anti-German atmosphere in New York was hardly conducive to the continuation of his military pictures. Forced to deny his affection for Germany and surrounded by a completely different visual environment, he abandoned the subject matter which he had spent over two years developing and turned to neutral still-life motifs (pl. 23). In a Synthetic Cubist mode, he accentuated the crisply demarcated forms of his German paintings, but he now completely rejected overlapping planes and coarse brushwork in favor of small, controlled maneuverings of the hand and a flat, iconic treatment.[122] The result is a remarkably simplified, frontal effect. In *One Portrait of One Woman* (pl. 23).—often considered a symbolic portrait of Gertrude Stein—the isolation of shapes on the picture surface and the strict symmetry of design accentuate this rigid frontality.

Three of these new paintings were included in "The Forum Exhibition of Modern American Painters" held in March 1916, along with three earlier paintings. The exhibition was organized by Willard Huntington Wright, a discerning critic who contributed a monthly art chronicle to *Forum* magazine, and by a committee of five which included Stieglitz. Their goal was to focus attention on contemporary American artists whose importance had been obscured by the hysteria surrounding the Armory Show's European section. Nineteen artists were represented in the exhibition and sixteen wrote an explanatory note for the catalogue. Hartley's statement admonished viewers not to focus on either subject matter or abstract, formal problems. He proposed instead that the artist's personal signature—the individual style in which an artist expressed himself, the personalized way in which forms and paint were handled—held the key to a picture. Subject matter was unimportant; objects were impersonal incidents which existed only to be observed and rendered through the artist's idiosyncratic

Plate 23 *One Portrait of One Woman*, 1916 (cat. no. 43)
University Gallery, University of Minnesota, Minneapolis;
bequest of Hudson Walker from Ione and Hudson Walker Collection

style of expression.[123] This position thus differed slightly from that presented in his 291 statement of 1914, where he had spoken of his art as a personal, spiritual "inner content in all things."

Apart from the paintings in the Forum exhibition, Hartley's German pictures were not seen in New York until his April 1916 exhibition at 291. Scheduled initially for February, delays in ocean transit caused by the German blockade had forced its postponement. In the accompanying exhibition catalogue, Hartley reiterated the position he took in the Forum exhibition catalogue — his paintings were completely autonomous visual entities. He further insisted that the abstract forms and military emblems he used as subject matter held no symbolic meaning: "The forms are only those which I have observed casually from day to day. There is no hidden symbolism whatsoever in them . . . things under observation, just pictures of any day, any hour. I have expressed only what I have seen. They are merely consultations of the eye . . . my notion of the purely pictural [sic]."[124]

Strictly speaking, the images in Hartley's paintings *were* derived from the visual world, as he himself acknowledged. His firm denial of any personal involvement with his subject matter, however, emanated from his desire to disavow pro-German sentiment. Given the anti-German mood of the country, Hartley had placed Stieglitz in a potentially explosive situation; only a strict denial of all symbolism and German affiliations prevented political repercussions. Even so, reviewers expressed doubts that Hartley's paintings held no hidden symbolism. Henry McBride, art critic for *The Sun,* wrote: "There are triangles which can be readily accepted as soldiers' tents, and there are rhythmic repetitions of horses and constant suggestions of uniforms, of dragons, banners, swords and all the pomp and circumstance of war. . . . But as to the exact episode or emotion that the artist portrays there will be less certainty, although Mr. Hartley says he has expressed only what he saw during his travels in Germany."[125] Charles Caffin, writing in the *New York American,* mentioned two paintings which he felt recorded Hartley's "sensation on hearing of the death of a friend's horse and on reading a friend's description of a dream."[126]

Hartley succeeded remarkably well in escaping the wrath of the press, a surprising development, considering that at his huge show in Germany only a year before, a *New York Times* correspondent had come close to accusing him of immortalizing the Kaiser's Royal Guards and of committing near treason for living in an enemy city.[127] But Hartley did not succeed in gaining critical acclaim for his works. In the end, the German military subject matter did affect the art community's judgment and, given the political atmosphere of New York City, it had been somewhat naive of Hartley to imagine otherwise. The lack of critical enthusiasm crushed his hopes of triumphantly returning to America as a great avant-garde artist. The German military paintings were among the most advanced and brilliant works produced by any American at the time — as Hartley himself knew. The lukewarm response of the American art community was a severe blow, accentuated more painfully for Hartley by the favorable attention and accolades the paintings had received in Europe. The exhibition generated few sales, forcing him, once again, to rely on Stieglitz for financial support.

In the summer of 1916, John Reed, who had recently finished his series of articles on Pancho Villa and the Mexican Civil War, invited Hartley to his rented house in Provincetown. Writers, painters, and actors from New York's Greenwich Village had begun to summer in Provincetown when war made travel to Europe impossible. The group included many of the political reformers and personalities from Mabel Dodge's New York salon: Hutchins Hapgood, Hippolyte Havel, Maurice Sterne, Marguerite and William Zorach, Max Eastman, and Leo Stein. In addition, Hartley mingled with Louise Bryant, the journalist who later married

Fig. 44 *Abstraction,* 1916. Oil on board, 61 × 50.8 cm (24 × 20"). The Solomon R. Guggenheim Museum, New York

Reed, Carl Sprinchorn, an artist who became one of Hartley's closest friends, Charles Demuth, and Eugene O'Neill, then a budding playwright writing his first plays. The mixture of personalities provided a whirl of social activities; Hartley later described it as "the Great Provincetown Summer."[128]

Hartley had a productive summer, but the adverse reaction to his German iconography left him without a subject matter to which he felt committed. Hence the expressive symbolism and mystical content of his German period gave way to purely formal concerns. What remained was the structural format of Synthetic Cubism. Hartley retained the tight brushwork and sharply delineated, flatly colored shapes of his simplified still lifes (pl. 23), but he had now reduced his elements to unified geometric shapes painted in pale, muted colors. With a vocabulary of arcs and triangular forms derived from sailboat motifs, these paintings constitute Hartley's most radical venture into non-objectivity (fig. 44). The flatness toward which he had worked earlier is now complete; each area of the canvas occupies the surface plane with equal intensity. Moreover, he rejected the all-over patterning of his later German military paintings, returning to the centralized format of his officer portraits. In their flatness and geometric simplification, these works come closer than before to classic Synthetic Cubism (fig. 45). Hartley had been the last American artist of his time to leave Europe, and he understood better than anyone in America the level of abstraction Cubism had attained. American information about European developments in painting had been impeded by the war and by the burgeoning isolationist attitudes of the art community. Even Stieglitz had lost interest in supporting European artistic developments after the Armory Show. Hartley's Synthetic Cubist works of the Provincetown summer were not only comparable to those being executed in Europe, but they would not be equalled by another American artist for ten years. They proved too advanced, however, for even the more sympathetic cosmopolitan admirers of his painting to fully appreciate. The lack of support from his peers and his removal from the stimulation of an advanced artistic milieu would eventually erode his confidence and lead him to abandon his avant-garde European style.

Fig. 45   Albert Gleizes. *Danseuse* ("Dancer"), 1917. Oil on canvas, 100.3 × 76.2 cm (39½ × 30"). Mr. and Mrs. Sidney E. Cohn, New York

Fig. 46   *Movement No. 10*, 1917. Oil on composition board, 38.7 × 49.5 cm (15¼ × 19½"). The Art Institute of Chicago; The Alfred Stieglitz Collection

Bermuda and Ogunquit: 1917

Reed closed his house in mid-September, leaving Hartley and Charles Demuth on the Cape for several additional weeks in a rent-free house they had found. Prompted by the pleasure of the Provincetown summer and the need for inexpensive accommodations, Hartley arranged to spend the winter of 1916–17 in Bermuda, where Demuth joined him for several months. The wartime mining of the harbors made Bermuda nearly deserted, and he and Demuth lived and painted on a surprisingly low budget.

This excursion marked the beginning of Hartley's separation from avant-garde issues and from a committed stylistic direction. His Provincetown paintings had been completely mature works, but they had not been generated by emotional experiences and lacked personal meaning for him. Removed from an environment which supported advanced painting and exposed daily to Demuth's more representational mode, Hartley's abstract style faltered.[129]

Nor was Hartley able to return to his pre-European expressionistic roots; his attitude toward nature had changed when he was abroad and he no longer viewed it as the embodiment of a transcendental vision: "You know my reverence for nature is not at all keen, not nature just for itself. Every artist is sure to outgrow that in time, and unless it symbolizes itself for him vividly in unusual images, it

Fig. 47 *Still Life No. 9, 1917*. Oil on beaver board, 61 × 50.8 cm (24 × 20″). University Gallery, University of Minnesota, Minneapolis; bequest of Hudson Walker from the Ione and Hudson Walker Collection

Fig. 48 *A Bermuda Window in a Semi-Tropic Character,* 1917 (see Plate 27)

Fig. 49 *Still Life with Eel,* 1917 (see Plate 28)

wearies the eye with so much of its commonness, or so much of its peculiarity, and that is so with all places where life is inclined toward phlegma."[130] Feeling this phlegma to characterize the Bermuda landscape, he turned to interior and still-life compositions. He began by applying the flat, uniform areas of muted color — derived from Synthetic Cubism and characteristic of his Provincetown paintings — to quasi-geometric still-life motifs (fig. 46). As the work evolved, he introduced organic curves reminiscent of the delicate sensuality of Demuth's flower arrangements (fig. 47). The two-dimensional organization of the field gradually gave way to more illusionistic depictions of interiors which frequently utilize the device of an open window, a favorite compositional technique of André Derain and Matisse (fig. 48).

The emotional intensity of Hartley's German works was replaced in these Bermuda paintings by a subdued quietude. Perhaps needing a relief from the turbulence of his Berlin experiences — and from the critical rejection they had generated — Hartley retreated from forceful expression and spiritual preoccupations.[131] This period marked his earliest formulation of the idea which would later dominate his thinking, that of wanting to eliminate his personality from his paintings. From here on, Hartley would increasingly disavow the personal and idiosyncratic in art. The idea may have been born out of a sense of self-protection. By claiming to withdraw himself from his art, Hartley made that self less vulnerable. He wrote that summer to Carl Sprinchorn: "I want my work in both writing and painting to have that special coolness, for I weary of emotional excitement in art, weary of episode, of legend and of special histories, which most painters occupy themselves with."[132]

Despite Hartley's ostensible retreat from emotional excitement in art, Bermuda pictures, such as *Still Life with Eel* (fig. 49), evoke a generalized sexual symbolism which did not go unnoticed. Although perhaps overly Freudian in his interpretation, the critic Paul Rosenfeld noted of Hartley's still lifes: "a cold and ferocious sensuality seeks to satisfy itself in the still-lives, with their heavy stiff golden bananas, their dark luscious figs, their erectile pears and enormous breast-like peaches."[133]

Hartley's Provincetown work was exhibited at 291 while he wintered in Bermuda. The exhibition was his last with the gallery, which closed permanently in the summer of 1917 after a Georgia O'Keeffe exhibition, signaling the end of an era in American art. Its closing came as a further blow to Hartley, leaving him not only psychologically demoralized, but without future financial support. Stieglitz continued to be Hartley's chief moral and financial advocate into the 1930s, serving as his major link with the New York art community.

In May 1917, Hartley left Bermuda for New York, where he had his appendix removed. He left for Lewiston soon after the operation and from there continued on to Perkins Cove, Ogunquit, Maine, arriving there in mid-July. A summer art colony had developed around the Ogunquit School of Painting and Sculpture, started in 1913 by Hamilton Easter Field and his protégé, the sculptor Robert Laurent. Field, a wealthy artist and patron who had been the art critic for the *Brooklyn Daily Eagle,* had built a cluster of houses at the cove in Ogunquit, which he offered to artists for a nominal charge, sometimes accepting a painting in exchange for rent. The lure of an inexpensive place to work undoubtedly attracted Hartley as did the presence that summer of Carl Sprinchorn and Maurice Sterne.

Hartley's major output that summer was a group of paintings on glass. His initial interest in the medium probably began with the Bavarian glass paintings he had admired and collected in Germany. This interest had undoubtedly been reinforced by Kandinsky's, Marc's, and Münter's experiments with the same technique. Hartley mentioned to Stieglitz that he had wanted to work with glass

Fig. 50 Artist unknown (European), probably 19th century. Oil on glass and gold foil, 23.7 × 17.8 cm (9-5/16 × 7″). Private collection, New York

Fig. 51 *Vase of Flowers*, 1917. Oil on glass, 33.7 × 22.4 cm (13¼ × 8⅞″) sight. The Carl van Vechten Gallery of Fine Arts, Fisk University, Nashville, Tennessee; Alfred Stieglitz Collection

Fig. 52 *New Mexico*, 1919. Pastel on paper, 43.2 × 69.9 cm (17 × 27½″). University Gallery, University of Minnesota, Minneapolis; bequest of Hudson Walker from the Ione and Hudson Walker Collection

for a long time and it might only have been his effort to differentiate his work as much as possible from Kandinsky's that kept him from trying out the medium earlier. Laurent later said that Hartley's desire to attempt glass painting arose from his exposure to early American mirrors and reverse paintings on glass in the Laurent collection.[134] Both Field and Laurent had become deeply interested in folk art; by the time Hartley arrived in 1917, Ogunquit was the center for a reborn enthusiasm about early American painting and furniture. Hartley's letters indicate that American glass painting and early American saloon windows were the motivations behind his own endeavors.[135]

The paintings themselves are distinct from anything that Hartley had ever done (fig. 51), although they do continue the still-life format and, on occasion, the curtain device developed in Bermuda. Deriving elements from both European and American folk art, Hartley isolated individual floral arrangements or ornamental studies of wheat or ears of corn against solid, unmodulated color backgrounds. His presentation of outlined symmetrical images relates directly to the American folk art tradition. But in technique Hartley's pieces draw on the German tradition, for the solid paint areas and blocky background divisions closely resemble German folk art (fig. 50), even though Hartley rejected the detailed representational compositions of Bavarian glass paintings, as well as those of the Blaue Reiter artists. The formal simplicity in Hartley's paintings and their occasionally crude executions were perhaps due to the difficulty of painting in reverse. Writing later to Rebecca Strand, Hartley noted the medium's extreme fragility and attendant difficulty, adding that "it nearly killed me and I never had the courage to take it up again."[136] That only a relatively small number of Hartley's glass paintings are extant is probably attributable to breakage.

In the fall of 1917, Hartley returned to New York where he stayed through the spring in a Brooklyn Heights apartment owned by Field, again exchanging a painting for rent. He continued painting on glass, executing several in Staten Island during visits with Robert Locher, Demuth's lifelong friend. Hartley's association with the New York literary community and his commitment to writing intensified that fall. From then until 1922, he augmented his meager income by contributing articles and poems to *The New Republic, The Dial,* and *Seven Arts.*

New Mexico: June 1918 – November 1919

Financial pressures continually plagued Hartley. In June 1918, the need to find inexpensive living accommodations lured him to Taos, New Mexico. According to his autobiography, his trip to Taos was initiated by a woman there who had offered to pay him for painting lessons, although he also told Harriet Monroe, editor of the vanguard magazine *Poetry,* that he was going for his health and for the peace and quiet.[137] In May Hartley reminded Charles Daniel, his dealer since the closing of 291, that in order to go West he needed the money Daniel owed him from the sale of a landscape.[138] He apparently was paid, for he arrived in Santa Fe on June 12, 1918, and was met by Mabel Dodge and her new husband, Maurice Sterne. Two days later Hartley went to Taos.

The Taos – Santa Fe area was a burgeoning oasis for avant-garde writers and artists. Mabel Dodge's arrival in 1917 prompted visits by many East Coast luminaries but even prior to that the area had attracted a diverse assortment of artists.[139] Hartley's experience there proved both exhilarating and disappointing. Apart from Dodge, Maurice Sterne and occasional visitors like Leo Stein and

Fig. 53 *Blessing the Melon. The Indians Bring the Harvest to Christian Mary for Her Blessing,* 1918 (see Plate 87)

Fig. 54 Artist unknown. *Nuestra Señora de la Candelaria,* n.d. Tempera and gesso on wood, 33.7 × 24.1 cm (13¼ × 9½"). The Santa Barbara Museum of Art, Santa Barbara, California; gift of Mrs. Bernhard Hoffman

Waldo Frank, Hartley failed to establish rapport with the Taos artists, who from his point of view tended to be cultish and inhospitable to newcomers. Describing Taos as the "stupidest place I ever fell into. . . . a society of cheap artists from Chicago and New York," Hartley claimed it had given him "the smallest vision I have had of the world so far."[140] He apparently had difficulty adjusting to the high altitude and felt "physically off" most of the time.[141] Hartley was not entirely blameless for his alienation from the community. He had arrived in Taos with a lingering sense of self-importance, and his arrogance and superior attitude may have contributed to his estrangement. Although his work barely supported him, Hartley alone among the Taos artists could boast major shows in Europe and glorious praise from the increasingly respected Gertrude Stein. Local Taos artists were not quick to recognize these laurels, and Hartley's attitude, however valid, undoubtedly made a few enemies.

His dislike of the Taos art community was offset by his total joy with the Indians and their dances, about which he wrote several articles during the next four years. He felt renewed by proximity to the culture which he regarded as embodying purity and essential truth. He was equally enchanted by the magnificence and austerity of the landscape, "any one of these beautiful arroyos and canyons is a living example of the splendour of the ages . . . and I am bewitched with their magnificence and their austerity; as for the colour, it is of course the only place in America where true colour exists, excepting the short autumnal season in New England."[142] Despite the landscape's appeal, it proved to be difficult subject matter for him;[143] not until he was removed from it was he able to translate its imagery into powerful compositions.

Hartley initially attempted to capture the landscape in pastels, feeling that the mood of the colors was not appropriate for oils. Working rapidly out-of-doors, first with blue and green pastels, then later in brown tones when the color changed, Hartley transcribed the shrubs, mountains, and arroyos of the desert with a higher degree of naturalism than he had attempted since his student days (fig. 52). While pleasant enough studies, these pastels display none of his expressive strength or abstract, decorative skills. Their almost direct transcription of landscape sites may have been Hartley's way of dealing with the total unfamiliarity and awesome power of the desert's vastness. Stuart Davis, who visited Taos–Santa Fe somewhat later, remarked that "the place itself was so interesting. I don't think you could do much work there except in a literal way, because the place is always there in such a dominating way. . . ."[144]

This period marked a shift in Hartley's goals as a painter, a shift that further contributed to the realism of these landscapes. The tentative formulations against personalized painting that he had made in Bermuda took precedence over other approaches. He now sought to render images dispassionately, without intruding his own feelings and emotions to the exclusion of objectivity. This was a direct retraction of the ideology behind his Intuitive Abstractions — that the painting represented the inner emotions of the artist without regard to external stimulus. He wrote that spring to Harriet Monroe of his preference for recognizable objective images, asserting that all art was swinging back to realism.[145] In this, Hartley was very much of his time: the American sense of disillusionment and isolationism that followed the war manifested itself artistically in a general retreat from abstraction and a return to more representational modes. As the cynicism about American participation in European affairs grew, involvement with European painting was supplanted by the desire to identify what was American and what constituted the American spirit. Hartley articulated this search for indigenous expression in an essay written the following summer for *Art and Archaeology,* in which he advocated that America create an aesthetic consciousness out of its own culture, which he proposed could be done by building on the foundation of American Indian aesthetics.[146]

Hartley's position was not evident in the group of interior still lifes he executed during this period based on the Mexican-American altarpieces known as *santos*, which were then common in the Southwest. Comprised of two types—the *retablo*, or flat wooden board (fig. 54), and the *bulto*, or carved figure (fig. 56)—*santos* were collected by, among others, Mabel Dodge, whose house in Taos Hartley used as a studio. By adopting his motifs directly from these painted or carved figures of saints, Hartley captured their primitive Christian mysticism. His paintings remain close in both image and format to the originals. In *Blessing the Melon* (fig. 53), the centralized, triangular figure flanked by candles and drawn drapes was adapted from a *retablo* like *Nuestra Señora de la Candelaria* (fig. 54); the nearly identical compositions of Hartley's *Virgin of Guadalupe* (fig. 55), and the *bulto Nuestra Señora de la Guadalupe* (fig. 56), further demonstrate his direct borrowing.

Hartley's attraction to the simple religious expressiveness of the *santos* altarpieces paralleled his earlier fascination with Bavarian glass paintings and votive pictures. Equally appealing was the visual relationship between the primitive character of the *santos* and that in American folk art. The flat design arrangements and religious imagery of Hartley's *santos* pieces recall his 1914 symbolic still lifes, although the impenetrable symbolism of his earlier pieces has been replaced by accessible Christian meaning. The simplified, hieratic figures in the majority of Hartley's *santos* paintings, silhouetted against monochromatic backgrounds, are stylistically linked to his glass paintings. In this regard, *El Santo* (pl. 32) is exceptional. Here Hartley eschews the two-dimensional, iconic treatment in favor of a more traditional academic approach to still life. The *retablo* is treated as only one of several objects in the composition, all of whose forms are modeled illusionistically to create the effect of spatial recession.

When a case of influenza was discovered in Taos late in October 1918, Hartley took the precaution of moving to Santa Fe, glad for an excuse to leave the area he later referred to as another spelling of "chaos."[147] Santa Fe was only slightly more comforting. He longed for the crowds of Germany and the anonymity and sense of participation that grand pageants gave him.[148] Although he attributed a feeling of inspiration and greater potentiality to the presence of the Indians, their ceremonies never truly allowed him to feel more than a spectator. The only thing that made Santa Fe livable, he wrote in March, was "that it is near the most beautiful subject matter of the South West."[149]

That winter was extraordinarily cold in Santa Fe. With money from the sale of *El Santo* to the New Mexico Museum, Hartley went to La Cañada, a new resort near Pasadena. Because he regarded California as a place where "there is no landscape there to speak of. Mostly scenery,"[150] he continued to work on pastels of New Mexico. But his principal involvements in Los Angeles were with the literary community. He had established something of a reputation as a poet through the publication of several of his poems in *Poetry* and two poetry associations asked him to give readings. Along with his own works, he read the aviation poems of the then fledgling poet Robert McAlmon in one of his programs and the two men became close friends. A year later, Hartley introduced McAlmon to William Carlos Williams, who joined forces with McAlmon to publish *Contact*, the influential poetry magazine of the 1920s.

In late June 1919, Hartley returned to Santa Fe from California feeling renewed. In addition to pastels, he executed five or six oil paintings in pink and red tones (fig. 57). Sketchy, naturalistic depictions of the desert, these paintings do little to suggest the power that he would bring to this subject matter after he returned to

Fig. 55   *Virgin of Guadalupe*, 1919. Oil on composition board, 78.7 × 60.6 cm (31 × 23⅞"). The Metropolitan Museum of Art, New York; The Alfred Stieglitz Collection, 1949

Fig. 56   José Rafael Aragón, attributed. *Nuestra Señora de Guadalupe*, between 1830 and 1860. Tempera and gesso on wood, 75.5 × 25 × 12.5 cm (29¾ × 9⅞ × 4-15/16"). Museum of New Mexico at the Museum of International Folk Art; gift of the Historical Society of New Mexico

Fig. 57 *New Mexico, Landscape,* 1919. Oil on canvas, 45.7 × 61 cm (18 × 24″). University Gallery, University of Minnesota, Minneapolis; bequest of Hudson Walker from the Ione and Hudson Walker Collection

New York.

Not wanting to face another Santa Fe winter, Hartley left in November 1919 for New York, where he began a series of New Mexico paintings (fig. 58) based on his pastels and paintings, and on his memory of the desert. Although derived from his pastels, the imagery in these paintings was simplified and stylized into decorative patterns — patterns which manifested Hartley's desire for impersonal realism. Stylistically these paintings differ from his earlier Synthetic Cubist work in dispensing with flat, discrete color areas and two-dimensionality. Instead, Hartley used modulated, overlapping forms to suggest spatial recession. Hartley's instinct for decorative arrangement and overall design was manifested here in repetitive, curvilinear patterns delineated by dark contour lines. The sensuality resulting from the rich, material quality of dry, chalky paint is amplified by Hartley's use of organic forms, noted by Paul Rosenfeld in his description of these paintings: "earth-forms fitting into each other like coupling organs; strawberry-pink mountains dotted by fuzzy poison green shrubs, recalling breasts and wombs of clay...."[151] Modeling the New Mexico mountains and arroyos into tense, muscular forms imbued them with a sculptural plasticity and swelling voluptuousness. This denseness and solidity reflect the highly structured compositions of Cézanne, but their sensuality is quite removed from the classical restraint of the French painter.

New York and Gloucester: 1920–1921

In June 1920, Hartley again retreated to a summer art colony away from the city, choosing this time to go to Gloucester, Massachusetts, where he spent time in the company of Elie Nadelman and his wife, and Stuart Davis. The summer marked yet another change in Hartley's painting style. In format, his paintings that summer generally presented isolated, vertical images of single vases of flowers on tabletops, rendered primarily in tones of green, tan and brown (fig. 60). Most often Hartley centralizes his images on flat, monochromatic backgrounds, although on occasion he fractures the entire structure into planar color areas (fig. 59). Shallow spatial recession is suggested through perspectively rendered tabletops and fabric. On the whole, the series lacks vitality, and this may reflect the absence of personal meaning these subjects had for Hartley. But he had matured into a masterful painter and the loose, painterly brushstroke which he introduces in some paintings evokes a richness unusual for such conventional formats. Thus, although many of Hartley's paintings from this summer continue the tight, controlled brushstrokes of his Provincetown series, a small group have the sensuous handling of pigment which became the sustaining quality of his work during the 1920s, a decade in which he did not otherwise reach the level of achievement he had attained earlier.

In his letters and work of that summer, Hartley formulated his belief that excellence in painting was equated with spontaneity and the rapid execution of fluid, painterly brushstrokes.[152] This exaltation of the bravura aspect of paint recalled the example of his teacher, William Merritt Chase, who was famous for completing a figure painting in three hours before the assembled student body. Hartley felt that one's entire physical being must be put into action when painting: "[Painting] is a medium for passion. . . . [153] [It] is essentially a paroxysm of intelligence coupled with orgiastic deliverance."[154]

From all accounts Hartley was a sexually alert, but often frustrated man who funneled his passions into art. He himself described the collection of natural

Fig. 58 *Landscape No. 3, Cash Entry Mines, New Mexico,* 1920 (see Plate 88)

Fig. 59 *The Rubber Plant,* 1920. Oil on canvas, 81.3 × 66 cm (32 × 26"). Yale University Art Gallery; gift of Collection Société Anonyme

Fig. 60 *Still Life,* 1920. Oil on wood panel, 50.8 × 40.1 cm (20 × 15¾"). Hirshhorn Museum and Sculpture Garden, Smithsonian Institution

Fig. 61 Richard Boix. *New York Dada Group,* ca. 1920. Brush, pen and ink on paper, 26.7 × 31.8 cm (10½ × 12½"). The Museum of Modern Art, New York; Katherine S. Dreier Bequest

objects which obsessed him as an adolescent in Cleveland as a sublimated sexual expression.[155] William Carlos Williams referred to Hartley's sexual loneliness and frustration when he recounted an incident that occurred on one of his visits to Hartley's 15th Street apartment. The two of them heard the young lovers next door, who were separated from Hartley only by a thin wall: "'Yes, they often entertain me at night,' he said. I felt sorry for him, growing old. That was the moment he took for his approaches. I, too, had to reject him. Everyone rejected him. I was no better than the others. One of our finest painters. He told me I would have made one of the most charming whores of the city. We were close friends until his death."[156] Williams noted that "Hartley's whole life had been a similar torment which painting alone assuaged."[157]

Hartley's period in Gloucester was spiritually empty. Although he tried to replace the vision of himself as a mystical artist with a commitment to painterly virtuosity, he had become a man without a direction and could find no fulfilling subject matter or style. The center and focus of his life seemed to have dropped away, and his letters turned bitter: "I should have written sooner but you understand too well all things that make up the insult called life in one like myself. I have achieved great mastery to my own thinking in that I have brought up the inevitable smile of satire on to my cheek after the years of hope and faith and love. I have dropped the two former and love has turned to a kind of devilish tenacity to keep from letting the whole thing die on one's hands like a sick lizard. I have worked hard the past eight weeks — painting and writing every day to keep the wolf of mediocrity from gnawing at the aristocratic vitals of true ambition."[158] Despite his bitterness, Hartley persevered in his quest for personal growth and authenticity: "I despise the American quest for symbol because it argues nothing but the vilest mediocrity. . . . I regret I am not the physical giant to practice all I comprehend. I consider it asinine to allow life to destroy me. One must destroy life and destroy it with images greater than itself. That is what [O'Keeffe] is on the verge of to my thinking. Naturally she is terrified. If you want to create origins of experience for yourself you have necessarily to face the holocaust and the typhoon. . . ."[159]

Upon his return to New York in the fall of 1920, Hartley took an apartment with the actor George di Winter. In May, Hartley had been appointed secretary of the Société Anonyme, founded that year by Katherine Dreier, Marcel Duchamp, and Man Ray for the purpose of promoting modern art through exhibitions, publications, and lectures. Hartley now became more involved with this tiny clique of American-based Dadaists. Encouraged by their example to embrace Dadaism, he wrote an article entitled "The Importance of Being 'Dada'."[160] He felt a level of energy in the group that he found lacking elsewhere in America, but he never fully identified with the movement's frivolity or its intellectuality, both of which allowed him little room for painterly expression.[161]

Hartley's depression and sense of emptiness went on unabated and he became increasingly desperate to return to the Continent and the places he associated with success. His work no longer sustained him or brought him into contact with the kind of social or artistic community he had found abroad. No longer the eager artistic hopeful that had been introduced to Stieglitz twelve years earlier, he now expected a level of respect and financial recognition that did not seem to be forthcoming. He felt estranged from America and considered himself "satisfied to be a visitor on a supposed home soil."[162] More and more he viewed Europe as the antidote to his spiritual emptiness, feeling that he needed it, "for the sake of rehabilitation in general."[163]

In the spring of 1921, Hartley informed Stieglitz that he was destitute and needed twelve hundred dollars to go to Europe. In Stieglitz's more melodramatic version of the incident, Hartley placed a penny under the dealer's nose, saying,

"This is all that stands between me and starvation."[164] When Stieglitz asked what Hartley intended to do, Hartley replied that he wanted to go to Florence, write a book of hate, have a hundred copies handsomely printed and sent to friends, then commit suicide. Stieglitz, who was having financial problems of his own that made it impossible for him to provide the money, asked Hartley if he would be willing to give up all his unsold paintings in storage for the freedom twelve hundred dollars would bring. When Hartley agreed, Stieglitz offered the entire group to Charles Daniel and N. E. Montross for that exact amount. Neither dealer accepted the proposition, however, and Stieglitz next approached Mitchell Kennerly of the Anderson Galleries and proposed an auction. Since the only available slot had already been assigned to James Rosenberg, a wealthy lawyer-painter, Kennerly scheduled a double auction for May 17, 1921. One hundred and seventeen of Hartley's 1908-21 paintings and drawings were hung for a one-week period prior to that date. The auction was a major event in the art world: not only was it the first time the contemporary art market had been tested at auction, but Hartley's financial dilemma and his reliance on this sale to pursue his career abroad piqued the curiosity of the art community. The sale proved a tremendous success, netting nearly five thousand dollars,[165] and freeing Hartley to return to Europe. "I was safe and sound once more and could go on with the education of an artist."[166]

Plate 24   *Boat (Black and White Hull)*, 1916
Oil on board, 40.6 × 29.8 cm (16 × 11¾″)
The Barnes Foundation, Merion, Pennsylvania
Photograph Copyright 1980 by The Barnes Foundation

Plate 25 *Elsa*, 1916 (cat. no. 39)
University Gallery, University of Minnesota, Minneapolis;
bequest of Hudson Walker from the Ione and Hudson Walker Collection

Plate 26 *Movement No. 8, Provincetown*, 1916
(cat. no. 41) Wadsworth Atheneum,
Hartford, Connecticut; gift of Mrs. Robert E. Darling

Plate 27   *A Bermuda Window in a Semi-Tropic Character*, 1917 (cat. no. 44)
The Fine Arts Museums of San Francisco;
Dr. T. Edward and Tulla Hanley Memorial Collection

Plate 28 *Still Life with Eel*, 1917
Oil on canvas, 75.7 × 63.5 cm (30½ × 25")
Museum of Art of Ogunquit, Maine; gift of Mrs. William Carlos Williams

Plate 29 *Red Calla in Blue Vase*, 1917 (cat. no. 45)
Mr. and Mrs. John Laurent, York, Maine

Plate 30 *Painting No. 69*, 1917
Oil on glass, 41.3 × 23 cm (16¼ × 9¼″) (sight)
The Carl Van Vechten Gallery of Fine Arts,
Fisk University, Nashville, Tennessee;
Alfred Stieglitz Collection

Plate 31   *Still Life*, 1917 (cat. no. 46)
Private Collection

Plate 32   *El Santo*, 1918 (cat. no. 48)
Museum of New Mexico, Santa Fe; anonymous gift

Plate 33 *New Mexico Landscape*, 1919–20
Oil on canvas, 76.2 × 91.4 cm (30 × 36″)
Philadelphia Museum of Art; The Alfred Stieglitz Collection

The Middle Years

Fig. 62   Marsden Hartley, Berlin, 1922

Paris and Berlin: 1921–1924

Hartley arrived in Paris in July 1921 and spent the summer indulging in café life and relishing being back in Europe. The city was teeming with American expatriate writers and he quickly found his way into the group that gathered at the Dôme and at the Rotonde. At forty-four, although not handsome, Hartley was still youthfully slender and his structured face and aquiline nose gave him a distinguished air (fig. 62). Never an extrovert, Hartley could yet be a gregarious, witty conversationalist who established contact with people easily. His fortuitous encounter with Louise Bryant, John Reed's former wife, then married to the future American ambassador, William Bullitt, was ultimately his most significant renewal of friendship.[167] Hartley became very close to the couple and on one of his visits, Bullitt proposed the idea of a syndicate which would provide Hartley's living expenses for a given number of years in exchange for paintings. This fund, formed a year and a half later through Bullitt's friend, William Griffin, allowed Hartley to remain in Europe longer than would otherwise have been possible.

In late November 1921, Hartley left Paris for his beloved Berlin, where he remained for more than two years. He found the city more decadent than he had remembered. "There was an air of abandon come over the place," he wrote. "Life was at the height of heights — that is, to the highest pitch of sophistication and abandon — none of us had seen anything quite like the spectacle. . . . The psychology was incredible."[168] The war had devastated Berlin's economy and foreigners rushed to the city to reap the benefits of the mark's fall. As Robert McAlmon recalled, "no one knew from one day to the next what the dollar would bring in marks, but everyone knew that, whatever happened, the dollar bought in Berlin as much as ten or twenty dollars would elsewhere."[169] Hartley quickly found his way into the social life of the city. In March he spent one thousand marks on an outfit for a costume party. He was quite pleased with his effect on the young men there, and wrote to his friend Mathilde Rice that one of them had said the only thing left was to put Hartley on an altar with his legs crossed. "Of course he was worshipping me," Hartley added.[170] Hartley's decadent behavior, however, was held back by a New England restraint: after attending a private costume party at which the host was attired in a flowing dress, he remarked that he disliked most effeminate aspects in men.[171]

The art world seemed to have changed less than Berlin's mood. Synthetic Cubism still reigned and Hartley informed Stieglitz that the whole city was "under cubist influence."[172] Something of Hartley's reputation had remained in Germany; sustained by that, he began working again. The bravura spontaneity and painterly expressiveness hinted at in his Gloucester still lifes now became dominant. As before, he worked rapidly, apparently telling a friend that if one could not complete a picture in a day, one should stop painting.[173] It comforted him that he could "go to the canvas and the work flows and is not a terrified question of escape as it has been so long."[174] His work moved quickly from cactus still lifes which, while more loosely painted, were otherwise close in spirit to his Gloucester

Fig. 63 *Still Life with Grapes*, 1922–23. Oil on canvas, 59 × 109 cm (23¼ × 43″). Columbus Museum of Art, Ohio; gift of Ferdinand Howald

Fig. 64 *Landscape Fantasy*, 1923. Oil on canvas, 72.4 × 104.1 cm (28½ × 41″). New York University Art Collection, Grey Art Gallery and Study Center; gift of Charles Simon

Fig. 65 *Seated Male Nude*, 1923. Sanguine on paper, 38.7 × 59.1 cm (15¼ × 23¼″). James F. Duffy, Jr., Detroit

series, into even more painterly Cubist still lifes (fig. 63). Compositionally, these still lifes are freer and more spatially plastic than the flat, decorative style of late Synthetic Cubism that prevailed in Berlin. Often outlined with dark contours, images of food, bowls and baskets on tabletops are rendered in distorted perspective. The rich harmonies of tans and browns which Hartley applied in creamy brushstrokes give these works their unique quality. Their coloristic unity and fluid, rich surfaces infuse them with a sensuous elegance that reflects Hartley's life in this period.

Spending time with Rönnebeck, whose atelier he shared, and visiting with his German friends in the cafés, continued to nourish Hartley's spirits. In September 1922, ten months after his arrival in Berlin, Hartley began work on his first major series of lithographs — heavy black contour drawings of bowls of fruit. This did not inhibit his painting schedule; by January 1923 he was able to boast that he had finished some drawings, as well as sixty canvases. Although elegant, none of these paintings achieved the expressive or formal power attained during his earlier Berlin periods. Having disavowed personalized expression and idiosyncratic art, he lacked a fixed direction about what to paint. Throughout the 1920s he would experiment with styles ranging from painterly Cubist still lifes to cleanly chiseled landscapes, but none bore the inner conviction or expressiveness of his early career. They contained instead an air of unrelieved hesitation which corresponded to Hartley's spiritually empty center. What linked them was Hartley's superb virtuosity as a painter.

By April 1923, Hartley felt he had exhausted the still-life theme, and he began painting recollections of New Mexico (pl. 35), turning to American themes as he had done earlier with his American Indian paintings. As he looked back on his New Mexico experience, his mood turned somber; these recollections bear no relationship to the pastels done *in situ* or to the New Mexico paintings done in New York (fig. 58). In place of the voluptuous, curvilinear quality of his first New Mexico series, Hartley now depicted the New Mexico landscape as a vast, horizontal void, wind-stripped of life. Laterally attenuated forms and broken, twisted foreground trees create a mood of blighted desolation — a Wuthering Heights such as Emily Brontë had not known.[175] The empty middle ground in these paintings serves as a fulcrum for the formal tension created by the inward and outward pull of foreground and background space. Even the paint — now thin and horizontally stretched instead of dense as in the earlier series — reinforces the bleakness of Hartley's remembered vision. In contrast to the decorative stylized patterning of his first New Mexico series, the Recollections are dominated by undulating forms which expressed what he felt were the "natural wave rhythms" of the Southwest.[176] In what were his most expressionistic and perhaps most successful New Mexico Recollections (fig. 64), Hartley turned these undulating forms into fanciful, turbulent landscapes infused with a brooding quality which corresponded to his current mood, as well as to his earlier experience of Taos — or "chaos," as he saw it.[177] Three months after beginning the New Mexico Recollections, Hartley augmented the series with a group of chalk life drawings of male and female nudes (fig. 65). Anomalous as subject matter, these large muscular figures would not become part of his pictorial vocabulary for fifteen years.

Despite the relative calm and peace Hartley experienced in Berlin, he felt restless. With the proceeds from the publication of his book *Twenty-five Poems* by Contact Publishing Company, he financed a trip to Italy in late October 1923. After first spending eight days in Vienna, he left for an eight-week stay in Florence, followed by Christmas in Rome with Maurice Sterne. The Renaissance paintings of Giotto, Masaccio, and Piero della Francesca which he encountered on this trip moved him deeply. In their works he saw the possibility of reconciling his shifting

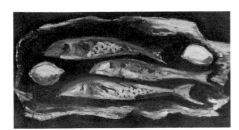

Fig. 66 *Three Red Fish with Lemons*, 1924. Oil on canvas, 34.3 × 64.8 cm (13½ × 25½″). University Gallery, University of Minnesota, Minneapolis; bequest of Hudson Walker from the Ione and Hudson Walker Collection

artistic credos — that of personal expressiveness and objectively painted depictions of reality. For the rest of his career, Hartley would struggle with the problem of uniting inner vision and external reality. This he felt the three Renaissance masters had accomplished, achieving an earth-bound spirituality through a union of objectivity and inner vision.[178]

At the end of his Italian sojourn in December, Hartley sailed for the United States in order to negotiate in person the details of the fund initiated in Paris by Bullitt. Financed by Bullitt's friend Griffin and three other businessmen, it promised to provide Hartley with three thousand dollars annually for four years in exchange for ten paintings per year.[179] His negotiations successfully completed, Hartley returned to Paris in the middle of the summer of 1924.

Hartley worked that season in the Paris studio of the American artist George Biddle. In addition to resuming his New Mexico themes, he worked on a group of fish still lifes which he called "Chez Prunier" after the fish he observed in Prunier's fish-market window (fig. 66). Seen from above and disposed vertically against a painterly background, the depictions of fish continue the style of the 1923 Berlin still lifes. The New Mexico Recollections executed this year (fig. 67) were dense and chunky compared to the thin horizontal undulations of the first group. In place of the blighted desolation of the earlier Recollections, Hartley introduced into this series houses, roads, and cemeteries. Thus, although darker and weightier, these works avoid the previous series' bleak vision. Their dominant thick plant stalks were worked into Hartley's next paintings, a group of Maine Recollections, known as Paysages (fig. 68), which recall his early Ryder-influenced Dark Landscapes (pl. 3). As with the 1909 series, spatial recession is tightly compressed between a foreground plane dominated by bulbous plant forms and a background plane in which the high horizon line of the mountain pushes claustrophobically against the upper boundary of the picture. The rapid succession of styles Hartley's work underwent this season suggested his lack of inner resolve and commitment. Despite the lofty aspirations that evolved from his exposure to the Renaissance masters, none of the approaches he tried seemed to offer a sustaining direction, and he began contemplating a change of environment.

Fig. 67 *Cemetery, New Mexico*, 1924. Oil on canvas, 80.3 × 99.7 cm (31⅝ × 39¼″). The Metropolitan Museum of Art, New York; The Alfred Stieglitz Collection, 1949

Southern France: 1925–1929

Hartley eventually decided he needed the countryside. In late August 1925, he went south and took up residence in Vence, in a four-room stucco house called La Petite Maison. The charm of Vence quickly wore off, despite pleasant excursions to Cannes and to Ville Franche, where he found an expatriate circle that included Monroe Wheeler, Glenway Wescott, and Paul Robeson. Hartley considered the landscape around Vence beautiful to look at but not to paint; several times he escaped to the Italian Alps for more suitable subject matter. Vence's lack of stimulating society added to his frustration, for he disliked the American tourists and found the native residents dull. "Vence is a truly agreeable place but it's always the same," he wrote to Gertrude Stein, noting reflectively that, "where one is is not the place one wants — for it's a few people one likes that make the place."[180] He even began thinking fondly again of America which, he conceded, at least had "elemental energy."[181] He found Vence so dull that if he had not already signed a lease and started to paint, he would have fled.

Even painting proved unsatisfying. His yearly ten-picture commitment to the syndicate began to weigh heavily on him as the November 15 due date approached. Unable to complete any work, he became panic-stricken and appealed

Fig. 68 *Paysage*, 1924. Oil on canvas, 80.9 × 80.9 cm (31 × 31″) (sight). New York University Art Collection, Grey Art Gallery and Study Center; gift of Leo M. Rogers

Fig. 69 *Vence, Landscape*, 1925–26. Oil on canvas, 81.2 × 80.3 cm (32 × 31⅝″). Tucson Museum of Art, Tucson, Arizona; The Lawrence J. Heller Collection

Fig. 70 *View Toward the Mediterranean*, 1926. Oil on wood panel, 34.8 × 45.7 cm (14½ × 18″). Present whereabouts unknown.

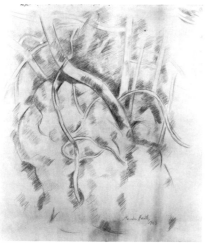

Fig. 71 *Trees and Rocks*, 1927. Silverpoint on prepared paper, 37.8 × 33 cm (14⅞ × 13″). The University of Michigan Museum of Art, Ann Arbor; bequest of Florence L. Stol, 1968

to Stieglitz to pacify his "angels."[182] By the end of a damp December, the new paintings still had not dried and Hartley asked Stieglitz to substitute ten works from those he had sent to New York in previous years — "not of the very best of course."[183] Having failed to make his quarterly installment to the syndicate, Hartley went through several months of worry as he waited for their check to come. He later reflected on the experience as a lesson from which he "learned that it [art] is an aristocratic privilege and it is all wrong to be driven to make a mercantile commodity of it."[184] Although he eventually received the syndicate's check, his confidence had broken and his spirits had plummeted. The depression continued into spring, aggravated by the first of frequent bouts of bronchitis which would plague him the rest of his life. By July, anxiously awaiting the expiration of his year's lease, he wrote to Stieglitz that "nothing has really gone right — nothing was as it promised and everything turned out to be as I had not expected or desired."[185]

As if reflecting his emotional depression and lack of focus, Hartley's paintings from this period seem forced and uncertain. In response to the landscape and light quality around Vence, he again abruptly shifted his style. Not only do these paintings bear little relationship to his preceding work, but even within the group itself his style forms no coherent statement. Instead, it varies from location to location. The landscapes resulting from his two brief trips to Gorges du Loup and Gattière in the Italian Alps are infused with a crispness unique in his work (fig. 69). Hartley renders these mountains and aqueducts in a chiseled, mannered style with sharp juxtapositions between tonalities rather than transitional passages of graduated color. For the first time, shadows and the play of light across surfaces are depicted as shapes in their own right, solid and clearly bounded. The massive quality of these paintings recalls the denseness of his second New Mexico series (fig. 67), but their broader areas of uniform color and lighter tan and green tones relate clearly to the sun-drenched landscape of southern France. In contrast to these weighty forms are the landscapes of the valley of Chevreuse, which he rendered with sketchy, rapid brushstrokes and a high-keyed palette (fig. 70). Hartley's third group of paintings from this period, his still lifes — which he regarded as more successful than the landscapes — are composed of solid, stable masses; forms are simplified and outlined with dark contours (fig. 74). The quasi-horizontal surfaces of his 1923 still lifes (fig. 63) have given way to crumpled fabric backdrops tilted parallel to the picture plane to create a relatively flattened space, which resembles the contemporaneous Synthetic Cubist compositions of Georges Braque. The creamy, expressive brushstroke of the 1923 series has been supplanted by massive durable forms and more solid color areas.

Hartley's lease on the house at Vence finally expired in September 1926. Free at last, he escaped with his two cocker spaniels to Aix-en-Provence, where he leased a house called Canto Grihet ("Song of the Cricket"). He was immediately enthralled by Provence, sensing there a peace he had not felt since Berlin: "It is the first spot on earth where I have felt right — in harmony — body, soul and mind — and if that can't be called a state of 'home' then nothing can. . . . I can't destroy the symbol of home in my mind and soul. . . ."[186]

That fall Hartley worked primarily on still lifes which, while abandoning the massive severity of the preceding group, retained their emphasis on stable, distinct forms instead of expressive, sensuous brushstrokes (fig. 72). Structurally, these paintings begin to reflect the influence of Cézanne (fig. 73), who had long abided in Aix and who would soon again dominate Hartley's thinking: the perspective is similarly "incorrect," and the ornamental background — which, like Cézanne's is broken horizontally into two distinct areas — is integrated with the three-dimensional shapes to create a rhythmic pattern. By emulating Cézanne's severe,

Fig. 72 *Peasant's Paradise*, 1926–27. Oil on canvas, 49.5 × 61 cm (19½ × 24"). University Gallery, University of Minnesota, Minneapolis; bequest of Hudson Walker from the Ione and Hudson Walker Collection

Fig. 73 Paul Cézanne. *Still Life with Apples and Peaches*, ca. 1905. Oil on canvas, 81.3 × 100.7 cm (32 × 39⅝"). National Gallery of Art, Washington D.C.; gift of Eugene and Agnes Meyer

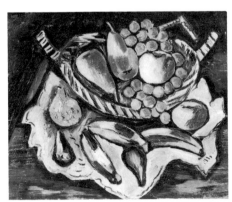

Fig. 74 *Still Life with Pears*, 1925–26. Oil on canvas, 50.2 × 60.9 cm (19¾ × 24"). Whitney Museum of American Art, New York; gift of Dr. Meyer A. Pearlman, 1964

classical style, Hartley tried to achieve a stable, timeless quality, and a clear sense of spatial order. He found the same characteristics in the work of Vermeer, whose "inexpressible quietude" he tried to evoke in his own paintings.[187]

Hartley's relief at finding "home" was more transitory than he first suspected, for his stay in Aix differed very little from other sojourns. His ebullience began to falter in late December when Canto Grihet was sold, forcing him into new quarters in a house called Maison Maria in the Château Noir forest. Disoriented both by the move and the trauma of turning fifty, Hartley entered another period of indecision and insecurity, which undermined his faith in himself as a painter and in his future. In late January he escaped to Paris, Berlin and Hamburg in search of inspiration and relief. He returned to Maison Maria in May 1927, still haunted by doubts about his career: "I dread the ensuing years," he wrote to Stieglitz shortly after his return, "for the quiet insinuation that will attend them of not having come through."[188]

Aix was permeated with the spirit of Cézanne. Not only had he lived in Aix most of his life and painted perhaps his best landscapes in the Château Noir forest, but for several years, Maison Maria had been his second studio and a frequent subject. In Hartley's search for some direction that might bring him much needed attention and emotional support, his imagination began to be dominated by Cézanne. Financially dependent on the syndicate, which he believed to be uninterested in his expressionist and abstract canvases, he turned to Cézanne. Whereas his earlier emulation of Cézanne had focused on still lifes, Hartley now looked to the landscape motifs Cézanne had preferred in his later years. As if in homage to the French master, he executed a whole series of Mont Sainte-Victoire paintings based on the same view of the mountain Cézanne had favored. He appropriated not only Cézanne's subject matter, but his style as well, although the broad parallel brushstrokes in Hartley's paintings and their raw primary hues were clearly post-Cézannean (pl. 39). Cézanne's goal had been to "make of Impressionism something solid and durable." In Hartley's decision to take up where Cézanne had left off,[189] he tried to push this goal even further. Hartley derived his basic technique of applying parallel striations of color from Cézanne, but by exaggerating the strokes and ordering them into distinct bands or registers, he created a remarkably architectonic effect. Although, like Cézanne, his color-strokes mix optically, in comparison to the architectural stability of Hartley's Mont Sainte-Victoire paintings, Cézanne's mountains appear diffused in shimmering light. A more direct appropriation of Cézanne's style occurred with Hartley's group of silverpoint landscapes from this same year—1927 (fig. 71). Here, neither a bright palette nor a style variation distinguishes Hartley's delicate parallel-line drawings from Cézanne's. Having found a direction, Hartley worked rapidly despite social isolation. By November he wrote that he was "working like a 'trooper' to get my pictures done so they can dry some before December 1."[190]

In his desire to follow in Cézanne's footsteps, Hartley adopted not only Cézanne's painting style, but his philosophical ideas as well. Just as in his earlier Cézannean period, when Cézanne's example had led him to abandon mysticism in favor of an objective, formal approach, Hartley now emulated Cézanne's elimination of all that was extraneous to the formal truths of his motifs, a position which implied expunging from painting every trace of personality, emotion, and literary or symbolic meanings.

When Hartley returned to the United States in January 1928 to attend his one-man exhibition at The Arts Club of Chicago, he publically articulated these theories in a poem, "The MOUNTAIN and the RECONSTRUCTION," printed in his exhibition catalogue. In the poem, he proposed that the artist should refrain from expressing a personal life by psychologically losing himself in the motif to be painted, identifying with it completely.

Hartley had struggled since 1916 to resolve the conflict between inner vision and objective depictions of reality. Apart from brief flirtations with formalism in 1910-12 and 1916, expressing personal vision had been paramount. This had been articulated in his letters and in the catalogue statements which accompanied the Forum exhibition and his 291 exhibitions of 1914 and 1916. From 1917 on, he had begun advocating the truthful representation of external reality. By the time his volume of essays, *Adventures in the Arts,* was published in 1921, he was writing of the limitations and false premises of the abstract styles of Futurism and Cubism and, in his essay "Whitman and Cézanne, " had disavowed the personal and idiosyncratic in art. These attitudes were most fully articulated in an article entitled "Art — And the Personal Life," which appeared in the June 1928 issue of *Creative Art.* He was interested solely in the craft of painting, "of how to make a better painting according to certain laws that are inherent in the making of a good picture. . . . I no longer believe in the imagination. . . . And when a painting is evolved from imaginative principles I am strongly inclined to turn away because I have greater faith that intellectual clarity is better and more entertaining than imaginative wisdom or emotional richness. . . . I have lived the life of the imagination, but at too great an expense. . . . I have made the complete return to nature. . . . I would rather be sure that I have placed two colors in true relationship to each other than to have exposed a wealth of emotionalism gone wrong in the name of richness of personal expression. . . . Art is not a matter of slavery — or to the aesthetic principles. It is a tempered and happy union of them all." [191] This article corresponded to the general orientation toward realism found in Hartley's paintings, yet it illustrates the contradictory and obtuse nature of the various credos he was forever professing. Perhaps because his art was built on other art, he felt the need to constantly define what he stood for at every moment. Luckily, his preconceptions did not govern the decisions he made in his art and he ignored or abandoned them when they no longer suited his needs.

Although Hartley's 1928 article had ended with a call to unite emotional wisdom, formal principles, and truth to external subject matter, its rhetorical thrust was toward the denial of imaginative, emotional principles. Since Stieglitz still believed vehemently that the expression of the artist's deepest feelings was essential to good art, this article — which appeared while Hartley was still in the United States — could well have deepened their growing estrangement. The beginnings of the rift had occurred earlier. Hartley was always fearful about his career and, at the same time, egocentric. Oblivious to his effect on people, he seemed to take from friends without giving, to be unable to acknowledge those around him or to successfully thank them for their efforts on his behalf. Although in his essays and letters he could be appreciative and admiring, in his life his emotional parsimony estranged his friends and led eventually to his break with Stieglitz. In 1923, Stieglitz had responded ferociously to a text of Hartley's in which Hartley apparently did not acknowledge Stieglitz or the role 291 had played in his career[192] — estrangement became inevitable.[193]

Hartley remained in America from January to August 1928. After attending his exhibition at The Arts Club of Chicago, he traveled to Denver to visit Rönnebeck, who had recently been appointed director of the Denver Museum; he then proceeded on to a comforting reintroduction to New England. This was only the second time Hartley had visited the United States since his departure in 1921. Unlike his previous homecoming, he spent little time in the cosmopolitan milieu of New York, preferring instead the comfort and quiet of friends and rural settings. During June and July he visited the Bullitts in Conway, New Hampshire, then went to Georgetown, Maine, for a two-week stay with Gaston and Mme. Lachaise, and Paul and Rebecca Strand. The warm nurture these friends provided offset the tension he felt at being back on native soil. Likening his condition to that of "an empty shell on a foreign beach,"[194] Hartley later told the Lachaises that he would not have remained a minute in New England but for their "gentle influence."[195] Capable of admiring his own country from the distance of Europe, Hartley felt alienated from it when he was actually there. Once back on the Continent, he wrote that he could not help finding New England "like a first wife that one cannot help revering and yet cannot possibly live with."[196] The visit, however, implanted the possibility of belonging to something, of being part of a country whose people spoke his language and shared his interests. Despite the pretense Hartley made of being indifferent, his estrangement from his native country had grown primarily out of the conviction that it had rejected him. Although he had felt himself an alien in America, when he returned to France in August 1928, Europe seemed stale.

He remained in Paris that winter and spring, claiming he could not "face the rain + chill + isolation [in Aix] altogether with no chance to work outside + no light to work inside."[197] However, the sense of uneasiness and isolation which he attributed to Aix was more internal than geographical, and Paris offered scarcely more sanctuary. He wrote to Rebecca Strand that he lived the life of a real New England recluse, with less social life than ever before.[198] Moreover, while Hartley always seemed to be suffering from some sickness, his health now began to show real signs of failing. In November he had an attack of grippe, which resulted in painful ear troubles that plagued him for the rest of his life. He spent Christmas alone in his room, contemplating the fact that he had no offspring to continue the family name; he was glad, he wrote, "to be the vicious period at the end of a very dull but virtuous sentence."[199]

Artistically, Hartley was equally isolated and out of harmony. His artistic reputation had fallen dramatically by the late 1920s. The vital link he had earlier had with Gertrude Stein no longer existed; he wrote cynically that she was "singling out young boys of flimsy talent which is natural because there are no older ones to discover."[200] He sensed that the Paris art world had lost its vitality. The kind of art that had previously inspired him had died, and he found it impossible to be enthusiastic about any of the postwar "isms," especially Surrealism, which he detested. Even if his own Intuitive Abstractions of 1912 had presented his internal emotional states and inner consciousness through a kind of free association, he now rejected the Surrealists' focus on unconscious revelations of the artist's inner life and strove instead to paint motifs existing in the world rather than in his mind. "It is the consuming ambition of my life now," he wrote in February 1929, "to remove all trace of 'inwardness,' to have the image revealed as an immediate experience + not by thought or reflective processes. Paris is so overrun with personal painting that it is sickening."[201]

Hartley remained confident of his theoretical position, but his recent travels and sense of displacement had unnerved him and he had not actually painted for a whole year—since the beginning of his visit to the United States in January of 1928. He likened his situation to a pianist who had not touched keys for a year, although his primary task, he realized, was to develop emotional tenacity in the face of an unresponsive or nonexistent audience. "The main struggle is to keep from having hardening of the spiritual arteries."[202] To recover from his malaise, he began painting still-life motifs, hoping that daily practice on stable models could get his "almost paralysed hand and eye back into health."[203]

By the end of January 1929, he had disciplined himself sufficiently to have completed fifteen canvases and was painting punctually from 11:00 in the morning to 12:30 in the afternoon, the hours he thought offered the only light in Paris. These still lifes (fig. 75) depict individual images of seashells, flowers, and fruits against monochromatic backgrounds, which Hartley attributed to the influence of Parisian light: "It is not to be wondered at that painters have found monochrome adequate to all their needs because there is no other kind of light here . . . and so of course all these canvases of mine are tinged with monochromatic emotions for the reason that pure light does not exist." [204] These canvases were more lush and delicate than anything he had ever painted: they abandoned the structural organization of his landscapes painted in Vence and Aix-en-Provence (pls. 37 and 39), and the heavy outlining and tan monochromes of his 1923 German still lifes (fig. 63). Not since his summer in Gloucester (fig. 60) had Hartley painted such sparse compositions, although in comparison, the Gloucester series is rigid and tight, whereas here, the structure and brushwork achieve a remarkable degree of fluidity. His new color adjustments contained no blacks or violent contrasts; in their place were light tones of pinks and blues mixed with white. Using a technique which created a jewel-like sparkle similar to that in his glass paintings, he tried to create an effect "almost as if the objects are seen through windows or by mirror reflection." [205] None of the paintings were larger than 20 by 24 inches since Hartley could neither afford materials nor believe that anyone in the United States wanted them larger: "If people are ever going to be interested in buying my things, small ones are more to the point." [206] Hartley was optimistic about the paintings and felt they presaged a new epoch in his career; in their lack of personal content, he felt he had achieved "almost selfless painting." [207]

Fig. 75 *Two Shells*, 1929. Oil on canvas, 50.2 × 61 cm (19¾ × 24″). Hirshhorn Museum and Sculpture Garden, Smithsonian Institution

This three-month period of enthusiasm ended abruptly. In January 1929, Hartley had exhibited his southern French landscapes and still lifes at The Intimate Gallery, which Stieglitz had opened in 1925. The idea for the gallery had grown out of a successful exhibition entitled "Seven Americans" that Stieglitz had organized in 1925 at the Anderson Galleries in New York. The new gallery's purpose was to provide a place where Stieglitz's core of seven artists — O'Keeffe, Dove, Marin, Strand, Hartley, Stieglitz and X (no. seven) — could have regular exhibitions. Although Hartley was considered part of the group, the four-year hiatus between The Intimate Gallery's opening and Hartley's first show there indicates Stieglitz's growing impatience with him. In the foreword to Hartley's exhibition catalogue, Lee Simonson commented favorably upon Hartley's retreat from personal expression, writing that Hartley's Mont Sainte-Victoire paintings represented a transference of self, an identification of the artist with an object: "In the interval between Maine and Aix, Hartley did, like Alice through the Looking Glass, seem to disappear for a while down Kandinsky's Kaleidoscope and be lost among its colored fragments. . . . Hartley after ten years of journeying has found his mountain again." [208]

Neither the critics nor the public shared Simonson's enthusiasm. The still lifes found guarded acceptance, but the landscapes met with complete rejection. By February, word of the show's near failure began to reach Hartley in Paris. On February 10, Stieglitz admonished him to return to the United States: "Eventually . . . you will have to face a reality which I fear you never tried to understand. You have really made no 'practical' contact in Europe and you are really without contact in your own country." [209] Sensing that his contract with the syndicate would not be renewed and that Stieglitz's evaluation of the situation was accurate, Hartley decided to repatriate himself the following year, a move toward which he was not altogether indisposed: "If my presence will affect anything I must be there on the ground. . . . From a human standpoint I am not at all against it — for I find life itself excessively dull over here — especially after my recent visit home." [210] Stieglitz responded favorably, though hardly optimistically, to his decision: "I think that is the only course you can follow. You might as well establish contact now if a contact is at all possible."[211] Hartley had no idea what he would be returning to, but he knew that Europe no longer provided him with inspiration or stimulus. The successes and friendships of his first glorious visit had vanished and he was unable to participate in the concerns of the succeeding generations of artists. He noted "how barren Europe is — of ideas — of belief in art — or even of spiritual prospect. It is a country of forgotten ideals esthetically speaking."[212]

But Hartley did not realize how changed was the America to which he would be returning, nor how drastically his artistic reputation there had fallen. On March 16 he received news that devastated him. Henry McBride, the art critic for *The New York Sun,* had written that Hartley's French landscapes were "disappointingly academic" and had accused Hartley of being an American who had turned his back on his native country.[213] And Stieglitz, who had become increasingly committed to an independent American vision, apparently agreed that Hartley's pictures were unsuccessful derivatives of European models. Hartley responded angrily: "McBride has now seen fit to spew forth vicious publicity on the expatriates, simply too filthy for words. . . . The talk is that I have gone down terribly in my painting in the last four years — [a woman friend] says it comes directly from Stieglitz but I will not believe he invented it — he with his heavy and distorted regard for the truth may have repeated it but you can see what a vicious spirit exists in New York at this time. . . . They respect nothing but money. Certainly no insignificant slug under an immovable rock like myself. The day *will come* when a change will take place."[214]

Despite the anger and momentary bravura, Hartley was psychologically destroyed by the rejection. Feeling that it made no difference whether he painted or not, he questioned whether he should burden himself with further humiliation, which he felt he had endured since childhood.[215]

Resolved to return to the United States, Hartley nevertheless had to remain in France until his lease in Aix expired the following November. But, unwilling to face the winter cold or isolation of Aix, he postponed leaving Paris until April 10. In the meantime, he tried rather heroically to marshal his emotional strength with the notion that "a failure is but a sign to begin again" and that "things cannot go lower than they already are."[216] The critical rejection of his exhibition had produced an uncharacteristic humility; he saw himself as a millstone around Stieglitz's "very tired neck," a situation he hoped to remedy upon his return to America.[217] He managed to continue painting during this period, and by the time he left Paris for Aix, he had finished enough paintings for another exhibition should Stieglitz want one.

In the depths of his depression, Hartley had looked forward to being in Aix in the warmer months, viewing it as a place which would offer some relief. Instead, the loneliness there proved dispiriting and he referred to Maison Maria as "this little house of detention."[218] "I prefer rough textures and solid substances than all this flayed and whipped sensuality the French call finesse."[219] The sense of "home" which had attended his first glimpse of Aix vanished; once again, Hartley saw himself as an uprooted orphan. "The little cluster of belongings that had come to represent home for me will have to be dispersed — and the symbol of homelessness is I suspect to be perpetuated forever."[220]

Hartley's work tempo slowed that summer and he painted only when it went easily and smoothly. He occupied himself with still lifes of flowers — not only because he considered the heat outdoors intolerable, but also because he was discouraged by the disappointing reception his landscapes had received in New York. Nevertheless, he maintained his stance — against imaginative criteria and for objectively rendered depictions of the external world: "mathematicians have it all over poets + philosophers because they get close to solid substances."[221] Yet Hartley's commitment to objectivity pertained only to his art; for the first time in ten years, he again began to read the metaphysical and mystical writers, perhaps seeking solace for his troubled soul. His letters refer to Santayana's *Plotinus and the Spiritual Life,* to the medieval mystics John Ruysbroeck and Meister Eckhart, and to Saint Teresa and Jacob Boehme.[222] His readings helped restore his equilibrium, so that by the end of the summer he could write that he liked himself a little better and felt he had come closer to what he wished to be.[223]

Hartley's lease expired on November 21 and he was finally able to leave Aix. After one last circuit through Paris, Hamburg, Berlin, and Dresden he sailed for the United States on March 5, 1930. Except for the six years from 1916 to 1921, Hartley had spent most of his adult life in Europe. Although there had seldom been a time he had not thought about the country of his childhood, the return to America late in middle age proved to be an ordeal.

New Hampshire: 1930

Hartley's second European sojourn and subsequent return to the United States followed a pattern of alienation and reintegration typical of American expatriates of the era.[224] On his first repatriation from Europe in 1915, Hartley had felt detached from his native background, an exile in America. When he went abroad again in 1921, it was with the intention of spending the rest of his life in Europe. Arriving there, however, he started to look favorably at America, albeit at a distance. Hartley, like the expatriate writers forced home in the 1930s by the deteriorating situation in Europe, would continue to think of himself as oppressed by American society and would remain spiritually distanced from it for the next seven years.

Hartley would eventually rediscover a sense of "home" in America. But when he arrived back in 1930, he found an art community that had turned from European models to American themes and American forms of expression. In such an atmosphere, his paintings were viewed suspiciously. Hartley's supporters, moreover, always believed that his true origins as a painter were to be found in Maine; indeed, Paul Rosenfeld's 1923 article had even proposed that only a return to Maine could again bring cohesion to his painting.[225] Hartley saw in these recommendations a way to win back public acceptance, but his bitter memories of Maine — of childhood loneliness and estrangement — prevented him from returning there. Unable to face North Lovell, he spent the summer across the state border in Sugar Hill, New Hampshire, in the Franconia Valley.

Through some friends, he rented a deserted house there for three dollars a week on Cooley farm, facing the western slope of the mountains he had painted from North Lovell. His first response to New England was enthusiastic. He and an unidentified Polish friend from Paris scrubbed the house and decorated it with geraniums, curtains, and a new tablecloth. Initially his letters were filled with ebullient descriptions of the wonderful pictorial motifs he had found in the chasms and boulders of the nearby Lost River region, but by the end of the summer things had soured. He complained of having "no social life. . . . All work and no play is turning this Jack into a duller boy than he has been for a long time. . . ."[226] New England, he felt, had sold out to the tourist trade and was filled with rich, idle parasites and parvenus; hundreds of parked cars lining the mountain tops spoiled the views, and the tourists snooping over his shoulder forced him to abandon several pictures.

Even New England's colors were disappointing that year. "The country turned into soup green with the usual summer ending condition—and I had to stop painting as without some sort of colour there is no use working." [227] "There will I expect be no relief for the rest of the season except the natural autumn colour and I wish it would hurry up and come in so I can get at it and through with it." [228] To find relief, he took up mountain climbing, but even this quickly lost its appeal—there was, he felt, nothing about the mountains viewed from the top that he could not see from the bottom and climbing them therefore never surprised or excited him. The final disappointment was that the brilliant autumn color he had anticipated for twenty years was spoiled by a drought. [229]

Fig. 76 *Beaver Lake, Lost River Region*, 1930. Oil on canvas, 88.9 × 76.2 cm (35 × 30″). Walker Art Center, Minneapolis; gift of the T. B. Walker Foundation

Fig. 77 *Mountains, No. 21*, 1930. Oil on canvas, 86.4 × 76.2 cm (34 × 30″). Whitney Museum of American Art, New York; gift of Mr. and Mrs. Herman Schneider, 1967

Hartley's paintings of that summer bear witness to his discontent with his subject matter; although they faithfully described the shapes and colors of the area, the majority have no real vitality. He attempted to transpose the parallel brushstroke technique of his Mont Sainte-Victoire paintings (pl. 39) to motifs derived from the Lost River region of Beaver Lake (fig. 76), and Franconia Notch, Mt. Lafayette (fig. 77). But he no longer applied brushstrokes in well-defined bands of color, so that the series lacked the earlier paintings' structural solidity. In place of distinct strokes of imperceptibly different colors which mix optically to create an overall tonality, Hartley now brushed the paint on thinly in relatively homogeneous color areas. The result—especially in his Franconia Notch paintings—is a flat, nonplastic effect. A more spatial quality informs the Beaver Lake paintings. Unlike the rest of the New Hampshire series, here Hartley dispensed with uniform areas of purple, blue and red in favor of more discrete parallel strokes, which create a greater spatial effect. Still, the green and black palette in these paintings does little to demonstrate Hartley's skill as a colorist.

By October, New England had taken its toll on Hartley's emotions. He felt "done in with this incarceration . . . no escape day and night from facing nature constantly . . . and now I am all garbage heap of nerves and weakness—mental, physical and spiritual—aches and pains in the flesh—and a vacuum in the soul. . . . But I've learned one thing—Never never never to turn north again as long as I live—I am so chilled psychologically that I wonder if I'll ever be able to get the damp out of me." [230] He was so severely depressed about the immediate future that he confessed, "I have lost most of my will power and moral courage for what remains to me of the thing called life." [231]

At the end of the month, he left New Hampshire for Brooklyn, intending to finish his summer paintings in a more hospitable setting, but he was so depleted on all fronts that he had neither the energy nor the money to retrieve his pictures from the freight company. [232]

That winter was to be emotionally enervating; if Hartley expected a welcome for the prodigal son, he was disappointed. Although he had understood the country's isolationist inclination, he had not realized just how chauvinistic and xenophobic America had become. Once again, he had returned to a society of which he was not a part. Not only was he unable to share its convictions, but he felt excluded: "The last months have been very hard for me," he wrote, "for I felt the force of certain (perhaps imaginary) repulsions toward me in some directions—for no other reason I can think of save that I have lived abroad." [233] Some of Hartley's anxieties may well have been brought on by his lingering sense of the futility of showing his pictures, and the dread of having to encounter McBride and those who had rejected him. Yet the fears that his New Hampshire paintings would receive the same degree of censure that had greeted the Mont Sainte-Victoire landscapes proved unfounded. His December exhibition at Stieglitz's newly formed gallery, An American Place, was sufficiently profitable to finance him for another year.

The rest of the winter of 1930-31 took a severe physical toll on Hartley. He became so debilitated by bronchitis that he could not go up and down the stairs and had to rely on friends to bring him food. During this time, Adelaide Kuntz, whom he had become friendly with in France, became his closest companion, contributing to his finances and taking care of him physically. She took him to an ear specialist who told her privately that injury to Hartley's mastoids had left him with only scar tissue from the outside of his ear to his brain.[234] The doctor suggested he must have suffered excruciating pain and gave him between two months and two years to live. Hartley lived for thirteen more years, but he could not have been completely unaware of his precarious condition; the following November he asked his niece to investigate the legal costs of cremation.

His illness and brush with death drove him toward the kind of self-assessment he had not taken in years. His health returned, as did the willpower and moral courage about life which he had lacked in New Hampshire. By the end of winter, he wrote optimistically: "I have learned much these past years. . . . Especially the past year has brought me to a better meaning of myself than I could have expected. . . . How to love life and to keep from being estranged from it — that is a problem and I am not interested in trivial existence."[235] Through his physical and emotional suffering, Hartley had begun a process of personal integration which would culminate in a more expressive and powerful art. From here on, the quality of his work began to improve, and the hesitancy of the preceding decade was left behind.

Fig. 78 *Blueberry Highway, Dogtown*, 1931. Oil on academy board, 46.1 × 61 cm (18½ × 24″). High Museum of Art, Atlanta, Georgia; museum purchase with bequest of C. Donald Belcher, 1977.49

Dogtown: 1931

Hartley was well enough by February to make summer plans. He was attracted to Gloucester, Massachusetts, specifically to an area outside the city called Dogtown Common, which he had been introduced to during his 1920 summer visit to Gloucester. Dogtown Common, a stark, ice-age moraine, had been a city of about forty families before it was abandoned in 1750. Little remained except large glacial boulders and a few crumbling, man-made stone walls. In Hartley's words, it was "a place so original in its appearance as not to be duplicated either in New England or anywhere else — and the air of being made for no one — for nothing but itself. . . . A sense of eeriness pervades all the place therefore and the white shafts of these huge boulders mostly granite — stand like sentinels guarding nothing but shore — sea gulls fly over it on their way from the marshes to the sea — otherwise the place is forsaken and majestically lovely as if nature had at last found one spot where she can live for herself alone. It takes someone to be obsessed by nature for its own sake — one with a feeling for austerities and the intellectual aloofness which lost lonesome areas can persist in. . . . No triviality enters such places as these. . . . [It is] a cross between Easter Island and Stonehenge — essentially druidic in its appearance — it gives the feeling that an ancient race might turn up at any moment and renew an ageless rite there."[236]

Fig. 79 Road in Dogtown, Cape Ann, Massachusetts

Arriving in Gloucester in early July after eight months of not painting, Hartley found it surprisingly easy to begin work. He existed in relative isolation that summer; although he maintained a copious correspondence with friends, he had little direct social contact. He divided his day, as he had done for years, into two parts — reading and writing in the mornings and painting in the afternoons. Too weak to transport his materials over long distances, he did most of his painting from memory or from sketches.[237] By late summer he had completely given up painting on site. Despite this removal from the actual landscape, he strove to objectively capture the quality of the area, "if only to get rid of the artistic aspect that pictures are so ridden with these days. . . . Art is so inclined to ape itself."[238] This anti-formalist sentiment — which restated the position articulated in his 1928 article — was echoed the following March in a letter to Harriet Monroe expressing his interest in the "objectivist" theme of her magazine: "I myself have returned to objective nature in painting during the past four years and I hope one day to be known as a fine realist. After all, the world is tired of subconscious extravagances and artists are finding it out very rapidly. The visible appearances are picturesque enough and no one cares what a private neurotic life divulges."[239]

Hartley successfully infused his Dogtown paintings with the stark monumentality of the area. His New Hampshire landscapes had emphasized the two-dimensionality of the canvas through tactile brushstrokes and through shapes and colors that reverberated across the field to create a unified pictorial plane. In these Dogtown paintings, the forms become truly sculptural — "painted sculpture + not ordinary painting" (figs. 78 and 80).[240] Hartley depicted the glacial boulders of Dogtown as dense, massive volumes. Rejecting surface detail in favor of simplified, severe forms, he created images of permanence and stability. His "objective" goal was not to transcribe the exact physical likeness of the area, but rather to capture the underlying geometric structure which remained after accidental appearances had been eliminated. In their immobility and lack of detail, Hartley's paintings evoked the Egyptian art which fascinated him that summer. The Egyptians, Hartley felt, replaced references to artistic personality with contemplative identification with their subject and thus achieved the kind of realism he himself was seeking.[241]

But Hartley's stated commitment to an objectivist principle once again pertained only to his art. That same summer his emotional focus shifted back to a more inner-directed awareness. He had begun moving in this direction in Aix after the devastating critical reception his 1929 exhibition at The Intimate Gallery had received. Both then and now at Dogtown, he read extensively from metaphysical and mystical writers.[242] Driving him back into himself, he laid the foundation for a new future, different from that of the past fifteen years, but as yet unknown. He felt he had given up old concepts and laid new principles of life for himself; he sought to clear his mind of art issues and to strive instead for simplicity and purity of vision in life itself. He attempted to return to the interior state that had existed up to 1915, but to incorporate the experiences and insights of the intervening years, so that his new subjective philosophy would be something more substantial than intellectual diversion.[243] It would take nearly five years for Hartley to assimilate these life goals to the point where they were reflected in either his daily habits or his art. When he did, his art would once again achieve an expressive intensity equal to that of his German military period.

By the end of December, Hartley finished the last of the summer's pictures and returned to New York, vowing to revisit Gloucester. Although his new philosophical attitudes were not yet apparent in his work, the psychological reassessment he had undergone that summer revived not only his faith in his inner vision, but also his faith in himself as a painter: he returned to the city feeling refreshed and renewed. He agreed to exhibit his Dogtown paintings at The Downtown Gallery that April, a move which further strained his relationship to Stieglitz. He accompanied the (unsuccessful) exhibition with a poem, "The Return of the Native," in which he declared himself a New England painter. The poem linked the philosophy he had developed over the summer with a return to Maine; by going back to his native land and renewing his earlier faith and ideals he would "make what was broken whole." Despite this affirmative posture, Hartley would not return to Maine for another five years.

Fig. 80 *In the Moraine, Dogtown Common, Cape Ann*, 1931. Oil on academy board, 45.7 × 61 cm (18 × 24″). Georgia Museum of Art, The University of Georgia, Athens; University Purchase, 1969

Plate 34   *Still Life*, ca. 1922–23 (cat. no. 52)
Mrs. Hazel B. Strand; courtesy of The Currier Gallery of Art,
Manchester, New Hampshire

Plate 35 *Landscape, New Mexico*, 1923 (cat. no. 53)
Babcock Galleries, New York City

Plate 36   *New Mexico Recollections No. 10*, 1923 (cat. no. 55)
Private Collection, Great Neck, New York

Plate 37   *Landscape, Vence*, 1925–26 (cat. no. 56)
University Gallery, University of Minnesota, Minneapolis;
bequest of Hudson Walker from the Ione and Hudson Walker Collection

Plate 38 *Purple Mountains*, 1925–26 (cat. no. 57)
Phoenix Art Museum; gift of Mr. and Mrs. Orme Lewis

Plate 39 *Mont Sainte-Victoire*, 1927 (cat. no. 59)
Des Moines Art Center; gift of Mr. and Mrs. Fred Bohen

Plate 40   *Mont Sainte-Victoire, Aix-en-Provence*, 1927 (cat. no. 60)
Mr. and Mrs. Carl D. Lobell, New York

Plate 41 *Mountains No. 19*, 1930 (cat. no. 61)
Private Collection

Plate 42   *Flaming Pool, Dogtown*, 1931 (cat. no. 62)
Collection of American Literature, Beinecke Rare Book and Manuscript Library,
Yale University, New Haven; gift of Adelaide Kuntz

Mexico: 1932

During the winter of 1930 Rebecca Strand had persuaded Hartley to apply for a Guggenheim Foundation fellowship, and before leaving for Gloucester he had received word he had won the award. The fellowship stipulated that work be executed out of the country; this requirement, coupled with his precarious health and fond memories of the Southwest's warmth and sunlight, led Hartley to choose Mexico. He embarked in March for Mexico City, where he spent the first two months studying the Aztec and Mayan cultures in the anthropological museum before relocating to Cuernavaca. He pursued his spiritualist interests with the help of a friend's library of occult books. "As a result," he wrote, "I am so much clearer about the superior aspect of introspection than I have ever been and I learn from men like Ruysbroeck, Rolle, et cet.—how much of a science introspection can be. . . ."[244]

In Mexico, Hartley found a microcosmic art and literary community: he variously encountered Paul Strand, Mark Tobey, Andrew Dasburg, John Evans (Mabel Dodge's son), and Hart Crane. Hartley had contacted Crane, whom he had known casually in Brooklyn Heights and southern France, shortly after his arrival in 1932. During the afternoon they spent together, Hartley felt they established a special rapport. Crane seemed slightly nervous and hysterical and Hartley believed he could help him. Hartley left the meeting reluctantly for another appointment, but made plans to get together with Crane the following morning. The rendezvous never took place. Soon after, Crane sailed from Mexico for the United States on the steamship *Orizaba* and committed suicide off the coast of Cuba by jumping overboard from the stern of the boat. Although Hartley did not have a close relationship with Crane, he felt a kinship with the poet, perhaps because both men harbored deep anxieties about their homosexuality, perhaps because Crane voiced so openly his fear that he had nothing left to say as an artist.

The shock of Crane's death did not, however, destroy Hartley's initial enchantment with Mexico, with what he considered the primitive energy of the Mexican people, and the noble, sculptural landscape. Yet in the end, the environment proved to be enervating. He finally concluded in his autobiography: "Mexico was a place that devitalized my energies—it was the one place I shall always think of as wrong for me. . . . It is a place all by itself and all for itself—left to come and go on a listless tide. . . . The light will wear you down, the air will fatigue—height will oppress. . . . Perhaps you can learn the secret of all the dark living but you will change your whole being to do it."[245]

But Mexico did stimulate his growing focus on the inner life. Encouraged by his readings in occult literature and by his fascination with the esoteric rituals of the Aztec and Mayan cultures, he wholeheartedly embraced the field of the imagination. "I have taken Blake's advice which I took years ago and was proceeding to follow it, when I slipped off into thinking that mind was everything when god knows it has proved itself an idiot often enough in these times. In other words I am really going to try to do now what I indicated in the 1913-1915 period when I swung off into space and made pictures of just shapes and movements which had a very definite approval at that time; I should have been less emotional when an occultist woman came to see my pictures, and said—you don't realize what you are doing in these pictures, they are full of cabalistic signs; I will now far better know what I am employing in the way of symbols when I use them."[246]

This letter foretold a radical shift in his painting style and a reversal of the "objectivist" philosophy of the past sixteen years. As the letter implied, the images of his Mexican paintings—like those in the Intuitive Abstractions and German

Fig. 81 *Eight Bells' Folly, Memorial for Hart Crane,* 1933 (see Plate 96)

Fig. 82 *Yliaster, Mexico,* 1932. Oil on cardboard, 63.5 × 72.4 cm (25 × 28½"). Babcock Galleries, New York

Fig. 83 José Clemente Orozco. *Zapatistas,* 1931. Oil on canvas, 114.3 × 139.7 cm (45 × 55"). The Museum of Modern Art, New York; given anonymously

military series — were not based on what he saw in the external world.

However, the images and symbols in the earlier work were invented through free association and represented no recognizable objects. Moreover, they were not intended to signify anything more than a generalized spiritual consciousness. In contrast, Hartley's Mexican paintings contain none of the linear pictographs or transparent washes with in the 1912-13 work suggested ethereal transcendence; instead, they use a palette of yellow, orange, and blue to present solidly rendered symbols with profound and specific meanings. The result is more cabalistic than cosmic. Hartley's intent to convey specific meanings through these symbols is particularly evident in *Eight Bells' Folly Memorial for Hart Crane* (fig. 81), of which he wrote: "It has a very mad look as I wish it to have — there is a ship foundering — a sun, a moon, two triangular clouds — a bell with '8' on it — symbolizing eight bells — or noon when he jumped off — and around the bell are a lot of men's eyes — that look up from below to see who the new lodger is to be — on one cloud will be the number 33 — Hart's age — and according to some occult beliefs is the dangerous age of a man — for if he survives 33 — he lives on — Christ was supposed to be 33. . . ."[247] The eight-pointed stars in the clouds and the numerological references to transcendence and regeneration recall his 1914-15 symbolic tributes to Karl von Freyburg. And while the massive, immobile forms in these Mexican works relate to Hartley's Dogtown series, their effect is no longer objectivist. Quite apart from the esoteric symbols scattered throughout the paintings, the naturalistic color and sculptural fullness of the earlier series is replaced with flat planes created by eliminating modeling and value contrasts, and with arbitrary areas of uniform color applied without regard to physical facts. Even paintings which include more traditional landscapes motifs, such as *Yliaster, Mexico* (fig. 82), are given a mystical character through this irrational color and space. Hartley's dramatic contrasts of intense yellows and oranges and severe, stylized forms recall the work of José Clemente Orozco (fig. 83), whose expressive compositions greatly impressed Hartley in this period. By adopting the flat, decorative quality of Orozco's murals, Hartley was able to appropriate the character of the Pre-Columbian art he had studied in the anthropology museum.

Garmisch-Partenkirchen: 1933 – 1934

Mexico had reawakened Hartley's mystical interests, but it had also devitalized him and he needed the familiar reassurance of Europe. On April 30, having completed his one-year commitment to the Guggenheim, he sailed from Vera Cruz to Europe, going immediately to Germany, lured by what he felt to be the naturally symbolist nature of the Germans.[248] After spending the spring and summer in the then flamboyantly decadent city of Hamburg, he settled in the more rural village of Garmisch-Partenkirchen in the Bavarian Alps. His economic situation deteriorated drastically as the last of the Guggenheim fellowship money was spent. He could not even afford the usual German coffee in the afternoon, nor could he buy canvas; he was forced to use cardboard as a substitute.[249] Equally distressing was his realization that his financial struggles might never be alleviated. His affiliation with The Downtown Gallery had been strained by the financial disaster of his 1932 exhibition there; at the same time, his relationship with Stieglitz was such that he could no longer count on the dealer's support. A large exhibition of Hartley's Mexican paintings had been held in Mexico City, but no sales had resulted. Given the pessimistic financial prospects and lack of sustained interest in his work, Hartley, once again, became despondent and questioned the value of painting at all. For the first time, however, his letters acknowledged that, despite the futility of his endeavors, he had no other option: he needed to paint for his own psychic survival.[250] This realization would gradually free Hartley to paint for himself rather than for external rewards, either financial or social.

The Garmisch-Partenkirchen years marked the beginning of Hartley's reconciliation of his belief in imaginative principles with his desire for objectivism in art. He continued his spiritual, intuitive pursuits, but tried to extend his consciousness beyond selfhood to achieve an empathetic identification with depicted motifs. On one of his walks, he had a mystical revelation of this psychic union: ". . . something came over me. . . . something whisked me away, completely enfolded me, I felt myself becoming everything — continuity, measure, surcease — I had become nothing and in that instant I saw myself saying to myself — wasn't it wonderful now we can begin again."[251]

Hartley attempted to apply these insights to his art by abandoning the personal, esoteric symbolism of his Mexican paintings, but retaining their commitment to intuitive principles. He wanted his paintings to reflect an understanding of his subject matter that went beyond intellectual knowledge. For role models he kept photographs on his table of pictures by Van Eyck, Piero della Francesca, and Dürer, feeling that their works embodied the principles of "perfect observation and perfect sensing of things" that he wanted in his own compositions.[252]

Hartley's Garmisch-Partenkirchen paintings were the first to hint at what would become the great landscape style of his late period. When he arrived in Garmisch, he started a series of landscapes lithographs. By late November, he began painting, turning his attention to the peaks of Alpspitz-Mittenwald and Dreitorspitz. As in Dogtown, he did not paint *in situ*, but instead would walk six or seven miles to make a drawing or absorb the scene and later paint it indoors from memory. "I have had to work that way for years," he wrote to his niece, "and it is my way of showing how much I have learned and absorbed of nature."[253] The natural world had become once again his point of departure, but he no longer rendered it with the cold, intellectual clarity that had characterized his southern French landscapes. In its place was an awesome grandeur which combined structural solidity with resonant color. Most of these paintings were completed by December 1933.[254] The bold black-and-white contrasts characterizing the series recall Hartley's 1909 Dark Landscapes. That Hartley went back to this mode indicates how much his vision was returning to the imaginative realism of his early career. The Bavarian Alps series is dominated by massive forms whose angular shapes are defined by heavy outlining and solid tonal areas (fig. 84). Hartley depicts these peaks as monuments towering above the surrounding ground. What makes them most suggestive of his late landscape period is their color and paint quality: although working within a dark tonal range, Hartley modulated his brushstrokes with subtle interweavings of closely related colors which maintain distinct tonal areas, while at the same time creating an immensely rich color effect.

Hartley's German sojourn ended after less than a year, but he had managed to paint abroad with a certain inner peace. This last trip to Germany played an important role in developing and restoring his emotional reserves; he later called it "the shrine of my delivery."[255]

Fig. 84 *Garmisch-Partenkirchen*, 1933. Oil on canvas mounted on board, 74.9 × 46.4 cm (29½ × 18¼"). Museum of Art, Carnegie Institute, Pittsburgh; gift of Mr. and Mrs. James H. Beal

New York and Gloucester: 1934

From Germany Hartley had written enthusiastically about the benefits of government support of the arts, considering himself a perfect "test case" for the recently formed Public Works of Arts Project in America. After his return to New York in mid-February 1934, he joined the project and remained with it until its dissolution at the end of May, grateful for the fifty-five-dollar-a-week salary.

Hartley's recent conviction that he psychologically needed to paint in order to function did not lessen his desire for external support from the art community. His French Provence work had been unfavorably received by the press and by Stieglitz, who had become so committed to an indigenous American vision and style that he was reluctant to exhibit Hartley's recent Garmisch-Partenkirchen landscapes. Still seeking an artistic mode which would generate respect, Hartley became obsessed with the desire to be known as a great regional painter of New England. Memories of his early hardships still kept him from returning to Maine, so he went again to Dogtown, vowing to make of this landscape something "as intense as Homer's Maine or Ryder's subjective N[ew] E[ngland]."[256]

In his second series of Dogtown paintings (fig. 85), Hartley abandoned the coldly defined massive volumes of both his alpine landscapes and his 1931 Dogtown series, replacing them with dense clusters of smaller forms. The broad expanses of closely modulated tones and uniform surface treatment gave way to either an overall scratching effect or thickly modulated paint. Hartley laid greater emphasis on the two-dimensional picture plane through this worked paint surface and through the perspectively "incorrect" tiering of forms as in *Sea View, New England* (fig. 86). These paintings have none of the austere monumentality or mythic qualities that Hartley had captured in his first Dogtown series. In general, they fall short of his goal — to make these landscapes as intense as those of Homer or Ryder.

In early winter, Hartley left Gloucester for New York, where crisis awaited him. It was the height of the Depression and money was universally scarce. The widening rift with Stieglitz left him without a committed dealer and therefore without any permanent source of income. His friend Adelaide Kuntz had agreed to help by paying twenty-five dollars a month toward a painting, but by November her affairs were so bad that she could no longer afford to advance the money. Other financial reversals were even more devastating. For many years, Hartley had kept his unsold paintings in Lincoln Warehouse in Manhattan, and he now owed two hundred and forty dollars in back rent. The company's threat to sell the stored pictures in a Bronx auction if Hartley could not pay his bill threw him into absolute panic, since he felt a sale would completely ruin his reputation. His initial attempts to raise funds failed; Steiglitz did not come through, and his Guggenheim fellowship was not renewed. Some of his friends — Ettie Stettheimer, for example — refused to see him because they regarded his recent tenure in Germany as a condonation of Hitler's anti-Semitic regime. He eventually managed to procure one hundred and fifty dollars from friends and make up the rest himself. Although the money covered his storage bill, it did not account for future costs, and Hartley had to reduce the number of paintings so that they could be stored in a single vault. His attempts to sell the paintings having failed, he saw no other alternative than to destroy them.

On his fifty-eighth birthday, in January 1935, Hartley went to the storage room and destroyed over one hundred paintings and drawings. His sense of helpless desperation was aggravated by the recent news that a poverty-stricken sister had died in Cleveland; during his mission of destruction, he carried the letter informing him of her death.

Fig. 85 *Dogtown*, 1934. Oil on masonite, 40.3 × 73 cm (15⅞ × 28¾"). University Gallery, University of Minnesota, Minneapolis; bequest of Hudson Walker from the Ione and Hudson Walker Collection

Fig. 86 *Sea View, New England*, 1934. Oil on academy board, 30.5 × 40.6 cm (12 × 16"). The Phillips Collection, Washington, D.C.

Hartley's disillusionment, which he had managed to suppress in Germany, increased now to near disastrous proportions. Before his rampage in the warehouse, he had been able to write: "All I want is to live modestly without terror of hunger and I can go on and produce quietly, for I am at my very best now for all reasons and it is important that I find a way to keep at work." [257] All this changed after he destroyed his paintings: "Anyone who thinks art is worth the tortures must be prepared. I have endured nothing but negation for two years which doesn't bring forth gusts of courage. I write a great deal because it helps me function. . . . I am in a state of crucifixion these days. . . . I don't think too well of anything or anybody — and if I had my way I'd never set foot in N.Y. again." [258]

Suicidal depression took over and for weeks he imagined writing suicide notes to be left on tables. He remained secluded, confessing later to Rebecca Strand that he had not had "the courage to face even those I love," and had felt he could resuscitate himself only by keeping off the "terrible" New York streets. [259] For the rest of the winter and spring he subsisted on sixty cents a day and ate only one real meal a week, which Stieglitz bought for him at the Shelton Hotel. This act of compassionate generosity indicates the complexity of their relationship. Stieglitz was no longer for Hartley the benevolent, emotional supporter or financial patron that he had been before or that he was to his other artists. However, although Hartley had drifted away and had sought patronage elsewhere, he had not been expelled from the gallery and he still retained a vestige of his ties with his early champion.

By pricing his paintings very low, Hartley managed to sell enough privately to skid through the summer, although he never had quite enough to eat. His doctor gave him tranquilizers, which calmed him and put him to sleep, a remedy he welcomed since depression and persistent bronchitis allowed him little real rest.

Fig. 87 *View from the Window,* 1935. Oil on board, 61 × 45.7 cm (24 × 18″). John and Jan Mackey, St. Louis

Bermuda and Nova Scotia: 1935

Forbidden by his doctor from going north that summer, but loath to remain in New York, Hartley booked passage to Bermuda. From the money acquired by the sale of a painting to his nephew, Theodore Newell, and a monthly stipend of fifty dollars which he received from an "angel," he managed to live as one of "the elegant poor" in a house on the north shore of Bermuda, rented for fifteen dollars a month. [260] The poverty and humiliation of the previous winter had exhausted him and he lived in comparative seclusion, writing each morning and painting after lunch. He read less and thought less, simply indulging in the luxury of the sun.

Hartley's paintings of that summer reflect his desire for quiet and calm. He concentrated on still lifes in order to avoid the serious contemplation necessary for "profound landscapes." Nevertheless he did complete several paintings from his last Dogtown series — a strange impulse considering how dissimilar his groups of paintings were from one another. In format, the Bermuda still lifes (fig. 87), recall the open-window paintings he had executed during his earlier trip to Bermuda (fig. 48). Hartley now reduced his imagery to broad expanses, painted in creamy tones of pale blue and white, which, when combined in a sparse, open composition, evoked the tranquility that Bermuda gave him that summer. As before, however, Hartley regarded the Bermuda scenery as too pretty and quaint for oil, and he rarely portrayed its landscape. The underwater scenery proved ultimately more stimulating, and the brightly colored fish seen on the fishing trips he took with the owner of his house appeared in a series of Bermuda paintings completed in New York the following spring (fig. 88).

Hartley vacated his house in early September. To avoid returning to New York, he decided to visit Lunenberg, a southern Nova Scotia town mentioned to him by his friend Pierre Coalfleet, the Canadian novelist.

From Coalfleet's description, Lunenberg seemed like a remote and inexpensive alternative to Gloucester, which he could no longer afford and where he dreaded contact with other local artists. He arrived in Lunenberg in late September 1935 and found the town completely unappealing. On the advice of a cab driver, he went up the coast to the small fishing community of Blue Rocks and there took a room.

The town's archaic severity and wildness immediately enchanted Hartley. He wrote Rebecca Strand that stories of the sea were told as if they were bus rides: "I get a thrill out of personal anonymity as if I were financially free."[261] A few days after his arrival, Hartley met Mrs. Francis Mason, a neighbor who came from a small offshore island to spin yarn at the house where he was boarding, and her calm spirit greatly impressed him. That evening he met her husband, and one of their huge and—according to Hartley—magnificent sons, Alty, who aroused his sexual interest by hugging him vigorously around the waist. Weighing a muscular two hundred and ten pounds, with dramatic black hair that shot up six inches above his forehead, thirty-one-year-old Alty appeared to Hartley as a vision of the perfect male.

Several days after their meeting, Alty invited Hartley to spend the afternoon with him and some friends, a meeting Hartley later described in an unpublished story: "There was a great deal of pornographic talk, many awkward passes, much freedom of expression . . . an intensely exciting and original day, the entire set up being so archaic and utterly different from all other qualities of life."[262] After meeting the second son, Donny, Hartley asked if he could live with the family on the island. This agreed to, Hartley moved into the Mason home on Eastern Points Island, where he received room and board for seven dollars a week.

The elemental quality of life on the island attracted Hartley immediately. "There is a touch of Christian martyrdom about the life anyhow, for they endure such hardships and hate any show of cheap affectation. . . . All this vital energy and force. . . . I have never been so near the real thing before."[263] Although he stayed there only six weeks, the Mason household—which included the parents, the two sons, and two daughters, one of whom lived in Halifax and was rarely home—had a profound effect on him. For the first time since his mother died he was accepted as a member of a family. Under the influence of their gentle humaneness and pervading kindness and affection, he felt a liberating sense of familial love and security; always more reverent about the world when he felt self-confident, Hartley now vowed, after years of rejection and self-doubt, to become "violently in love" with life again.[264]

Although his primary attraction was to the physical magnificence and comradeship of the two sons, Hartley was greatly drawn to the simple dignity and direct faith of the mother and father. He particularly revered Francis Mason, whom he described as "one of the greatest men I have ever known."[265] After seeking the glamour and mannered finesse of Europe for most of his life, the unpretentious piety and epic simplicity of the Masons' lives inspired him; as he came increasingly to value these qualities, his art grew spiritually richer. Hartley would not translate these feelings into paint for over a year, but when he did, the resulting compositions were among his most expressive and powerful.

New York and Nova Scotia: 1936

With the onset of winter, Hartley had to leave Eastern Points, but he made plans to return the following summer for six months. Back in New York that December of 1935, he retreated again into seclusion as fear of rejection and memories of the humiliation of the previous winter resurfaced.[266] He heard little encouraging news about anyone upon his return, and felt New York called for an emotional endurance he was not certain he could summon. He loathed the city, but did not have the money to go elsewhere, and needed to maintain what meager business and social contacts he had.

Hartley received some financial support beginning in late January from the Works Project Administration.[267] But he had to delete the clause that required artists to sign in at nine A.M. for four days a week because another siege of bronchitis forced him to rest in bed in the morning "till normalcy is achieved."[268] Despite this preferential treatment, he terminated his contract in May, incensed by bureaucratic red tape and beset by a feeling that his work was not appropriate for the large mural commissions being offered.

What Hartley did produce for the WPA were paintings devoted to the flower and fish motifs begun earlier in Bermuda. Because flowers had been scarce there, Hartley had invented his own floral motifs. He described the resultant brightly colored fantasies as imaginative portrayals of things "seen or sensed in Bermuda."

The most striking feature of these Bermuda Fantasies (fig. 88) is their color range, more brilliant now than any of Hartley's work since his 1908-9 Neo-Impressionist landscapes. To describe the brightly colored fish he had seen in Bermuda, Hartley abandoned the restrained earth tones of recent years for a palette of high-keyed pinks, blues, and reds. As with his fish still lifes painted in Paris in 1924 (fig. 66), he dispensed with illusionistic spatial representations in favor of bird's-eye views or profiles. But now he also dispensed with the loose, spontaneous brushwork and creamy brown tones of the Paris series. Instead, he applied dabs of brilliant color over the entire canvas surface to create a speckled, ornamental effect which visually unites the disparate, otherwise unrelated forms of the composition. Noting that his paintings were "all gay—no more dark pictures now," Hartley attributed their jubilance to "a Spiritual rebirth, etc."[269] These paintings were the first pictorial manifestation of his new ebullient attitude toward life which had developed during his six-week stay with the Masons. At the same time, they reflect his continuing commitment to avoid profound subject matter. "For with flowers," Hartley explained, "one escapes into simplicity without mood."[270]

Hartley re-established contact with Stieglitz that winter and became a habitué of Stieglitz's new gallery, An American Place, which had opened in 1930, a year after The Intimate Gallery closed. Hartley felt a genuine warmth toward Stieglitz, whom he described as "dearer than ever—quite a halo emanates from his smile these days."[271] He somehow convinced Stieglitz to show his work again and in March 1936 opened his exhibition consisting of what he called "Fantasies" and "Romantic Intervals" of Bermuda, and landscapes from Garmisch-Partenkirchen. Two weeks before the opening he was still finishing paintings. Although the exhibition produced several sales, the Alpine vistas were not well received. The critical hostility to the German subjects convinced Hartley of the necessity of returning to Maine and establishing his identity as a Maine artist: "I propose a 100% Yankee show next year," he confided angrily to Adelaide Kuntz, "to cram that idea down their throats till it chokes them even."[272]

Hartley found relief from the pressure of criticism when he returned to Nova Scotia in July. The Mason family welcomed him back warmly and he once again

Fig. 88 *Sunken Treasure*, 1935–36. Oil on board, 45.1 × 60.3 cm (13¾ × 23¾"). Mr. and Mrs. Carl D. Lobell, New York

Fig. 89 *Braided Rope and Shells*, 1936. Oil on board, 61.3 × 46 cm (24⅛ × 18⅛"). Present whereabouts unknown

Fig. 90 *The Old Bars, Dogtown*, 1936 (see Plate 50)

Fig. 91 Winslow Homer. *The Gulf Stream*, 1899. Oil on canvas, 71.1 × 124.5 cm (28 × 49"). The Metropolitan Museum of Art, New York; Wolfe Fund, 1906

felt "more at home than I have felt anywhere." [273] He renewed his attachment to the sons, particularly Alty, with whom he developed a strong, probably sexual relationship. For fifty-nine-year-old Hartley, Alty offered a unique association with youth and hedonistic physicality. "He lives," Hartley wrote of Alty, "utterly for the consummate satisfaction of the flesh, the kind of flesh making no difference. . . . You must be prepared for the eruption of his vesuvius, for his laval heats and flows will inevitably inundate your careful and calm city. . . . He has no common code, no inhibitions. He will give as much love to a man as to a woman . . . . Because he was thrown over by the first woman, I think he has transferred his affections to his men friends for he loves them. . . ." [274] Hartley had rarely been so happy; with the Masons' encouragement, he considered building a house on the island to share with Alty so that he could stay indefinitely.

In response to the Nova Scotia light, Hartley's paintings that summer reverted from the colorful palette of his Bermuda still lifes to what he called "the poetical sense of low tones." [275] For subjects, he turned to the artifacts of fishing life — sea shells, bleached crabs, corkfloats, and coils of rope. He began by adopting the format used in his Bermuda fish fantasies — rendering basically unrelated, often disproportionally scaled elements against a homogeneous background (fig. 89) or in an outdoor setting. The amplification of linear details in these still lifes differentiates them from Hartley's work of the preceding years, where he avoided embellishments in favor of simplified, massive forms. The only other time Hartley adopted a drawing approach was in his 1934 Dogtown series (fig. 85). However, unlike the two-dimensional emphasis created by the linear markings in this series, the linear elements in the Nova Scotia paintings actually contribute to their high degree of naturalism. As before in Hartley's career, naturalism — the "objective" approach — reflected his desire to eliminate his emotions from his art. The interest in introspection and the inner consciousness which he had renewed in Aix, Gloucester, and Mexico apparently evaporated after his return to the United States in 1934. His decision to unite the imaginative with the objective, formulated in Bavaria, no longer seemed a consideration. Instead, he returned that summer to simple and relatively uninspired objective painting. "If there is a hint of the abstract in the result," he wrote to Stieglitz of these paintings, "it is the quality of nature itself that rules for I want to have no emotion of my own." [276] In addition to these naturalistic still lifes, Hartley executed his third series of Dogtown themes that summer, using the crumbling stone walls he had seen in the Commons as motifs (fig. 90). These paintings share with preceding work the heavy-bodied application of paint, but by structuring the composition around the dramatic play between black and white, Hartley achieves a massive, weighty quality, suggested but not fully exploited in his Bavarian landscapes. Even his first Dogtown series seems dainty when compared to the density of these images. This quality was to become the hallmark of Hartley's late style.

Tragedy suddenly ended the peace that Hartley found in Nova Scotia. On Saturday, September 19, Donny and his cousin Allan went to Lunenberg to meet Alty, who worked there as a mechanic during the week. That evening a fierce North Atlantic storm swept the area. Knowing the danger and the boys' bravado, Allan's father tried to telephone the mainland to have Alty's punt hidden, but high winds had blown down the wires. By ten the following morning, the storm had passed, but the boys had not returned home. A search party eventually located the punt twenty miles down the coast, still loaded with the boys' belongings and the Sunday groceries. Their bodies were found nearly two weeks later. [277]

The tragedy devastated the family. To maintain some continuity in their lives, they asked Hartley to remain on Eastern Points until December, which he agreed to do. Deeply shaken by the event, he wrote to Rönnebeck that "life here has been

Fig. 92 *Northern Seascape, Off the Banks,* 1936–37 (see Plate 98)

Fig. 93 Albert Pinkham Ryder. *Toilers of the Sea,* n.d. Oil on wood, 28.9 × 30.5 cm (11⅜ × 12″). The Metropolitan Museum of Art, New York; George A. Hearn Fund, 1915

Fig. 94 *The Wave,* 1940. Oil on composition board, 76.8 × 103.8 cm (30¼ × 40⅞″). Worcester Art Museum, Massachusetts

made empty, without the boys. . . . I haven't felt anything like it since the death of Karl von F[reyburg]."[278] As with von Freyburg, the family became a powerful symbolic image in Hartley's imagination. From the tragedy emerged a series of the most intense and emotional paintings he had attempted since his German officer portraits.

His first response to the catastrophe was a group of dark marine studies which portrayed the violence and lonely force of the sea. Painted while he was still in Nova Scotia, compositions such as *Northern Seascape, Off the Banks* (fig. 92) incorporate the vision of Ryder (fig. 93) with the pessimistic attitude about man's helplessness against nature expressed in late Winslow Homer (fig. 91). Of the two, Ryder's vision in particular dominated Hartley's consciousness. His second essay on Ryder, written later that year, stated that Ryder was the one foundation upon which an indigenous American art could be built. As Hartley turned back toward his own roots, Ryder increasingly became the image that he had earlier described as "emblazoned on the body of my belief like a symbolic form of heraldry."[279] The expressive quality manifested in these Northern Seascapes is attributable to the successful reconciliation of Hartley's desire for a detached, objective realism with personally significant themes that embodied his ideas about the meaning of life. As in his earlier Ryderesque series, the Dark Landscapes (pl. 3), these paintings explore the relationship between nature and mankind. But in contrast to the passive, suffocating effect of the youthful work, these seascapes invoke the ominous threat of a crushing sea. Nature is indifferent to man in both cases, but in the Dark Landscapes it evokes a psychological depression through its bleakness and loneliness. In the Northern Seascapes, its threat has become a matter of life and death. The claustrophobic pressure of dominant foreground shapes and a high horizon line in the Dark Landscapes has been supplanted by a spatially open composition whose centered horizon line suggests at once infinite expanse and two-dimensionality. Although governed by black-and-white contrasts, as is the Dogtown series of that summer, a brushed surface treatment replaces the earlier distinct delineation between smooth color areas. The image of a lone ship on a foreboding sea haunted Hartley's imagination. In the following years he executed variations on this theme, often reworking the exact motif or focusing on isolated elements such as the crashing foreground waves (fig. 94).

From Eastern Points, Hartley returned to New York, where he finished the Nova Scotia paintings, and in April 1937, he hung his last exhibition with Stieglitz at An American Place. Because of criticism leveled at his German landscapes the year before by Stieglitz and the press, he declared himself in the foreword to the exhibition catalogue to be the painter from Maine: "This quality of nativeness is colored by heritage, birth, and environment. . . . And so I say to my native continent of Maine, be patient and forgiving, I will soon put my cheek to your cheek, expecting the welcome of the prodigal. . . ."[280] However, he returned to the fold too late for Stieglitz, who had grown impatient with Hartley's self-centeredness and what he considered a lack of direction; with this exhibition, Hartley and Stieglitz parted ways forever. O'Keeffe, Marin, Dove, and Strand had come to embody true American art for Stieglitz, and he had scheduled Hartley's exhibition more out of a sense of past responsibility than of true commitment to Hartley's work. Elizabeth McCausland, reviewer for the *Springfield Republican,* recalled that Stieglitz followed her around the exhibition, disclaiming Hartley's importance as an artist.[281] Ironically, Hartley's break with Stieglitz occurred just at the moment when his vision had shifted back to that imaginative expressiveness with which Stieglitz would have been sympathetic; as he had declared but not implemented in 1932, Hartley was now ready to return to Maine and to the earlier conditions of his inner life.

Financially the exhibition at An American Place was an utter failure and Hartley, who had not sold anything in over a year, faced what he considered complete annihilation. In a series of pitiful letters pleading for money, he compared his condition to the circumstances surrounding the suicides of Vachel Lindsay and Hart Crane.[282] He wrote to Lloyd Goodrich, curator of the Whitney Museum of American Art: "I have fought a heavy battle, and am on the outside of my private problem now, and I know that from now on the pictures will be clear, straight, and completely revealing." He appealed to Goodrich "to help me out in any way you can to get out of the worst hole in all my life."[283] His utter desperation proved an effective entreaty; the Whitney purchased *The Old Bars, Dogtown* for eight hundred dollars, the only sale he made that year.

Although unable to maintain sustaining, long-term relationships, Hartley always seemed to find someone to help him either financially or emotionally. Hudson Walker's interest in him, after Stieglitz's disaffection, followed this pattern. Walker, a young dealer who opened his own gallery in 1936, expressed interest in Hartley's work during the 1937 exhibition. Stieglitz gladly relinquished to Walker all responsibility for Hartley's career. Completely committed to Hartley's work, Walker remained a friend and supporter even after his gallery closed in 1940. The gallery was new, however, and did not have the same reputation or clientele as Stieglitz's. Walker was also thirty years Hartley's junior and, although supportive, could not fill Stieglitz's mentor role. Hartley's correspondence with Walker reveals the bitter, complaining personality of an artist with a somewhat imperious attitude toward his new dealer.

Hartley's health failed badly that winter and again he considered arranging his affairs in the event of sudden death. His hearing deteriorated to such an extent that conversation became difficult; he was overweight and the gradual loss of his teeth gave his face a sunken, sorrowful expression. According to Walker, Hartley's toothlessness embarrassed him so much that he rarely laughed without putting his hand over his mouth. Partly because of poor health and criticism toward his paintings, and partly because his experience in Nova Scotia had reconnected him with an epic simplicity reminiscent of Maine, the cosmopolitan, cultured world he had so long pursued lost its appeal. As he grew increasingly detached from it, returning to his homeland became less of an emotional ordeal.

Plate 43 *The Mountain of the North*
(After Design of Cosmas the Monk, 900 A.D.), 1932 (cat no. 66)
Mr. and Mrs. Alan Schwartz, New York City

Plate 44   *Earth Warming, Mexico*, 1932
Oil on board, 64.8 × 84.5 cm (25½ × 33¼″)
Robert Miller, New York City

Plate 45 *Garmisch-Partenkirchen*, 1933 (cat. no. 70)
Milwaukee Art Center Collection; bequest of Max E. Friedman

Plate 46   *Bavarian Alps, Garmisch-Partenkirchen*, 1933 (cat. no. 67)
Private Collection

Plate 47 *Whale's Jaw, Dogtown Common, Cape Ann*, 1934 (cat. no. 74)
Yale University Art Gallery; gift of Walter Bareiss, B.A. 1940

Plate 48 *Dogtown, The Last of the Stone Wall*, 1934 (cat. no. 71)
University Gallery, University of Minnesota, Minneapolis;
bequest of Hudson Walker from the Ione and Hudson Walker Collection

Plate 49 *New England Sea View—Fish House*, 1934 (cat. no. 72)
Mrs. Hudson D. Walker, Forest Hills, New York

Plate 50   *The Old Bars, Dogtown*, 1936 (cat. no. 76)
Whitney Museum of American Art, New York; purchase, 1937

Plate 51   *The Last Stone Walls, Dogtown*, 1936 (cat. no. 75)
Yale University Art Gallery; gift of Walter Bareiss, B.A. 1940

Return to Maine

Georgetown: 1937–1938

Hartley had attempted to establish a regional character for his career in the 1932 exhibition at The Downtown Gallery. Entitled "Pictures of New England by a New Englander," the exhibition had been accompanied by Hartley's poem proclaiming the "Return of the Native." Even while still in Europe, few painters wrote or said more about the country of their childhood than did Hartley. It was not until June 1937, however, that he actually returned to Maine. He accompanied Mme. Lachaise to Georgetown, Maine, that summer, with the intention of spending the next six months there in order to establish residency.

Hartley's paintings that summer (fig. 95) develop stylistically out of the elegiac seascapes he had executed in Nova Scotia following the deaths of Alty and Donny Mason (fig. 92). The dramatic contrasts of black against white and the creamy, heavy-bodied paint texture of the Nova Scotia works are exploited even further in these new compositions. The soft forms which characterized the seascapes are now simplified into broadly organized, chunky shapes which, in the black-and-white color scheme, create a greater sense of weight and density than Hartley had previously achieved. In place of the open areas of sky and expansive sea, Hartley now focused on enlarged, dominating foreground forms which have certain affinities with the close-up, cropped photographs of Stieglitz and Paul Strand. Maine's severity and rugged simplicity permeates these paintings. Determined to become the state's "first painter," he stressed that "Maine is a strong silent country and so I being born there am able to express it in terms of itself with which I am familiar."[285]

Fig. 95 *Granite by the Sea, Sequin Light, Georgetown*, 1937–38. Oil on academy board, 50.8 × 71.1 cm (20 × 28"). Neuberger Museum, State University of New York, College at Purchase; gift of Roy R. Neuberger

Vinalhaven: 1938

Hartley's return to Maine proved more difficult than he had anticipated. He had spent the summer and winter of 1937–38 among friends in the relatively harmonious and cosmopolitan communities of Georgetown and Portland, but when the summer of 1938 arrived, he moved to Vinalhaven, an island fifteen miles off the Maine coast, where he lived on a dollar a day from July through mid-November of 1938. All of his life, Hartley had been plagued by dichotomous needs: a longing for crowds and, when painting, a desire for solitude and stark stretches of landscape. When he was in cities, he yearned for seclusion, yet when he was removed from the urban pulse, he found the isolation dispiriting. This had become especially apparent after his return to the United States in 1930, but Maine further exacerbated the contradiciton. Hartley was simply not the same person that had left Maine twenty-five years earlier; although he had gone back geographically, he would never be able to bridge the gulf that existed between him and the common life of the Maine community. He considered the Vinalhaven people one-dimensional and wrote that he had never suffered so miserably "in

Plate 52   *Fox Island, Georgetown, Maine*, 1937
Oil on board, 54.6 × 71.1 cm (21½ × 28″)
Addison Gallery of American Art, Phillips Academy,
Andover, Massachusetts

Plate 53   *Robin Hood Cove, Georgetown, Maine*, 1938–39 (cat. no. 85)
Mrs. Hudson D. Walker, Forest Hills, New York

Plate 54 *Fishermen's Last Supper*, 1938 (cat. no. 82)
Mrs. Hudson D. Walker, Forest Hills, New York

Plate 55 *Fishermen's Last Supper*, 1940–41 (cat. no. 91)
Roy R. Neuberger, New York

Fig. 96　Alty Mason

Fig. 97　*Adelard the Drowned, Master of the Phantom*, 1938–39 (see Plate 102)

Fig. 98　Francis Mason family

both the physical and spiritual sense."[286] "After awhile it gets to be one of those things sitting in a room away from life — and I crave the feel and texture of life so — all right to be sentimental about the homeland and all that — but it provides no stimulus."[287] After five months of listening to "bucolic platitudes of people who never think above the surface," Hartley doubted whether he could continue to spend his summers in Maine.[288] The utter disregard and occasional hostility with which the island's inhabitants viewed art and its practitioners increased his isolation and he felt "flattened out spiritually" the whole summer.[289]

Despite Hartley's isolation from the community, his art grew richer and more expressive. The landscapes drawn from sites around Vinalhaven (pl. 101) contain a gentleness not present in his more aggressive Georgetown depictions. In composition, the paintings still have the dominant foreground forms of the Georgetown landscapes, but the latter's strong black-and-white contrasts have yielded to a richer, softer palette and more tranquil mood, as if Hartley were now beginning to find nature moving and endearing rather than threatening. These compositions embody the solemnity and restraint that had come to characterize his personality.[290] As in Garmisch-Partenkirchen, he strove for the "perfect observation" of his chosen themes and was pleased when two local people who saw one of his paintings knew exactly what view it represented.

In Hartley's main body of work that summer, he dramatically altered his subject matter to create a group of Archaic Portraits that translated his feelings for the Mason family. To protect their anonymity, he gave them French-Canadian names both in the paintings and in the unpublished story, "Cleophas and His Own." To capture the archaic severity and elemental strength of the Masons' life in Nova Scotia, he abandoned elegance and refinement in favor of raw immediacy, deliberately simplifying form for the sake of emotional content. In so doing, he aligned himself once again with the Expressionist tradition. As an embodiment of dignity and an affirmation of faith, the family represented for Hartley a kind of contemporary religious myth. He had been so moved by the piety and love expressed at family dinners that even as early as 1936 he said that if he ever painted murals he would depict the family at supper or noon meal.[291] He turned now to the subject in paintings such as *Fishermen's Last Supper* (pl. 54) — intended as a preliminary study for a mural he hoped to paint for a fishermen's bethel in Maine — as a means of depicting the family's simple, direct faith. As with his German officer series of 1914-15, actual details from the environment formed the basis of the composition. The large physiques of the family members and their straight-up hair, albeit exaggerated, referred to concrete physical characteristics, as did accessory details such as the rose which Alty often wore behind his ear (depicted in his portrait, *Adelard*; fig. 97). Although individualized, these portraits are not intended to be naturalistic. Rather, as with other artists, like Georges Rouault and Gauguin, who attempted to depict religious faith and renewal in contemporary terms, Hartley was inspired by pre-Renaissance sources. It is as if Hartley's geometrically severe, flat designs and the symbolic shorthand were intended to create contemporary icons. Hartley eliminated modeling and three-dimensional space for a solemn, frontal presentation from which movement was excluded. He had favored abstract rigidity and a mannered, stylized effect in his Mexican paintings, but the deliberately primitive manner with which he depicts these figures is unique in his career (figs. 99 and 100). This primitivism, combined with glowing colors, black-bordered shapes and close-cropped figures, also recalls Rouault's religious pictures — to which Hartley was particularly drawn in this period.

Hartley intended *Fishermen's Last Supper* to be a symbolic epic. In the first version of the painting, executed that summer in Vinalhaven (pl. 54), the eight-pointed star above the two sons' heads signified those who would not return and, in Hartley's personal lexicon, referred to transcendence. Of the three chairs on the table's empty side, two were for the sons—whose deaths were noted with wreaths—and one was for Hartley, who had always sat between the boys at dinner. The words "mene mene," written on the table cloth, derived from the Biblical passage in which Daniel interpreted the handwriting on the wall—*mene, mene, tekel, upharsin* ("numbered, numbered, weighed, divided")—to mean that God had weighed Belshazzar, found him lacking, and would destroy him. In Hartley's painting, the passage alluded to the numbered days of the boys, who had not heeded the warning about rowing home. However, no judgment is implied, since only the words "mene, mene" appear. In another painting from the period, *Give Us This Day* (fig. 102), Hartley uses an allegorical mode to invoke a religious faith and an acceptance of the natural cycle of which the death of the three boys is a part.

Hartley worked on depicting the boys' death through Christian symbols for the next three years. In the second version of *Fishermen's Last Supper*, executed in 1940-41 (pl. 55), the eight-pointed stars were replaced with halos. In the memorial painting, *The Lost Felice* of 1939 (pl. 104), the brothers are marked by halos, and all three figures hold fish, a symbol of Christ. This painting adopts a more mannered, geometric style than the Mason portraits of the preceding year and recalls to a greater extent the flat, stylized vocabulary of Orozco (fig. 83). Hartley also painted in 1938 a portrait from memory of Albert P. Ryder (fig. 101). The painting is a solemn, majestic tribute to the artist whose aesthetic vision he had begun again to emulate after the Mason sons' tragic deaths. Just as Hartley had embraced Cézanne for most of the 1920s, Ryder's art now became paramount in his imagination. That the painting is executed in a completely personal style indicates that Hartley had finally assimilated Ryder's imaginative realism.

Fig. 99 *Cleophas, Master of the Gilda Gray,* 1938–39. Oil on academy board, 71.1 × 55.9 cm (28 × 22″). Walker Art Center, Minneapolis; gift of the T. B. Walker Foundation

Fig. 100 *Marie Ste. Esprit,* 1938–39. Oil on academy board, 71.1 × 55.9 cm (28 × 22″). University Gallery, University of Minnesota, Minneapolis; bequest of Hudson Walker from the Ione and Hudson Walker Collection

West Brookville and Bangor: 1939–1940

The Archaic Portraits were exhibited in March 1939 at the Hudson Walker Gallery in New York. The exhibition succeeded critically, but was a financial failure, netting a mere one hundred dollars. Critical success, so long in coming, thus seemed a hollow victory. "I am too aware of the American art game after long experience to be thrilled by words of praise—as after all—the wherewithal to live is all that can possibly interest me because + only because I have a human stomach + fame will not fill it."[292] Hartley's single triumph of the season was cosmetic. Walker managed to trade one of Hartley's paintings for a set of teeth and the artist, before leaving for Maine in late June, was outfitted with dentures.

After several weeks in Portland he received a welcome offer from John and Claire Evans, Mabel Dodge's son and daughter-in-law, to be their guest in West Brookville, Maine. Hartley was grateful for the lodgings, but with virtually no money, his attitude toward art became intensely bitter. The hostility generated by his inability to eke out even a meager existence through his paintings was aggravated by the Maine residents' complete disdain of the art profession. Hartley told friends that if he had his life to live over again, he would never be an artist. At sixty-two he was no longer equipped to live at the poverty level that had earlier seemed adequate. Having failed to attain the prominence and financial security his early successes had promised, his rancor grew—along with the dichotomy between the worth he saw in his work and the treatment he received in society. He wrote that he was a "first class hater now," hating life and hating art, which he compared to a wife he had lived with too long to tolerate anymore.[293] And yet

Fig. 101 *Portrait of Albert Pinkham Ryder,* 1938–39 (see Plate 103)

Fig. 102 *Give Us This Day,* 1938–39. Oil on canvas, 76.2 × 101.6 cm (30 × 40"). Fine Arts Work Center, Provincetown, Massachusetts

painting had become his only option; as before when financial or critical rejection had driven him to question the value of continuing to paint, he realized he had "no other social gesture to make."[294]

The Evans' hospitality provided some relief from financial anxiety, and his poems and articles provided a modicum of emotional stability since their activity was not open to financial reward or rejection. Unlike painting, they thus did not create neurosis: "In poetry there is no 'pain' like with painting. . . . It can't be sold for it isn't bought — or very little. . . ."[295] Because of this Hartley allotted more time to his literary efforts. Despite the generosity of the Evans and the security of having a place to live and work, West Brookville was unsatisfying. Hartley felt he needed more "vital stuff" than just pleasing experience and West Brookville proved neither stimulating nor paintable.[296] The few paintings he worked on that summer stay with the simplified shapes and contained color areas of the preceding Georgetown landscapes, but lack the massive, geometric forms and weighty presence of the earlier group.

In September, John and Claire Evans left for the Southwest, and Hartley went to Bangor, where he continued his pattern, begun in Berlin in 1922, of reading and writing in the morning and painting in the afternoon. His finances completely depleted, he lived on seventy-five cents a day. "I am not well. Nerves. Everything so uncertain."[297] More significant now than anger and humiliation at the New York art community's rejection was the very real threat of hunger, which had haunted him all his life. He wrote that he was "worried to death" and hated art because it made him suffer so.[298]

Hartley augmented his meager funds that winter by teaching painting at the Bangor Art Society, to pupils he initially described as "pathetic old ladies who have passed their menopause."[299] Some financial relief arrived in October when Dorothy Norman sent him a check for thirty-five dollars for his contribution to the periodical *Twice a Year,* which she edited. Ignoring his precarious economic situation, Hartley decided to use the money to finance a trip to Mt. Katahdin, Maine's highest mountain. He desperately needed a relief from Bangor society and felt the trip would be a good investment: painting the mountain promised to generate publicity for his image as a Maine artist, a concern which had become so important for him that he even viewed his teaching position in Bangor and occasional dinners with faculty from the nearby college as contributing to his regional image. He arranged with Caleb Schriber, a game warden friendly with Carl Sprinchorn, to meet him at the train station in Millinocket and drive him to the base of Katahdin, where he began the four-mile walk to Cobb's Camp, his pre-arranged destination. The trek was extremely arduous; although only sixty-two, Hartley was not in good physical condition. The journey was further complicated by darkness and rain, and several times Hartley stumbled into mud holes. But the eight-day visit proved immensely rewarding. He wrote glowingly after his return: "I have achieved the 'sacred' pilgrimage to Ktaadn [*sic*]. I feel as if I had seen God for the first time — I find him so nonchalantly solemn."[300]

Back in Bangor, the memory of Katahdin and the experience with nature rekindled an enthusiasm toward life that he had not felt since Nova Scotia, and momentarily eased his loneliness and hostility. Hartley felt that he had emerged from "some awful valley of shadows" which he had wondered earlier if he could conquer, but which, having survived, he felt had taught him a great deal. He came to believe that his psyche had shifted to that part of his heritage which was aligned with imaginative rather than with intellectual wisdom. Hence, he expressed pride in that portion of his English background which had spawned the romantic vision of the Brontës and the mystic poets Francis Thompson and Richard Rolle, and was delighted by the recent discovery that his mother was part Irish, since he felt the Irish were closer than other races to imaginative principles.[301]

Hartley began a series of Mt. Katahdin paintings and by February 1, 1940, had finished eighteen, all of the same view, but depicting different weather conditions and moods. He painted several scenes of the snowstorm he had experienced during his visit, but in general these early Katahdin scenes were given strong autumn colors and clean outlines (fig. 103). As with his Archaic Portraits, Hartley simplified form into large shapes delineated by discrete areas of color, but he dispensed with the deliberately primitive style and black contour lines of the figure paintings. Now the design is less mannered, with a richer scale of intermediate shades of bounded color. Although the frontal, iconic treatment of the Archaic Portraits was replaced by a more realistic, three-dimensional depiction, Hartley was more intent on imbuing these "portraits" with a sense of the solemn, religious grandeur he felt the mountains embodied, than with faithfully describing their external appearance. Hartley continued painting Katahdin for the next two years, noting that if Hiroshige could do eighty Fujiyamas he could do eighty Mt. Katahdins. With each portrait of the mountain he felt "nearer the truth — even more so than if I were trying to copy nature from the thing itself."[302]

Interspersed among the Katahdin portraits that season was a new group of figure paintings. In one series, called Madawaska figures, Hartley abandoned his habit of painting from memory to work directly from his subject, a French-Canadian light-heavyweight boxer he had met (pl. 56). These portraits, as well as his concurrent depictions of Lincoln (pl. 58) and John Donne (fig. 104) continue the severe iconic treatment of the earlier Archaic Portraits. In the John Donne likeness, Hartley introduced a practice he would adopt with greater frequency in later years, that of deriving motifs from reproductions, in this case an etching.

Fig. 103   *Mount Katahdin, Autumn No. 2,* 1939–40. Oil on canvas, 76.2 × 101.6 cm (30 × 40"). Mr. and Mrs. Milton Lowenthal, New York

Fig. 104   *The Last Look of John Donne,* 1940. Oil on board, 77.1 × 59.1 cm (30⅜ × 23¼"). The Brooklyn Museum; gift of Mr. and Mrs. Milton Lowenthal

Corea and New York: 1940–1943

By 1940, Hartley had resigned himself to the necessity of living in Maine for part of the year and had accepted the propaganda value of identifying himself with the Maine-painter role, but he had found no location that satisfied his needs. The idea of a home, which had eluded him most of his life, had briefly materialized in Nova Scotia, only to be crushed by the tragic deaths of the Mason boys; in Maine, he sought some comparable situation. During the summer of 1939, the painter Waldo Peirce had driven Hartley to Corea, a small lobstering community on the Maine coast. Located on the southern edge of a harsh climatic zone, Corea's landscape of stunted forests and broad expanses of barren rock provided a dramatic change from the lush forests of the coast farther south. Hartley saw in Corea a lyric version of Nova Scotia, not as "epic" or as wild, but with something of its archaic simplicity.[303]

In August 1940, Hartley returned to Corea and rented the upper floor of Forest and Katie Young's home; the top floor of the church across the street became his studio. The Youngs valued Hartley as a person and treated him with the kind of human compassion he had known in Nova Scotia. Always comfortable around people who appreciated and loved him, Hartley began to view Corea as a symbol of home. He wrote to Mme. Lachaise, "I know this is the place I want to stay in and I am so sick of roaming around."[304]   To establish some stability in his transient patterns of living, he envisioned setting up a permanent residence in Corea and drew up plans for the house he would build "as a symbol of continuity."[305]

Hartley liked the family, particularly Mrs. Young and the son Joe, but he had little in common with them and did not admire them as deeply as he had the

Plate 56 *Madawaska—Acadian Light-Heavy (2nd Arrangement)*, 1940
(cat. no. 89) A. James Speyer, Chicago

Plate 57   *Sustained Comedy—Portrait of an Object*, 1939 (cat. no. 87)
Museum of Art, Carnegie Institute, Pittsburgh, Pennsylvania;
gift of Mervin Jules

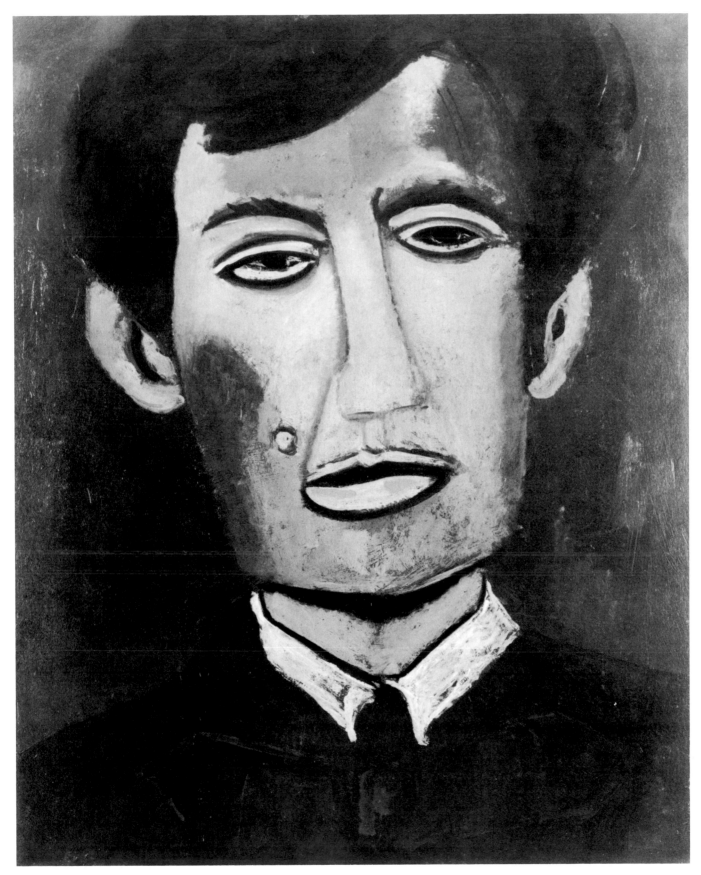

Plate 58 *Young Worshipper of the Truth*, 1940 (cat. no. 90)
Nebraska Art Association, Nelle Cochrane Woods Collection;
courtesy of the Sheldon Memorial Gallery, Lincoln

Masons. He generally avoided family conversations, ate most of his meals alone in the restaurant that Katie Young ran during the summer, and when it closed, chose to eat in the dining room while the family ate in the kitchen. Forest Young recounted that he never saw Hartley's paintings before his death, and did not care for them once he did see them.[306] Still, Hartley's relationship with the Youngs provided his only sense of home and community. He never mingled with the local people: his humanism and humility had not been particularly enriched by the tragedies he had suffered, and his personal reserve and arrogance toward the other townspeople precluded local friendships; when artists approached him in the Youngs' restaurant he would hold up his nose with his finger and walk away.[307] Most of Hartley's charm and social involvements were reserved for his correspondence, which often ran five or six pages per letter. As his isolation continued, he developed the peculiar habit of writing chatty, personal letters to people he knew only casually.

Hartley's health deteriorated as the winter approached, and his vision became such a problem that he refrained from typing in order to protect his eyes. He worked in the upper story of the church until the cold forced him to move his studio into the restaurant. This move proved equally untenable because of the cold and in January 1941 he returned to Bangor, where he remained until the middle of March, finishing the summer's canvases.

Fig. 105 *The Lighthouse*, 1940–41 (see Plate 61)

Several of these paintings, such as *The Lighthouse* (fig. 105), employ the impastoed surface and massive, black-bordered images of waves crushing on rocks that recall the foreground motifs of his 1936 Ryderesque seascapes (fig. 92). In both instances, the liberal use of white pigment gives the surface a chalky texture. The majority of Hartley's paintings that year, however, were figure groups of fishermen (fig. 108), or sunbathers, whose youthful beauty had entranced him on his frequent visits to Old Orchard Beach, Maine, the previous spring (fig. 107). These figures are less severe and massive and their features less individualized than those of previous years, despite the compositions' greater preponderance of contextual details. Combining a proliferation of references to the setting with a reduced figure scale allowed Hartley to shift the focus from the individuals themselves to the context. This shift was equally noticeable in those works which dealt with Christian themes. In contrast to the specificity with which he had responded to the Mason boys' deaths, these new paintings are not so much memorials to them as they are broader portrayals of Christian faith. His second version of *Fishermen's Last Supper* was painted in this period (pl. 55), along with works such as *Christ Held by Half-Naked Men* (fig. 106), which uses the recovery of Donny's body from the sea to allude to Christ being carried to the tomb. Strangely, this infusion of patently Christian themes into Hartley's art seems to have been generated less by mystical readings, as had been typical of his spiritual excursions in the past, than by the remembered dignity and faith of the Mason family in the face of devastating loss.

Fig. 106 *Christ Held by Half-Naked Men*, 1940–41. Oil on fiberboard, 101.9 × 76 cm (40⅛ × 30). Hirshhorn Museum and Sculpture Garden, Smithsonian Institution

Hartley was back in New York in the spring of 1941. Unable to afford a studio, he worked principally on his writing, which now constituted his major psychological support. The previous year's publication of his book of poems, *Androscoggin*, and the publication that year of *Sea Burial*, contributed to his feeling that writing benefited him more than painting, for painting kept him "in a kind of hot water all the time by virtue of its very nature."[308]

The extreme poverty of the past two winters had taken a severe psychological toll on Hartley; on one occasion when the Youngs took him to dinner, he had even surreptitiously picked up the tip.[309] When financial change finally came, Hartley was unprepared. Hudson Walker had closed his gallery at the end of the 1940 season, arranging before his departure for the Macbeth Gallery to represent

Fig. 107 *Canuck Yankee Lumberjack at Old Orchard Beach, Maine,* 1940–41. Oil on masonite, 101.6 × 76.2 cm (40 × 30"). Hirshhorn Museum and Sculpture Garden, Smithsonian Institution

Fig. 108 *Lobster Fishermen,* 1940–41. Oil on composition board, 75.6 × 103.8 cm (29¾ × 40⅞"). The Metropolitan Museum of Art, New York; Arthur H. Hearn Fund, 1942

Hartley. But neither the efforts of Walker nor the Macbeth Gallery had improved Hartley's finances. Financial independence became a possibility in the spring of 1941, when Walker purchased twenty-three paintings for five thousand dollars. For the first time since his 1921 auction, Hartley had some economic security. Ironically, his habits had become so entrenched and his pessimism so complete that he was unable to believe that the money offered freedom and the opportunity for change. He deposited the money in the National City Bank and never drew on it.

In June 1941, Hartley returned to Corea and converted a chicken brooder near the Youngs' house into a studio. Initially relieved to be out of New York and painting again, by August he had grown annoyed at the isolation. This pattern — hating crowds yet hating their absence — was, of course, not new, but now even nature no longer provided compensatory satisfaction. "I cannot live on just nature alone," he wrote. "This scene tightens and tightens and there is no human stimulus at all. And so I sit like a turnip in the ground hoping to grow another root before I am ploughed under or fed to the pigs. . . . I grow to want people more and more — just nature is not enough.[310] The bleak landscape and the coastline's granite severity failed to inspire new work: "There will be no new landscapes — as I am tired of this country and anyhow I have done my bit for Maine. . . . I am so sick of granite and balsam and fir and whatever that I could scream almost."[311]

Hartley's work pace also slowed down because of his poor health. Extremely high blood pressure and an enlarged heart caused his doctor to counsel him against any "physical, mental or spiritual excitement."[312] Hence, by October he had finished only eight paintings. He wrote that he hoped to pull out of the condition and avoid catastrophe, but his letters expressed a resigned attitude which suggested that illness had worn down his expectations about another full year of painting. "If not — well, all in all, I've had a good time and done the best I could — my name will live forever in American art history and I suppose that is something."[313] Hartley's vision, moreover, was so bad that he refrained from painting in high-key colors, claiming that his eyes could not tolerate the vibrations of bright red and yellow. "They actually ache," he wrote, "so I have resorted to chromatic monochrome of late."[314]

Both in style and quantity, Hartley's paintings that summer reflect his failing health. Although his subject matter varies, most of the paintings are characterized by a low-keyed palette and an absence of strong color contrasts. Rather than locate colors within clearly prescribed areas as he had done in preceding series, brushed shapes are now delineated by thinly impastoed, fuzzy brushstrokes within close-toned ranges of deep, rich color. The variation and modulation of such resonant color tones is a distinctive feature of Hartley's late work, in contrast to his middle period, where massive, severe forms predominate over subtle harmonies. Having grown tired of the landscape, he turned to still lifes for subject matter, depicting birds or flower studies, either isolated against dark monochromatic backgrounds (pl. 68) or in front of an open window overlooking the sea (fig. 109). In addition, he continued his Mt. Katahdin motifs, adopting the same view as before, but abandoning the crisply outlined, bright color areas and clearly defined solid shapes for a softer, more luminous treatment (fig. 110).

Hartley was now producing work whose level of richness and achievement equalled if not exceeded that of his German military paintings. Still, the art community was slow to recognize his contribution. Excluded from the Carnegie Institute International exhibition that spring, Hartley wrote to Walker: "There'll be a reckoning one day and so help me god if I don't nip the pants off that ilk that continue to insult me . . . and no one who has [not] been all but nailed to the cross for an ideal can ever know what the pain is."[315] His anger was partly assuaged by an exhibition of his post-1937 paintings which Walker had organized for travel to five museums during 1940, and by a joint exhibition at the Cincinnati Modern Art Society with the highly respected Stuart Davis.

Asked to contribute a catalogue statement for the Cincinnati exhibition, he prepared an essay entitled "Pictures," in which he repeated an earlier view that subject matter was irrelevant and that he was interested solely in the performance of painting: ". . . I have no interest in the subject matter of a picture not the slightest. A picture has but one meaning — it is well done, or it isn't. . . . I want the whole body, the whole flesh, in painting. Renoir said that he painted with all of his manhood, and is it not evident?"[316]

This obvious contradiction between Hartley's intellectual posture and his actual paintings had existed throughout his career. He had disavowed the importance of subject matter in his statements issued at the time of his 291 exhibition in 1916 and the Forum Gallery exhibition that same year, claiming that the artist's personal signature rather than subject matter or formal problems held the key to a painting. In actuality, the power of his German military paintings depended specifically on his emotional involvement with the subject. In the 1920s and early 1930s, he had renounced imagination and had stressed the desirability of an objective interpretation of images. Ironically, it was the lush, painterly execution that sustained the quality of his work during this period, rather than formal structure and intellectual clarity. At the end of his 1928 article "Art — And the Personal Life," he had suggested the necessity of combining subject matter, objectivity, and imagination, but in his personal quest for order, which had driven him all his life as a result of the uncertainty and chaos of his childhood, he had constantly championed one over the other. For all of his theorizing, Hartley was basically an expressionist and his work achieved its fullest strength when he was personally entangled with his subject. This occurred in both his early and late work. What in fact made his paintings of the intervening years less successful was precisely that he chose emotionally neutral themes.

Hartley traveled to Cincinnati in December 1941 to deliver a lecture in conjunction with his exhibition at the Cincinnati Museum, and from there went on to Cleveland to visit his sister's family for Christmas. As in the past, the success and vindication of his reputation, which he felt attended his Cincinnati exhibition, gave him a renewed optimism and changed perception of his relationship to society. He returned to New York from Cleveland in January 1942, exhilarated by the city for the first time in years. His flair for nature somewhat cooled, Hartley found himself caught up in the energy of New York. He expressed his new feelings in an essay entitled "Falling in Love with New York."[317] Despite the money from Walker's purchase of his paintings, he continued to live in a cheap hotel and painted in the studio of his friend, the photographer George Platt Lynes. Hartley mingled comfortably among the bohemian intelligentsia of Greenwich Village and established a circle of acquaintances, including Glenway Wescott and Monroe Wheeler, both of whom he had known casually in southern France, Sally and Milton Avery, the antique dealer Dikran Kelekian, Alfredo Valente, and George Platt Lynes. The insecurity and fears of earlier years had mellowed. The piercing intensity and edgy quality captured in early photographs had given way to a fleshy, slow-moving frame. Lacking a family, his friends became especially important; in their presence, he was a quiet, warm listener who contributed witty, truculent comments to conversations. Although no longer physically flamboyant, he wore rings and concocted perfumes as a hobby.[318] Hartley also returned to his adolescent passion for collecting beautiful objects, and had acquired an assortment of fabrics, shells, artifacts, and jewelry which he kept in his room at the Youngs' house.[319] His expansive attitude did not, however, extend to Maine

Fig. 109 *Windy Day, Maine Coast,* 1941. Oil on canvas, 51.4 × 41 cm (20¼ × 16⅛"). Munson-Williams-Proctor Institute, Utica, New York; anonymous gift

Fig. 110 *Mount Katahdin,* 1941. Oil on masonite, 55.8 × 71.1 cm (22 × 28"). Mr. and Mrs. P. J. Schrag, New York

residents with whom he had little in common and from whom he kept a haughty distance. Since even the stark Maine landscape no longer provided stimulation, he became less interested in returning to Corea.

Hartley's renewed fondness for New York did not prevent him from leaving for the summer. Although he now possessed the financial resources to travel to the Southwest or to Florida (which he wanted to visit for several years), ingrained habits took him back to the Youngs' house in Corea in mid-July. His health was poor and the lethargy induced by his high-blood pressure pills continually interrupted his painting. Severely overweight, he walked with difficulty; in October he fell on the coastal rocks and was bedridden for weeks. His career, however, seemed to flourish. In August, the prestigious Paul Rosenberg Gallery had asked to represent him, an offer he compared to marrying an angel. At almost any other time in his career, his injuries and illnesses would have curtailed his production, but the promise of financial and critical success induced him to persevere. That fall he worked optimistically for a new show of his Maine paintings, and by October had finished three new portraits of Mt. Katahdin.

Fig. 111 *Flowers by the Sea*, 1942. Oil on masonite, 71.1 × 55.8 cm (28 × 22"). Babcock Galleries, New York

Fig. 112 *End of Storm, Vinalhaven, Maine*, 1937–38. Oil on masonite, 76.2 × 101.6 (30 × 40"). The Benton Collection; courtesy of The William Benton Museum of Art, Storrs, Connecticut

These late Katahdin portraits (pl. 107), as well as his concurrent landscape paintings (pl. 109), continue themes he had developed in previous seasons (fig. 112). Executed in tones of reds and purples, the variations and modulations of these deep, resonant harmonies create subtle, atmospheric inflections unequalled in Hartley's oeuvre. Their rich tones reflected Hartley's close study of Coptic textiles, several examples of which he had procured through trades with Kelekian, who greatly admired his paintings: "The Coptic textiles have done much for me in my work. . . . I have chosen mine for their color value. They help me enormously to live." [320] Hartley also produced in this period a number of figure paintings employing Christian themes, which return to single figures whose shapes, delineated again with dark contour lines, are less atmospheric than the concurrent Katahdin portraits. The contemporary group of still lifes of fish, birds, or flowers (fig. 111) was more similar to the Katahdin paintings. Rendered as isolated images against seascape backgrounds, these still lifes did not differ significantly from the style of the preceding season. Throughout his career, Hartley did not imbue his floral still lifes with the same emotional presence as that contained in his landscapes or figure paintings. They were simply vehicles for the sensuous presentation of his broad, fluid treatment of paint. From Bermuda in 1936, he had written that flowers were a means of escaping into simplicity without mood. He now came to also regard them as more commercially viable; he confessed that he thought it "a good idea to always have a number of flower things as people don't have to think or worry about them as to 'meanings.'" [321] This was not true of the group of moving portraits of dead birds from 1942, which display a compassion and tenderness rare in his work (fig. 113). Executed in a subtly modulated palette of browns and tans, these portraits eliminated the strong contrasts of light and dark that characterized his other still lifes.

Hartley's attitude remained exuberant as his failing health was balanced by further success. In December 1942, he won a two thousand-dollar fourth prize in The Metropolitan Museum's "Artists for Victory" exhibition. This belated triumph and his new alliance with the Paul Rosenberg Gallery promised a brighter future than he had imagined for many years; with his typically indefatigable vanity, he wrote jubilantly to his niece that month: "My name will register forever in the history of American Art." [322]

He remained in Corea through Christmas, which he spent with the Youngs. Returning to New York, ailing but optimistic, he felt rejuvenated by the same crowds he had shunned a few years before, and he proclaimed that he loved New York above all other places in the world. In preparation for an exhibition

Fig. 113 *Dead Plover*, 1942–43. Oil on masonite, 40.6 × 50.8 cm (16 × 20"). Private collection

Fig. 114 *Fisherman's Family*, 1943. Oil on canvas, 101.6 × 76.2 cm (40 × 30"). Present whereabouts unknown

scheduled by the Rosenberg Gallery for February of 1943, he arranged to work several hours each afternoon in George Platt Lynes' studio in exchange for a painting. The show succeeded beyond Hartley's expectations, both financially and critically — he had not received so much favorable attention since his 1913 show at 291. Establishing a place for himself amongst a circle of writers and artists, he engaged in the kind of social life he had nearly forgotten existed in almost twenty years of anxious doubts about his career.

Loath to leave the success and excitement he had coveted for so long, Hartley postponed his summer departure to Corea until late July. He knew he needed rest and a period of seclusion, but the transition to Maine's slow pace was too abrupt. The utter lack of stimulation and companionship in Corea once again disheartened him, and he wrote to a friend, "I can't tell you how I suffered since I came back here — nothing but rocks — the ocean — seagulls. I just hated to leave the beautiful scene of Broadway at night . . . knowing it was the last I should see of the white splendor until next spring and summer." [323]

Hartley's health was wretched. Before he left New York he had admitted that he was totally exhausted, but in Corea he was even too tired to paint. Mrs. Young later recalled that when he arrived he "looked and acted so different from his usual self." [324] Restless and fitful at night, he slept during the day, often falling out of his chair. Without exercise, his blood circulation problem increased and at times his hands and feet became so swollen that he could not tie his shoes. In August he wrote a "Document of Identification" designating that his niece Norma Berger, his nephew Clifton Newell, and Hudson Walker should be notified in the event of his death. The Youngs helped him up and down the stairs to his room, but as he weakened further he had to be carried, and they reluctantly acknowledged that he needed hospital attention. At sixty-six, Hartley was virtually alone in the world; he had friends, but no close relationships other than with the Youngs. He vehemently protested hospitalization and, once there, refused to let anyone but the Youngs touch him or help him. The family remained with him that first day but left in the evening after promising to return the next morning. Hartley's heart failed during his sleep on September 2 at 6:30 A.M. His body remained at the funeral home for several days until proper authorization arrived for the cremation he had insisted upon, after which it was taken to Boston, where the nearest crematorium was located.

Hudson Walker later remarked that he believed Hartley had eaten himself to death, driven by a fear of dying in poverty, instilled by his father. [325] It is more likely that years of inadequate nutrition, marginal medical assistance, and unresolved nervous anxieties hastened his death. His financial troubles and the haunting threat of hunger subsided in his last two years, but even belated success never altered his meager living habits or calmed his fears. At the time of his death, he had five hundred dollars in cash and ten thousand in savings. [326]

The public triumph of Hartley's final season provided a brief respite from virtually twenty years of depression and insecurity. Despite his miserable health, he had optimistically anticipated the coming year. That spring he had written to Henry Wells, who had proposed editing a book of his poetry: "There is so much that is calling on me from within that I don't know how I will get it all done. . . . So you can see what I have ahead of me — a new exhibit, a new book of verse — a new book on the circus — and a new story of myself a tall summer I call it — but I have five months to count on deep rich quietude and some of it will get done I know." [327]

Plate 59   *Log Jam, Penobscot Bay*, 1940–41 (cat. no. 93)
The Detroit Institute of Arts; gift of Robert H. Tannahill

Plate 60 *On the Beach*, 1940–41 (cat. no. 94)
Suzanne Vanderwoude, Great Neck, New York

Plate 61 *The Lighthouse*, 1940–41 (cat. no. 92)
Mr. and Mrs. William A. M. Burden, New York

Plate 62   *Evening Storm, Schoodic, Maine, No. 2*, 1942
Oil on board, 76.2 × 101.6 cm (30 × 40″)
Mr. and Mrs. Milton Lowenthal, New York

Plate 63 *Off to the Banks at Night*, 1942 (cat. no. 100)
The Phillips Collection, Washington, D.C.

Plate 64   *Summer Sea Window, Red Curtain*, 1942 (cat. no. 103)
Addison Gallery of American Art, Phillips Academy, Andover, Massachusetts

Plate 65 *Sea Window, Tinker Mackeral*, 1942 (cat. no. 101)
Smith College Museum of Art, Northampton, Massachusetts; purchased, 1947

Plate 66   *White Cod*, 1942 (cat. no. 104)
Mr. and Mrs. Milton Lowenthal, New York

Plate 67 *Mount Katahdin*, 1941 (cat. no. 96)
Hirshhorn Museum and Sculpture Garden, Smithsonian Institution

Plate 68   *Black Duck No. 1*, 1941 (cat. no. 95)
The Detroit Institute of Arts; gift of Robert H. Tannahill

Plate 69   *Gull*, 1942–43 (cat. no. 105)
Mr. and Mrs. Milton Lowenthal, New York

Notes

1 Most of the information about Marsden Hartley's early life derives from his unpublished (and unfinished) autobiography, *Somehow a Past*, which was written in the late 1930s or early 1940s. The manuscript exists in three variant unpaginated drafts, all of which are in the Beinecke Rare Book and Manuscript Library, Yale University, New Haven, Connecticut (hereafter cited as Yale).

2 See Hartley's "Family Album in Red Plush," in *Selected Poems*, ed. Henry W. Wells (New York: The Viking Press, 1945), pp. 13–15.

3 Hartley's father eventually abandoned cotton spinning in favor of the less demanding job of posting bills for a relative's theater.

4 The official records of Lewiston, Maine, indicate that Hartley's mother died on March 4, 1885. Hartley himself was inconsistent about this date. He wrote at various times and in various versions of his autobiography that he was eight when she died (1885), that she was buried on the inauguration of President Garfield (1881), and that she died March 4, 1888.

5 Hartley, *Somehow a Past*, Yale.

6 From the first draft of "Somehow a Past," it appears that Martha Marsden was living in England. Hartley mentions that when he was eleven his father went there on a visit and spent most of his time with her.

7 Hartley, "Concerning Fairy Tales and Me," *Adventures in the Arts* (New York: Boni and Liveright, 1921), p. 3.

8 Hartley, *Somehow a Past*, Yale.

9 Between the time Hartley began lessons with Semon and the time he enrolled in the Cleveland School of Art, he seems to have taken other art classes. I.T. Fran wrote to Elizabeth McCausland that he had been in a sketching class with Hartley in Cleveland during this period. The class was conducted by Caroline Sowers in her house and consisted of six to eight students; see the McCausland Papers, Archives of American Art, Washington D.C. (hereafter cited as AAA), letter to McCausland dated October 22, 1951.

10 Although early drafts of Hartley's autobiography confirm that he took the class with Yates before entering the Cleveland School of Art, a later draft suggests that the Yates class occurred the summer following his entrance. As with his recollections about the year of his mother's death, Hartley's memory was not always reliable and the latter sequence of events seems improbable.

11 Hartley wrote that the book confirmed in him, "all the things I was made to know and out of which the substance of my being was fed"; see *Somehow a Past*, Yale.

12 Hartley soon gave up Dumond's composition course because of the three-dollar-a-week fee. In his first year, he also spent a month of afternoons at the Art Students League, where he had criticisms from Kenyon Cox.

13 Hartley, *Somehow a Past*, Yale.

14 Hartley to Richard Tweedy, May 27, 1900, Yale; copy at the AAA.

15 Ibid.

16 Hartley to Richard Tweedy, November 1900, Yale; copy at the AAA.

17 In addition to Jones, Hartley's instructors at the Academy were Edgar Ward, Maynard Dielman, and J. Scott Hartley.

18 On Saturday afternoons, Farrar opened her studio as a gathering place for artists. It was here that Hartley first met his future close friend, the poet Wallace Gould.

19 Hartley to Richard Tweedy, July 10, 1901, Yale; copy at the AAA.

20 For example, see Robert McAlmon, *Post-Adolescence* (Paris: Contact Publishing Co., n.d.)

21 To Hartley's acquaintance with the works of Emerson and Thoreau should also be added his familiarity with the writings of Walter Pater and Maurice Maeterlinck. Among Hartley's possessions at the time of his death was a handwritten letter by Whitman which Traubel had given him.

22 Letter to Seumas O'Sheel (who later adopted the spelling "Shaemus"), December 25, 1906, Yale; copy at the AAA.

23 Hartley adopted the name Edmund Marsden Hartley when he returned to Lewiston in 1906. Late in 1907 or early in 1908, at the suggestion of two friends in New York, he dropped the name Edmund altogether and used Marsden Hartley for the rest of his life.

24 According to Tweedy, Hartley had told him that he had met George Inness. In *Somehow a Past*, Hartley describes being taken to Inness' studio by J. Scott Hartley, Inness' son-in-law and a teacher at the National Academy. However, since Inness died in 1894 when Hartley was only seventeen and had not yet become involved with art, the meeting seems unlikely.

25 [Unsigned]. "Edmund Marsden Hartley of Lewiston, A Student and Painter of Nature." *Lewiston Saturday Journal*, December 29, 1906, p. 9. In addition to describing several last paintings from this early period, the article is illustrated by a half-tone reproduction of *Storm Clouds, Maine*. Previously dated 1908,

this work appears in a slightly unfinished state with the title *A Study of Speckled Mountain, Lovel* [sic], *Maine*, thus redating this work to 1906–7.

26 Samuel Kootz, *Modern American Painters* (New York: Brewer and Warren, 1930), p. 40. Hartley wrote in *Somehow a Past*, Yale, that the reproduction "was to prove the greatest... help to me and sent me spinning on my way."

27 Hartley had apparently quoted a price of two hundred dollars for the painting, and Fitzgerald gave him four hundred; *Somehow a Past*, Yale.

28 Hartley to Richard Tweedy, October 25, 1900, Yale.

29 The patterning and curvilinear form in these paintings also relates to Japanese prints which, according to Tweedy, Hartley was interested in after he left the Academy.

30 Hartley to Norma Berger, September 1924, Yale.

31 Hartley, "On the Subject of Mountains," unpublished essay, Yale.

32 Hartley to Seumas O'Sheel, October 19, 1908, Yale; copy at the AAA.

33 From *Somehow a Past* and his letters, it is clear that Hartley worked on these paintings until March 1909. Thus they should be dated 1908–9 rather than 1908, as they have been previously ascribed.

34 According to Hartley in *Somehow a Past*, Davies purchased four frames for him. Sloan's comments appear in his diary, *John Sloan's New York Scene* (New York: Harper & Row, 1965), p. 303.

35 Dorothy Norman, *Alfred Stieglitz: An American Seer* (New York: Random House, 1973), p. 101.

36 Hartley, *Somehow a Past*, Yale.

37 Hartley saw *The Tempest* (now in the collection of the Detroit Institute of Arts) and *Macbeth and the Witches* (The Phillips Collection, Washington, D.C.); see *Somehow a Past*, Yale.

38 Hartley, *Somehow a Past*, Yale. Hartley referred to this series as the Dark Landscapes, although they were also called the Dark Mountains.

39 Hartley, *Somehow a Past*, Yale.

40 The paintings were executed in a corner of the room of Hartley's friend Ernest Roth, an etcher. Stieglitz noted on the back of one of them: "Hartley undoubtedly was on the verge of suicide during the summer which brought forth this picture."

41 Two important exhibitions of Rodin drawings were also held at 291 during this period (January 2–21, 1908, and March 31–April 18, 1910), but they did not capture Hartley's imagination.

42 Hartley to Norma Berger, July 11, 1910, Yale.

43 John Marin later achieved a relatively high degree of gestural abstraction, but his work remained more referential than Hartley's most abstract 1910 paintings.

44 Stieglitz to Hartley, October 23, 1923, Yale.

45 Maurice Prendergast was a devoted admirer of Cézanne's work and was probably the first person to mention the painter's name to Hartley.

46 Hartley also based his paintings on photographs of Cézanne's work which he asked for and received from Stieglitz during the summer.

47 Hartley to Stieglitz, July 1911, Yale.

48 Hartley to Stieglitz, August 20, 1911, Yale.

49 Hartley to Stieglitz, September 1911, Yale. Despite Hartley's preoccupation over the summer with formal explorations stimulated by Cézanne and Picasso, his emotional fascination with mysticism continued, and on August 20, 1911, he wrote to Stieglitz that he felt he was standing continually "at a sort of Maeterlinckian threshold" (Yale).

50 Hartley, *Somehow a Past*, Yale.

51 Hartley apparently established an immediate rapport with Stein when he asked to borrow her copy of *Varieties of Religious Experience* (1902) by William James, with whom she had studied at Harvard.

52 Hartley to Rockwell Kent, August 12, 1912, Rockwell Kent Papers, Archives of American Art, Washington, D.C.

53 Hartley to Stieglitz, July 1912, Yale.

54 Hartley postcard to Stieglitz, September 1, 1912, Yale.

55 Max Weber, "Chinese Dolls and Modern Colorists," *Camera Work*, no. 31 (July 1910), p. 51.

56 Hartley's still-life paintings were the first works he executed when he began working in Paris in June. By August, his interest had shifted towards a modified Cubist approach, as in *Still Life with Fan*, indicating that *Indian Pottery, Paris* was done during June or July of 1912.

57 He wrote to Stieglitz that he was, "taking a very sudden turn in a big direction owing to a recent visit to the Trocadero. One can no longer remain the same in the presence of these mighty children who get so close to the universal idea in their mud-baking—The results in me are proving themselves and I am showing a strength unknown in past efforts. These revolts... must be revolts of the soul itself if they are to mean anything other than intellectual imitation..."; Hartley postcard to Stieglitz, September 1, 1912, Yale.

58 Hartley to Rockwell Kent, September 1912, Rockwell Kent Papers, AAA.

59 Hartley to Stieglitz, September 1, 1912, Yale.

60 Hartley, postcard to Stieglitz, October 9, 1912, Yale.

61 Hartley to Stieglitz, October 1912, Yale.

62 Hartley to Stieglitz, February 1913, Yale. The idea that Picasso's work represented essentially psychic or spiritual responses to subject matter had been suggested by Marius de Zayas in a statement issued in a brochure for Picasso's 1911 exhibition at 291 and later quoted by Arthur Jerome Eddy in *Cubists and Post-Impressionism* (Chicago: McClurg, 1914).

63 Ibid.

64 Hartley to Stieglitz, early November 1912, Yale.

65 Hartley to Stieglitz, early November 1912, Yale.

66 See the copy of the Armory Show catalogue annotated by Zigrosser, now in the Carl Zigrosser Collection, Rare Book Collection, University of Pennsylvania Library, Philadelphia.

67 Hartley to Stieglitz, November 25, 1912, Yale.

68 Hartley to Stieglitz, February 1913, Yale. Hartley also wrote to Stein that Cézanne gave him the "most inspiration for expressing the color and form of new places"; Hartley to Stein, October 1913, Yale.

69 Hartley to Stieglitz, received December 20, 1912, Yale.

70 Letter to Stieglitz, February 1913, Yale.

71 Hartley to Stieglitz, February 1913, Yale. Earlier in December of 1912, Hartley mentioned reading Maurice Bucke's *Cosmic Consciousness*, and finding stimulation in the translated fragments of the German mystic Jacob Boehme.

72 Hartley, *Somehow a Past*, Yale.

73 Ibid.

74 "It's a new theme I'm working on—did you ever hear of anyone trying to paint music—or the equivalent of sound in color—doubtless you have heard singers speak of the color of tones.... Well I am working on this plan and some of the artists say I am original in it.... There is only one artist in Europe working on it and he is a pure theorist and his work is quite without feeling—whereas I work

wholly from the intuition and the subliminal. . . ." Hartley to Norma Berger, December 30, 1912, Yale.

75 Hartley later wrote that he was "with" Redon at that time; Hartley to Mathilde Rice, March 11, 1922, AAA.

76 Hartley to Stieglitz, February 1, 1913, Yale.

77 The date of this meeting is found in Rönnebeck's diary (Yale), although he does not recount it in detail.

78 Hartley to Stieglitz, February 1913, Yale.

79 Ibid.

80 Hartley to Stieglitz (another letter), February 1913, Yale.

81 Hartley to Stieglitz, February 1913, Yale. The phrase "das Geistige in der Kunst" refers to Kandinsky's *Über das Geistige in der Kunst* (Munich, 1912), brief excerpts from which were printed in *Camera Work*, no. 39 (July 1912), p. 34.

82 Hartley, *Somehow a Past*, Yale.

83 "I have somewhat the same feeling toward the number 27 [rue de Fleurus — Stein's address] that I have toward the number 291 — They both have a magic of their own — 291 is in every way an oasis in a great place — and once one gets there — into this room the size of a kitchenette one gets in touch with currents that give one a great deal — And so with 27 I like what I get there — I feel as if I were really 'in' somewhere — whereas most places one goes one remains forever at the gate — "; Hartley to Stein, 1913, Yale; reprinted in Donald Gallup, "The Weaving of a Pattern: Marsden Hartley and Gertrude Stein," *Magazine of Art* 41 (November 1948), p. 257.

84 Ibid., p. 259: "In his painting he has done what in Kandinsky is only a direction. Hartley has really done it. He has used color to express a picture and he has done it so completely that while there is nothing mystic or strange about his production it is genuinely transcendent. Each canvas is a thing in itself and contained within itself, and the accomplishment of it is quite extraordinarily complete. There is another quality in his work which is very striking and that is the lack of fatigue or monotony that one gets in looking at his things. In some way he has managed to keep your attention freshened and as you look you keep on being freshened. There is not motion but there is an absence of the stillness that even in the big men often leads to non-existence. I don't know whether I am giving you any idea of his work but knowing him as well as you do you probably can see what I mean. He seems to me to be

entirely on the right track. He is the only one working in color, that is considering the color as more dominant than the line, who is really attempting to create an entity in a picture which is not a copy of light. He deals with his color as actually as Picasso deals with his forms."

85 "Kandinsky volunteered a discourse on the law of form. . . which however left me unmoved — most friendly of course — It was an interesting conference — the one a complete logician trying so earnestly to disperse with logic + I a simple one without logic having an implicit faith in what is higher than all intellectual solutions — knowing that intuition if it be organized has more power to create truly than all the intellect ever can — . . . I have no knowledge — only an organized instinct — Kandinsky has a most logical and ordered mind which appeals so earnestly to the instinct which has been overmastered — In other words in my heart of hearts I think he is not creative — I think he is an interpreter of ideas — He knows everything + that simply must not — cannot be in real creation — This is itself illogical. Gertrude Stein is right when she says that true art cannot explain itself — that Cézanne could not Picasso cannot — that I cannot — that Matisse's pictures now are studied logic + studied simplicity. Kandinsky also — all legitimate enough naturally — but not products of creation — that element of life which insists on self-expression before the mind has power — However — we had a fine day + they finished by saying that what they admired so much was the intensity of personality in them — the sense of truth they give and their real naiveté of spirit — "; Hartley to Stieglitz, May 1913, Yale.

86 Ibid.

87 Hartley transcribed the complete letter from Marc in a letter to Stieglitz of late May or early June 1913, Yale.

88 "It provided the sense of home always so needed in my life. . . . Rönnebeck knew of my love for any kind of pageantry — all coming from early boyhood and big days of the year — the coming of the circus to Lewiston — the real Barnum's circus — and the annual state fair — and remaining forevermore a living issue in my life. . . . I could always know that I was quite like other people when I was with a lot of people — it would take me out and make me feel outward and that has always been necessary for it is a very bad thing to live inside so much — as no one has learned better than myself. So at last I could have all I wanted of

crowd parade pageantry public glamour — and the like. There was always a parade of some kind coming down the Unter den Linden. . . . So of course there was always the changing of the watch before the castle every morning between 10:30 and 11:00. . . . It was of course the age of iron — of blood and iron, every bone in Germany was made of it — or had new iron poured into it — the whole scene was fairly bursting with organized energy and the tension was terrific and somehow most voluptuous in the feeling of power — a sexual immensity even in it — when passion rises to the full and something must happen to quiet it"; Hartley, *Somehow a Past*, Yale.

89 Hartley to Rönnebeck, November 8, 1936, Yale.

90 Hartley to Stieglitz, March 15, 1915, Yale.

91 Hartley to Mathilde Rice, March 11, 1922, AAA.

92 Hartley to Gertrude Stein, October 18, 1913, Yale.

93 Hartley to Gertrude Stein, April 1913, Yale.

94 Ibid.

95 Hartley, postcard to Stieglitz, June 28, 1913, Yale. He repeated this thought to Gertrude Stein, June 1913, Yale: "I was told before I came to Berlin to look for 8 pointed stars — and I am seeing them everywhere — on the foreheads of hundreds of people — on the breasts of some and on two I have seen them on the crown of the head — the Kaiser wears it always — Frederick the Great did also — over the heart — the occult say it has a deep symbolism — but I don't know so far as that — I only know it is a much prettier star than the American five-point — much more radiant and life giving — and in the sunlight on all the hundreds of foreheads it looks like real fire — yellow + white fire — not red ever. . . ."

96 References to the symbolism of numbers appear in Hartley's letters through the summer and fall. In August 1913, he wrote to Stieglitz, "I find it [Berlin] full of mystical ideas + colors + I have begun to paint them" (Yale). In June he wrote to Stein, "I wish we had some wireless all our own so I could send down a shaft from 4 and you could send up some from 27 [rue de Fleurus]. 4 is my house number. I must learn what 4 means" (Yale). In August he wrote again to Stein, "I like what your Spanish waiter said about the numbers. I have seen some wonderful ones here, especially a green 3" (Yale).

97 Hartley to Stieglitz, late August 1913, Yale.

98 Ibid.

99 Corinne Heline, *Sacred Science of Numbers*, 4th ed. (Los Angeles: New Age Press, 1977), pp. 65–66.

100 In late September Hartley told Stieglitz that colors were pure mystical expressions, but that his color explorations differed from Kandinsky's in rejecting specific associations between color and image. Hartley to Stieglitz, September 28, 1913; Yale.

101 He wrote to his young niece, Norma Berger, on June 26, 1913 (Yale) that he had shown his work to "some critics in Paris and the artists in Germany who all speak of its originality. Little they know the cost of production to the author!"

102 This drawing was one of the six exhibited in the Armory Show. As Stein had not been able to afford to buy one of the four paintings that she had hung in her apartment, she insisted on paying for the drawing, even though Hartley had been willing to give it to her. The two agreed, therefore, that the money would be held by Stein as an emergency fund for Hartley. The present location of this drawing is unknown.

103 Stieglitz to Hartley, October 20, 1913, Yale.

104 Hartley to Stieglitz, October 22, 1913, Yale.

105 Hartley to Stieglitz, October 31, 1913, Yale.

106 "I am homeless here. . . . It is a deadly place." Hartley to Gertrude Stein; quoted in Gallup, "The Weaving of a Pattern," 1948, p. 259.

107 Hartley to Gertrude Stein, January 16, 1914, Yale.

108 Hartley to Stieglitz, received May 14, 1914, Yale.

109 Stieglitz to Hartley, May 26, 1914, Yale.

110 Hartley, postcard to Stieglitz, postmarked May 15, 1914, Yale.

111 Hartley, postcard to Stieglitz, dated July 31/August 1, 1914, Yale. The same sentiment is mentioned in a letter to Stieglitz dated September 2, 1914, Yale.

112 Hartley to Stieglitz, November 12, 1914, Yale. Hartley misdated the letter November 12, 1913.

113 "I sit alone much the spectator of the great tragedy of the heart + soul of mankind—I cannot set up and work—for something that happens [*sic*] has an effect on me and it often takes weeks to feel things out clearly"; Hartley to Stieglitz, October 23, 1914, Yale.

114 Hartley to Mathilde Rice, March 11, 1922, AAA.

115 Six months after von Freyberg's death, Hartley wrote to Stieglitz, "You know what friendships are to me—how slowly I make them and when once made how I almost worship them. . . . Friendship is for me my only notion of the marriage state spiritually speaking whether it be a man or a woman—"; Hartley to Stieglitz, March 15, 1915, Yale.

116 Hartley, "Letters Never Sent," unpublished essays, Yale. The same sentiment was also expressed in an unpublished poem, entitled "Karl von Freyburg," also at Yale.

117 Hartley to Stieglitz, November 8, 1914, Yale.

118 Arnold Rönnebeck wrote a rebuttal to Duncan Phillips shortly after Phillips had published an article on Hartley ("Marsden Hartley," *Magazine of Art* 37(March 1944), pp. 82–87). Rönnebeck felt that Phillips had completely misunderstood the symbolic content of the painting *Portrait of a German Officer* (fig. 41), explaining that he was actually one half of the "officer" represented in the painting. He wrote that the "E" came from the epaulettes of his full dress uniform, and the long tassels represented those he wore as an aide-de-camp in the Royal Guards (Rönnebeck to Phillips, after March 1944).

119 Hartley to Stein, October 18, 1913, Yale.

120 Mabel Dodge Luhan, *Movers and Shakers* (New York: Harcourt, Brace, & Co., 1941), p. 460.

121 Ibid.

122 Hartley wrote to his niece that he was sending seven paintings to the Forum Exhibition: "Three that I have done since my return—one I brought with me and three from two years ago." Hartley to Berger, March 9, 1916, Yale. Matching this description with the six paintings listed in the checklist for the Forum exhibition indicates that these simplified Synthetic Cubist still lifes were painted after Hartley's return to the United States and thus should be dated 1916 rather than 1912 as previously ascribed. Hartley's documentation in his letters to Stieglitz of his 1912 paintings also indicates that he could not have painted these works in 1912. Their stylistic and technical similarity to his German paintings of 1914–15 and to his subsequent Provincetown paintings further corroborates 1916 as the correct date.

123 Hartley, "Explanatory Note," *The Forum Exhibition of Modern American Painters*, exhibition catalogue (New York: The Anderson Galleries, 1916), p. 54.

124 Hartley, "Foreword" to *Paintings by Marsden Hartley*, exhibition catalogue (New York: Photo-Secession Galleries, 1916).

125 Henry McBride, review in the *New York Sun*; reprinted in *Camera Work*, no. 48 (October 1916), pp. 58–59.

126 Charles H. Caffin, review in *New York American*; reprinted in *Camera Work*, no. 48 (October 1916), pp. 59–60.

127 [Unsigned], "American Artist Astounds Germans," *The New York Times*, December 19, 1915, p. 4.

128 Hartley, *Somehow a Past*, Yale.

129 Albert Gleizes was also in Bermuda at the time of Hartley's visit, but there is no indication from Hartley's letters that the two ever met.

130 Hartley to Carl Sprinchorn, Winter 1917, AAA.

131 "I think that I am rapidly outliving mysticism and hope one day to extinguish it all together; that is from the esthetic point of view." Hartley to Stieglitz, February 8, 1917, Yale.

132 Hartley to Carl Sprinchorn, Winter 1917, AAA.

133 Paul Rosenfeld, "American Painting," *The Dial* 71(December 1921), p. 658.

134 Laurent made these remarks in a discussion with Thomas N. Armstrong, III on August 20, 1968. The notes taken by Laurent are filed in the Whitney Museum of American Art, New York.

135 "What I most wanted to do was to paint some scenes in black and gold that one sees in early mirrors." In the same letter he referred to early American saloon windows "with glorious weavings of wheat and malt blossoms." Hartley to Sprinchorn, Summer 1917, AAA. In 1929 he referred to these same images in a letter to Rebecca Strand, January 1929, AAA.

136 Hartley to Rebecca Strand, January 1929, AAA.

137 Hartley to Harriet Monroe, March 17, 1918, Library of the University of Chicago; on microfilm at AAA.

138 Hartley to Charles Daniel, May 16, 1918, Yale.

139 By the end of 1920s, those who had made the trip to Taos-Santa Fe included the painters Andrew Dasburg, John Sloan, John Marin, Edward Hopper, Georgia O'Keeffe, and the writers Walter Lippmann and Paul Rosenfeld, as well as Leo Stein. See Sanford Schwartz, "When New York Went to New Mexico," *Art in America* 64(July-August, 1976), pp. 53–97.

140 Hartley to Harriet Monroe, August 22, 1918, AAA; Hartley to Carl Sprinchorn, mid-

September, 1918, AAA.

141 Hartley to Harriet Monroe, August 22, 1918, AAA.

142 Hartley to Harriet Monroe, September 13, 1918, AAA.

143 In describing the New Mexican landscape to Stieglitz, Hartley noted, "This country is very beautiful and also difficult. It needs a Courbet with a Renoir eye. . . ." Hartley, postcard to Stieglitz, August 26, 1918, Yale.

144 Schwartz, "When New York Went to New Mexico," p. 95–96.

145 Hartley to Harriet Monroe, November 27, 1918, AAA.

146 Hartley, "Red Man Ceremonials: An American Plea for American Esthetics." *Art and Archaeology* 9(January, 1920), pp. 7–14.

147 Hartley to Rebecca Strand, AAA.

148 "All I need is a town of more or less size or a city where I have the pageant or spectacle as something to go to and come from." Hartley to Harriet Monroe, November 27, 1918, AAA.

149 Hartley to Stieglitz, March 14, 1918, Yale.

150 Hartley to Harriet Monroe, July 3, 1919, AAA.

151 Paul Rosenfeld, "Marsden Hartley," *Port of New York* (New York: Harcourt, Brace & Co., 1924), p. 92.

152 Hartley to Kenneth Hayes Miller, June 20, 1920, Hartley files, Whitney Museum of American Art.

153 Hartley to O'Keeffe, January 14, 1920, reprinted in Robert Northcutt Burlingame, *Marsden Hartley: A Study of His Life and Creative Achievement* (Dissertation: Brown University, Providence, Rhode Island), 1934, p. 46.

154 Hartley to Kenneth H. Miller, June 20, 1920, Hartley files, Whitney Museum of American Art.

155 Hartley, *Somehow a Past*, Yale.

156 William Carlos Williams, *Autobiography* (New York: Random House, 1951), pp. 172–73.

157 Ibid.

158 Hartley to Stieglitz, August 2, 1920, Yale.

159 Hartley to Stieglitz, August 12, 1920, Yale.

160 Hartley, "The Importance of Being 'Dada'," *Adventures in the Arts* (New York: Boni and Liveright, 1921) pp. 247–54. Printed in a slightly different version in *International Studio* 74 (November 1921), p. LXIII.

161 Hartley's involvement with the Société Anonyme was also motivated by the hope that he would be sent to Europe as the group's foreign correspondent.

162 Hartley to Kenneth H. Miller, June 10, 1920, Hartley files, Whitney Museum of American Art.

163 Hartley to Stieglitz, September 1920, Yale.

164 Dorothy Norman, *Alfred Stieglitz: An American Seer* (New York: Random House, 1973), p. 165.

165 *The New York Herald*, May 18, 1921, reported that the auction netted $4,912. According to Hartley, he only received $3,900 and the remaining money was taken up in costs.

166 Hartley, *Somehow a Past*, Yale.

167 William Bullitt was American ambassador to Russia from 1933 to 1936; to France from 1936 to 1941; and at large from 1941 to 1942.

168 Hartley, *Somehow a Past*, Yale.

169 Robert McAlmon, *Being Geniuses Together*, revised with supplementary chapters by Kay Boyle (New York: Doubleday & Co., 1968), p. 106.

170 Hartley to Mathilde Rice, March 11, 1922, AAA.

171 Ibid.

172 Hartley to Stieglitz, November 30, 1921, Yale.

173 Related by Djuna Barnes to Elizabeth McCausland, McCausland Papers, AAA.

174 Hartley to Stieglitz, January 1, 1923, Yale.

175 Elizabeth McCausland, "Return of the Native." *Art in American* 40(Spring 1952), p. 65.

176 Hartley to Stieglitz, May 23, 1923, Yale.

177 Hartley to Rebecca Strand, AAA.

178 Hartley, *Somehow a Past*, Yale.

179 Each member of the syndicate put up seven hundred and fifty dollars a year and drew lots for his painting.

180 Hartley to Gertrude Stein, December 27, 1925, Yale.

181 Hartley to Mathilde Rice, January 27, 1926, AAA.

182 Hartley to Stieglitz, December 25, 1925, Yale.

183 Ibid.

184 Hartley to Carl Sprinchorn, 1919, AAA.

185 Hartley to Stieglitz, July 20, 1926, Yale.

186 Hartley to Carl Sprinchorn, AAA.

187 Hartley to Stieglitz, November 19, 1926, Yale.

188 Hartley to Stieglitz, May 16, 1927, Yale.

189 McCausland Papers, AAA.

190 Hartley to Mathilde Rice, November 10, 1927, AAA.

191 Hartley, "Art—And the Personal Life," *Creative Art*, 2(June 1928), pp. xxxi–xxxiv.

192 Stieglitz to Hartley, October, 1923; reprinted as "From a Letter to a Painter," *Twice a Year*, no. 1 (Fall-Winter 1938), pp. 99–102.

193 Hartley's constant need for financial aid contributed as much as his ingratitude to their estrangement.

194 Hartley to Rebecca Strand, October 1928, AAA.

195 Hartley to Mme. Lachaise, 1928, AAA.

196 Hartley to Adelaide Kuntz, June 30, 1928, AAA.

197 Hartley to Rebecca Strand, October 1928, AAA.

198 Hartley to Rebecca Strand, January 6, 1929, misdated January 6, 1928, AAA.

199 Ibid.

200 Hartley to Rebecca Strand, February 7, 1929, AAA.

201 Ibid.

202 Hartley to Rebecca Strand, January 6, 1929; misdated January 6, 1928, AAA.

203 Ibid.

204 Hartley to Rebecca Strand, January 26, 1929, AAA.

205 Hartley to Rebecca Strand, February 7, 1929, AAA.

206 Ibid.

207 Ibid.

208 Lee Simonson, foreword to *Marsden Hartley*, exhibition catalogue (New York: The Intimate Gallery, 1929).

209 Stieglitz to Hartley, February 10, 1929, Yale.

210 Hartley to Rebecca Strand, March 6, 1929, AAA.

211 Stieglitz to Hartley, March 22, 1929, Yale.

212 Hartley to Rebecca Strand, March 27, 1929, AAA.

213 McBride, Henry. "Attractions in the Galleries." *The New York Sun*, January 5, 1929, p. 12.

214 Hartley to Adelaide Kuntz, March 29, 1929, AAA.

215 Hartley to Rebecca Strand, March 27, 1929 and April 3, 1929, AAA.

216 Hartley to Rebecca Strand, April 3, 1929, AAA.

217 Hartley to Adelaide Kuntz, March 29, 1929, AAA.

218 Hartley to Adelaide Kuntz, July 21, 1929, AAA.

219 Ibid.

220 Hartley to Rebecca Strand, March 6, 1929, AAA.

221 Hartley to Rebecca Strand, November 19, 1929, AAA.

222 Hartley to Adelaide Kuntz, August 29, 1929, AAA.

223 Hartley to Rebecca Strand, August 19, 1929, AAA.

224 See Malcolm Cowley, *Exile's Return* (New York: The Viking Press, 1951), pp. 289–291.

225 Rosenfeld, "Marsden Hartley," *Port of New York* pp. 99–100.

226 Hartley to Rebecca Strand, August 1930, AAA.

227 Hartley to Rebecca Strand, September 30, 1930, AAA.

228 Ibid.

229 Hartley to Rebecca Strand, October 11, 1930, AAA.

230 Ibid.

231 Ibid.

232 Rebecca Strand told Elizabeth McCausland that it was Georgia O'Keeffe who eventually paid to have Hartley's paintings released by the freight company; AAA.

233 Hartley to Rebecca Strand, winter, 1930, AAA.

234 Interview with Hudson Walker by Elizabeth McCausland, AAA. Printed in *Journal and Archives of American Art* 8(January 1968), pp. 9–21.

235 Hartley to Rebecca Strand, Winter 1930, AAA.

236 Hartley, *Somehow a Past*, Yale.

237 "I go alone empty handed and sit in 'Dogtown Common'," he wrote. "I look at it and register it and the two [paintings] I have home are I think very speaking likenesses of the place. Very stark, very mythical. . . . I made many studies in Dogtown and as usual—and [as] I always have to do about a place—see it—and think nothing else"; Hartley to Rebecca Strand, late summer 1931, AAA.

238 Ibid.

239 Hartley to Harriet Monroe, March 1932, AAA.

240 Hartley to Rebecca Strand, September 31, 1931, AAA.

241 Hartley to Rebecca Strand, August 3, 1931, AAA.

242 This summer he read particularly from Boehme and Cardinal Newman.

243 These new ideas were articulated in a letter to Rebecca Strand, September 31, 1931, AAA, and to Carl Sprinchorn, September 6, 1931, AAA.

244 Hartley to Adelaide Kuntz, April 1932, AAA. Hartley describes using the library of mystical literature belonging to May Ostlund. "Rolle" refers to Richard Rolle, a fourteenth-century English mystic who he particularly liked.

245 Hartley, *Somehow a Past*, Yale.

246 Hartley to Adelaide Kuntz, February 17, 1933, AAA.

247 Hartley to Adelaide Kuntz, December 5, 1932, quoted in Burlingame, *Marsden Hartley*, p. 335.

248 Hartley to Adelaide Kuntz, April 1933, AAA.

249 Hartley to Norma Berger, September 20, 1933, Yale.

250 Upon reaching Germany he had written that he saw no reason to paint, "but as it is my necessary psychic gesture I must do it in order to function"; Hartley to Adelaide Kuntz, May 27, 1933, AAA. To his niece he confided that he was working on pictures even though he knew that no one would want them: "Every so often I get into the rut of thinking that—why all this bother about art anyhow, it is so useless by all the meanings and interpretations of life these days and there is no reason why it should be done and then I know it has because I am—done because it has to be done"; Hartley to Norma Berger, November 13, 1933, Yale.

251 Hartley to Adelaide Kuntz, July 19, 1933, AAA.

252 Hartley to Adelaide Kuntz, December 12, 1933, AAA.

253 Hartley to Norma Berger, November 27, 1933, Yale.

254 Hartley to Norma Berger, December 30, 1933, Yale.

255 Hartley to Stieglitz, November 21, 1934, Yale.

256 Hartley to Adelaide Kuntz, May 27, 1933, AAA.

257 Hartley to Louis Shapiro, January 2, 1935, AAA.

258 Hartley to Rebecca Strand, July 29, 1935, AAA.

259 Ibid.

260 Ibid.

261 Hartley to Rebecca Strand, October 18, 1935, AAA.

262 Hartley, "Cleophas and His Own," unpublished story, Yale.

263 Hartley to Adelaide Kuntz, November 4, 1935, AAA; Hartley to Kuntz, November 6, 1935, AAA.

264 Hartley to Adelaide Kuntz, November 4, 1935, AAA.

265 Hartley to Arnold Rönnebeck, November 8, 1936, AAA.

266 "I am sitting in my room a great deal now to escape what I call the malice of the cities," he wrote to Rebecca Strand. "It is astonishing how well off one is 'alone'"; Hartley to Rebecca Strand, January 5, 1936, AAA.

267 His salary on the project was $95.44 per week.

268 Hartley to Rebecca Strand, undated, winter, 1936, AAA.

269 Hartley to Rebecca Strand, March 7, 1936, AAA.

270 Hartley to Rebecca Strand, undated winter 1936, AAA.

271 Hartley to Rebecca Strand, undated, early winter, 1936, AAA.

272 Hartley to Adelaide Kuntz, possibly late May 1936, AAA.

273 Hartley to Rebecca Strand, AAA.

274 Hartley, "Cleophas and His Own," Yale.

275 Hartley to Adelaide Kuntz, July 29, 1936. AAA.

276 Hartley to Stieglitz, August 24, 1936, Yale.

277 In his unpublished story, "Cleophas and His Own," Hartley describes the tragedy, aspects of which were to appear in memorial paintings: how shopkeepers in Lunenberg related that Alty, Donny and Allan, true to the local habit, had been drinking in the pubs up and down the mainland that Saturday night. The three boys had been warned not to attempt to return home that evening, but Alty, apparently sensing another chance to dramatize himself, had insisted on rowing back to the island in the punt. The entire community joined forces to drag the ocean, but after three days of searching, they finally gave up. Almost two weeks later, the bodies of Alty and Allan were found, badly mutilated by the rocks, and their flesh eaten away by fish. The day of the funeral, Donny's torn body was discovered.

278 Hartley to Arnold Rönnebeck, November 8, 1936, AAA.

279 Hartley, "Albert P. Ryder," *Adventures in the Arts*, 1921, p. 41.

280 Hartley, "On the Subject of Nativeness—a Tribute to Maine," *Marsden Hartley: Exhibition of Recent Paintings, 1936* (New York: An American Place, 1937), p. 5.

281 McCausland Papers, AAA. "Marsden Hartley," *Journal of Archives of American Art* 8(January 1968), pp. 9–21.

282 "I am at the end of things and do not know which way to turn to find my way out of this awful predicament. . . . Can it be possible that there is no way of keeping an artist like myself alive to go on with his work? . . .";

Hartley to Edith Bry, May 11, 1937, AAA.

283 Hartley to Lloyd Goodrich, Whitney Museum, Goodrich papers.

284 Interview with Hudson Walker, AAA. Reprinted in "Marsden Hartley," *Journal and Archives of American Art* 8(January 1968), pp. 9–21.

285 Hartley to Rogers Bordley, 1939, AAA.

286 Hartley to Hudson Walker, October 8, 1938, AAA.

287 Ibid.

288 Hartley to Nick Brigante, November 14, 1938, Yale.

289 Hartley to Hudson Walker, October 8, 1938, AAA.

290 This comparison was proposed by Sanford Schwartz, "A Northern Seascape." *Art in America* 64 (January-February, 1976), pp. 72–76.

291 Hartley to Rebecca Strand, November 6, 1935, AAA.

292 Hartley to Hudson Walker, August 14, 1939, AAA.

293 Hartley to Hudson Walker, 1939, AAA.

294 Hartley to Carl Sprinchorn, February 13, 1940, AAA.

295 Hartley to Carl Sprinchorn, AAA.

296 Hartley to Rogers Bordley, late 1939, AAA.

297 Hartley to Rogers Bordley, September 30, 1939, AAA.

298 Hartley to Hudson Walker, September 9, 1939, AAA.

299 Hartley to Monica O'Shea 1939, AAA. Hartley taught four classes a week at the Bangor Art Society, for which he received a salary of $12.50 a week.

300. Hartley to Adelaide Kuntz, February 2, 1940, AAA. Hartley preferred the Indian spelling of Katahdin, "Ktaadn." This was also the spelling Thoreau used.

301 Ibid.

302 Hartley to Carl Sprinchorn, October 23, 1942, AAA.

303 Hartley to Adelaide Kuntz, September 4, 1940, AAA. Hartley wrote to Hudson Walker in August 1940, that Corea "is so like Nova Scotia where I was—it is difficult to believe it isn't—just another tempo of the same thing."

304 Hartley to Mme. Lachaise, August 1940, AAA.

305 Hartley to Hudson Walker, October 1940, AAA.

306 Forest Young, interview with McCausland, AAA.

307 Joseph Young, interview with author, August 1978, Corea.

308 Hartley to Hudson Walker, January-February 1941, AAA.

309 Joseph Young, interview with author, August 1978, Corea.

310 Hartley to Hudson Walker, August 23, 1941, AAA.

311 Hartley to Hudson Walker, October 1941, AAA.

312 Ibid.

313 Hartley to Hudson Walker, November 4, 1941, AAA.

314 Ibid.

315 Hartley to Hudson Walker, October 28, 1941, AAA.

316 Hartley, "Pictures," *Marsden Hartley/ Stuart Davis*, exhibition catalogue (Cincinnati: Cincinnati Modern Art Society, 1941), pp. 4, 6.

317 Hartley, "Falling in Love with New York," unpublished manuscript, Yale.

318 [Unsigned]. "Maine Morning" *Time*, November 20, 1944, p. 50.

319 This collection was among Hartley's personal possessions at the time of his death. It was given to Bates College, Lewiston, Maine, along with a group of drawings as the Marsden Hartley Memorial Collection.

320 Hartley to Arnold Rönnebeck, October 14, 1942, AAA.

321 Hartley to Hudson Walker, August 31, 1942, AAA.

322 Hartley to Norma Berger, December 20, 1942, Yale.

323 Hartley to Richard Sisson, August 3, 1943, AAA.

324 Letter from Mrs. Young to Hudson Walker, undated, AAA.

325 McCausland's interview with Hudson Walker, McCausland Papers, AAA.

326 Information from the Hartley Estate Records, related to the author by G. Allen Chidsay, executor of the Hartley Estate.

327 Hartley to Henry Wells, spring 1943, AAA.

Plate 70   *Storm Clouds, Maine*, 1906–7 (cat. no. 1)
Walker Art Center; gift of the T.B. Walker Foundation

Plate 71 *Cosmos*, 1908–9 (cat. no. 3)
Columbus Museum of Art; gift of Ferdinand Howald

Plate 72 *Landscape*, 1910 (cat. no. 8)
Fogg Art Museum, Harvard University, Cambridge, Massachusetts;
gift of James N. Rosenberg

Plate 73   *Musical Theme (Oriental Symphony)*, 1912–13 (cat. no. 14)
Brandeis University Art Collection, Rose Art Museum, Waltham, Massachusetts;
gift of Samuel Lustgarten, Sherman Oaks, California

Plate 74 *Painting No. 1*, 1913 (cat. no. 18)
University of Nebraska, Lincoln Art Galleries; F.M. Hall Collection

Plate 75   *Movements*, 1913 (cat. no. 17)
The Art Institute of Chicago; The Alfred Stieglitz Collection

Plate 76 *Indian Composition*, 1914 (cat. no. 27)
Vassar College Art Gallery; gift of Edna Bryner

Plate 77 *Portrait Arrangement*, 1914 (cat. no. 31)
The McNay Art Institute, San Antonio, Texas

Plate 78   *Painting No. 4 (Black Horse)*, 1914 (cat. no. 29)
Philadelphia Museum of Art; The Alfred Stieglitz Collection

Plate 79 *Flower Abstraction*, 1914 (cat. no. 24)
Mr. and Mrs. Meyer P. Potamkin

Plate 80   *The Aero*, 1914 (cat. no. 22)
National Gallery of Art; Andrew W. Mellon Fund, 1970

Plate 81   *Painting No. 49, Berlin*, 1914 (cat. no. 30)
Barney A. Ebsworth, St. Louis, Missouri

Plate 82 *Portrait of a German Officer*, 1914 (cat. no. 32)
The Metropolitan Museum of Art; The Alfred Stieglitz Collection, 1949

Plate 83   *The Iron Cross*, 1914–15 (cat. no. 34)
Washington University Gallery of Art, St. Louis, Missouri

Plate 84 *Handsome Drinks*, 1916 (cat. no. 40)
The Brooklyn Museum; gift of Mr. and Mrs. Milton Lowenthal

Plate 85 *Movement No. 9*, 1916 (cat. no. 42)
Walker Art Center; gift of the T.B. Walker Foundation

Plate 86 *Abstraction, Provincetown*, 1916 (cat. no. 38)
The Art Institute of Chicago; The Alfred Stieglitz Collection

Plate 87 *Blessing the Melon. The Indians Bring the Harvest to Christian Mary for Her Blessing*, 1918 (cat. no. 47)
Philadelphia Museum of Art; The Alfred Stieglitz Collection

Plate 88   *Landscape No. 3, Cash Entry Mines, New Mexico*, 1920 (cat. no. 50)
The Art Institute of Chicago; The Alfred Stieglitz Collection

Plate 89 *Landscape, New Mexico*, 1919–20 (cat. no. 49)
Whitney Museum of American Art, New York; gift of Frances and Sydney Lewis, 1977

Plate 90 *Still Life with Pears*, 1921 (cat. no. 51)
Helen and George Ratkai, New York City

Plate 91 *New Mexico Recollections*, 1923 (cat. no. 54)
William H. Lane Foundation, Leominster, Massachusetts

Plate 92 *Mont Sainte-Victoire*, 1927 (cat. no. 58)
Mr. and Mrs. Harry W. Anderson, Atherton, California

Plate 93   *Summer Outward Bound, Dogtown*, 1931 (cat. no. 64)
Private Collection

Plate 94   *Rock Doxology, Dogtown*, 1931 (cat. no. 63)
Private Collection

Plate 95   *Earth Cooling, Mexico*, 1932 (cat. no. 65)
Amon Carter Museum of Western Art, Fort Worth, Texas

Plate 96 *Eight Bells' Folly, Memorial for Hart Crane*, 1933 (cat. no. 68)
University Gallery, University of Minnesota, Minneapolis;
gift of Ione and Hudson Walker

Plate 97 *Garmisch-Partenkirchen*, 1933 (cat. no. 69)
Mr. and Mrs. William J. Poplack, Birmingham, Michigan

Plate 98 *Northern Seascape, Off the Banks*, 1936– 37 (cat. no. 77)
Milwaukee Art Center Collection; bequest of Max E. Friedman

Plate 99 *Smelt Brook Falls*, 1937 (cat. no. 78)
The St. Louis Art Museum; purchase: Eliza McMillan Fund

Plate 100   *Rising Wave, Indian Point, Georgetown, Maine, 1937–38*
(cat. no. 80) The Baltimore Museum of Art;
The Edward Joseph Gallagher III Memorial Collection

Plate 101   *Camden Hills from Baker's Island, Penobscot Bay*, 1938 (cat. no. 81)
Stedelijk Museum, Amsterdam

Plate 102   *Adelard the Drowned, Master of the Phantom*, 1938–39 (cat. no. 83)
University Gallery, University of Minnesota, Minneapolis;
bequest of Hudson Walker from the Ione and Hudson Walker Collection

Plate 103 *Portrait of Albert Pinkham Ryder*, 1938–39 (cat. no. 84)
Mr. and Mrs. Milton Lowenthal, New York

Plate 104   *The Lost Felice*, 1939 (cat. no. 86)
Los Angeles County Museum of Art; Mr. and Mrs. William Preston Harrison Collection

Plate 105 *Mount Katahdin, Autumn No. 1*, 1939– 40 (cat. no. 88)
University of Nebraska, Lincoln Art Galleries; F.M. Hall Collection

Plate 106 *Evening Storm, Schoodic, Maine*, 1942 (cat. no. 97)
The Museum of Modern Art, New York; acquired through the Lillie P. Bliss Bequest, 1943

Plate 107 *Mount Katahdin*, 1942 (cat. no. 99)
National Gallery of Art; gift of Mrs. Mellon Byers, 1970

Plate 108 *Summer Clouds and Flowers*, 1942 (cat. no. 102)
Mr. and Mrs. Milton Lowenthal, New York

Plate 109 *Hurricane Island, Vinalhaven, Maine*, 1942 (cat. no. 98)
Philadelphia Museum of Art; gift of Mrs. Herbert Cameron Morris

Chronology of Hartley's Life and Work

Marsden Hartley, age seven

Only major exhibitions of Hartley's work are included here. A complete list of exhibitions begins on p. 194.

1877

January 4. Edmund Hartley born in Lewiston, Maine, to Thomas and Eliza Jane Hartley.

1885

Spring. Mother dies on March 4. Youngest sisters are sent to Cleveland, Ohio, to join a married sister. Edmund remains with his father and another married sister in Auburn, Maine.

1889

Summer. Father marries Martha Marsden on August 20 and joins the family in Cleveland. Edmund is left with his sister in Auburn.

1892

Winter. Leaves school to work in a shoe factory.

1893

Joins family in Cleveland and takes a job in a marble quarry.

1896

Begins weekly art classes with John Semon, a local Cleveland painter.

1898

Spring. Goes on a two-week trip with Semon to Semon's country place in southern Ohio; loses job at the quarry as a result.

Summer. Takes an outdoor painting class with Cullen Yates, a local Impressionist painter.

Fall. Enters the Cleveland School of Art (now The Cleveland Institute of Art) on a scholarship.

1899

Spring. Receives from Anne Walworth, a trustee of the Cleveland School of Art, an annual stipend of $450 for five years to pay for art study in New York City.

Fall. Enters the Chase School, New York City, which he attends for one year.

1900

Summer. Returns to Lewiston, Maine.

Executes delicate botanical drawings (now lost).

Fall. Transfers to the National Academy of Design, New York City, where he studies for the next four years.

1901

Summer. Stays at a Utopian commune run by Charles Fox and Curtis Perry in North Bridgton, Maine.

Fall. Attends National Academy of Design.

1902

Spring. Awarded Honorable Mention in composition and the Suydam Silver Medal for still-life drawing at the National Academy.

Summer. Stays in Center Lovell, Maine.

Fall. Attends National Academy of Design.

1903

Summer. Returns to Center Lovell, Maine.

Fall. Attends National Academy of Design.

1904

Summer. Stays in North Lovell, Maine.

Fall. Stipend from Anne Walworth runs out in November. Takes a part-time job as an extra with Proctor's Theater Company, New York.

Marsden Hartley, ca. 1903

Marsden Hartley, Sarah Farmer, and two unidentified friends, Green Acre, Eliot, Maine, 1907

Marsden Hartley, 1909

1905

Continues to work with the theater company. Tours during the summer.

Painting in the style of academic realism (fig. 3; p. 12).

1906

Summer. Tours with theater company.

Fall. When the tour closes outside Boston, returns to Lewiston, Maine, hoping to teach painting.

Adopts his stepmother's maiden name, Marsden; calls himself Edmund Marsden Hartley.

1907

Winter. Impressionist landscape paintings (fig. 6; p. 13).

Summer. Goes to Green Acre, a mystical-intellectual retreat in Eliot, Maine.

Fall. First exhibition of his work is held in Eliot, Maine, at the home of Mrs. Ole Bull.

Moves to Boston.

1908

Winter. Drops his first name; calls himself Marsden Hartley.

Impressionist landscapes become brighter, and the application of paint thicker (fig.8; p. 14).

Spring. Exhibits one painting at the Rowlands Gallery, Boston. Meets Desmond Fitzgerald, an important Boston collector of Impressionist work, who buys a painting.

Fall. Returns to North Lovell, Maine.

Neo-Impressionist paintings and drawings (figs. 10, 11; p. 17), which he works on through March 1909.

1909

Spring. Visits Boston in March and shows paintings to Maurice and Charles Prendergast, who write letters of introduction on his behalf to William Glackens. Takes paintings to New York City, where Glackens arranges to show them to members of The Eight at his Washington Square studio. The works receive mixed reactions from the group.

Meets Alfred Stieglitz in April through Seumas O'Sheel.

First one-man show in New York opens in May at 291, Stieglitz's gallery.

N. E. Montross, a dealer, introduces him to the work of Albert Pinkham Ryder.

Summer. Dark Landscape series, influenced by Ryder (pl. 3; p. 19).

Receives a $4 per week stipend from Montross for the next two years.

Fall. Returns to Lewiston, Maine, in late November.

1910

Winter. Returns to New York City.

Becomes a regular member of Stieglitz's circle in New York.

Summer. Returns to North Lovell, Maine.

Fauve landscapes (figs. 13, 14; p. 21).

Winter. Returns to New York in December.

1911

Winter. Enters the hospital in January with scarlet fever; hospitalized for five weeks.

Spring. Visits Baltimore in April in an unsuccessful attempt to sell works through a private collector, Robert Frank Skutch.

Experiments with abstract compositional techniques derived from Picasso (figs. 15, 17; p. 22).

Summer. Returns to North Lovell, Maine, in June.

Cézannesque still lifes (fig. 19; p. 22).

Fall. Returns to New York City in November.

In late 1911 or early 1912, through Arthur B. Davies, sees original works by Cézanne for the first time (in the Havemeyer Collection, New York).

1912

Winter. Second one-man show at 291 opens in February.

Spring. Arrives in Paris on April 11, his first trip abroad. Quickly becomes part of the artistic community.

Summer. Moves into Lee Simonson's studio at 18 rue Moulin de Beurre in June and begins painting.

Back row, from left to right: Marsden Hartley, Lawrence Fellows, John Marin; front row: Jo Davidson, Edward Steichen, Arthur B. Carles. Inscribed by Hartley below the photograph, "a group of young American artists of the modern school. 1911."

Still lifes in a Matisse-Cézanne style (fig. 20; p. 26).

As the summer progresses, paintings take on a more Cubist character (fig. 21; p. 26).

Introduced in late August to *Der Blaue Reiter* and to Kandinsky's book *Über das Geistige in der Kunst* ("On the Spiritual in Art"), both of which generate interest in primitive culture and spiritual approaches to art.

Fall. Begins a series of abstract drawings in mid-October.

In November begins painting Intuitive Abstractions, referred to also as Subliminal or Cosmic Cubism (fig. 25; p. 28). Finishes six by early December.

Travels to London in mid-November to place several of the Matisse-Cézanne still-life paintings at the Chenil Gallery, run by Augustus John. Visits the British Museum to see the Egyptian and Assyrian art.

Winter. Becomes a regular visitor to the Stein salon.

Marsden Hartley in an Arabian Nights costume for the Quatres Arts Ball, Paris, 1912

1913

Winter. Leaves on January 3 for a three-week trip to Berlin. On return trip to Paris, stops in

Munich, where he meets Kandinsky and Gabriel Münter on January 24.

Reaches Paris in late January.

Intuitive Abstractions become more influenced by Kandinsky. (fig. 28; p. 30).

Gertrude Stein visits his studio and selects four paintings to be hung in her apartment.

Spring. Leaves Paris in late April for Berlin. Stops in Sindelsdorf to stay with Franz Marc for a few days.

Stops briefly in Munich in early May to arrange an exhibition at the Galerie Goltz. Kandinsky, Münter, Franz Marc and Albert Bloch meet with him to discuss his paintings.

Arrives in Berlin on May 17.

Summer. Resumes painting in mid-July for the first time since leaving Paris.

Paintings of pre-war pageants incorporating military and mystical subject matter (figs. 30, 31; p. 32).

Fall. Five Intuitive Abstractions are included in the *Erster deutscher Herbstsalon* ("First German Autumn Salon") in Berlin, which opens in September.

Sails for New York City on November 15 to bring his work back for an exhibition at 291. Arrives on the 23rd.

1914

Winter. Third one-man show at 291 opens on January 12.

In February, spends ten days in Buffalo during an exhibition of his work at the home of Nina Bull.

Spring. Returns to Germany in March via London and Paris, arriving in Berlin by April 30.

Paints emblematic color abstractions (fig. 35; p. 42).

Summer. By early August, completes four Amerika paintings based on American Indian imagery (fig. 36; p. 42).

After declaration of war on August 3, works on symbolic still-life paintings with red, yellow, and blue color scheme (fig. 38; p. 43). Continues with this series into early October.

Fall. Learns in late September of his father's death on August 4.

Karl von Freyburg, a young lieutenant for whom Hartley had deep affection, is killed in battle on October 7.

Begins German Military paintings in early November. First paintings in series are German officer portraits (fig. 41; p. 44).

1915

German officer portraits become increasingly less symbolic and more decorative (figs. 42, 43; p. 45).

Stepmother, Martha Marsden, dies in May.

Fall. Exhibition at the Münchener Graphik-Verlag, Berlin, in October: forty-five paintings and a group of abstract drawings done in Europe, as well as early 1908 drawings. The only major one-man show Hartley would ever have in Europe and, for its size and content, one of the most important shows of his life.

Winter. Sails for New York City on December 11.

1916

Winter. Remains in New York City except for a short stay in February with Mabel Dodge in Croton-on-Hudson, New York.

Paints simplified, frontal still lifes in Synthetic Cubist style (pl. 23; p. 53).

Spring. Exhibits six paintings and three drawings in the Forum exhibition at the Anderson Galleries, New York, March 13-25.

Summer. Arrives in Provincetown, Massachusetts on July 13 to spend the summer as a guest of John Reed.

Paints Provincetown abstractions based on geometric forms derived from sailboat motifs (fig. 44; p. 54).

Fall. Shares a rent-free house in Provincetown with Charles Demuth in September and October after Reed gives up his summer house.

Returns to New York City in November and stays with Robert Locher on Staten Island.

Winter. Travels to Bermuda in December; takes a room in a boarding house in Hamilton.

1917

Paintings become more representational (figs. 47, 48; p. 56).

Spring. Leaves Bermuda for New York City in May. Has appendix removed.

Summer. Goes to Lewiston, Maine, in June, then on to Ogunquit, Maine, where he stays at an art colony founded by Hamilton Easter Field.

Paintings on glass (fig. 51; p. 57).

Fall. Returns to New York City and lives in an apartment in Brooklyn Heights owned by Field.

1918

Summer. Arrives in Taos, New Mexico, on June 14 after stopping for a few days in Santa Fe.

Pastels of the New Mexico landscape in blues and greens, and a series of paintings based on *santos*, some of which were painted in Mabel Dodge's Taos house (figs. 53, 55; pp. 58, 59).

Fall. Moves to Santa Fe on November 6.

1919

Winter. Visits Carl Sprinchorn in La Cañada, California in February, where he meets Robert McAlmon and Arthur Wesley Dow. Also visits San Francisco.

Summer. Returns to Santa Fe on June 24.

Begins second series of pastels of the New Mexico landscape, now brown in tone, and paintings of the New Mexico desert (figs. 52, 57; pp. 57, 60).

Winter. Leaves for New York City via Chicago on November 19.

Works on more paintings of New Mexico based on the pastels, which he continues through the following spring (fig. 58; p. 60).

1920

Spring. On May 4, appointed first Secretary of the Société Anonyme, Inc., founded by Marcel Duchamp, Katherine Dreier, and Man Ray.

Summer. Leaves in June for Gloucester, Massachusetts, where he spends the summer. Elie Nadelman and Stuart Davis are also there.

Painterly still lifes of single vases of flowers (figs. 59, 60; p. 61).

Fall. Returns to New York City in October.

1921

Spring. Gives lecture on April 1 entitled "What is Dada?" at the Société Anonyme.

Along with Henry McBride, Katherine Dreier, and Mina Loy, gives a reading of works by Gertrude Stein, which takes place on April 30 at the Société Anonyme for "The First Birthday Party — An Evening with Gertrude Stein."

Auction of 117 of his works at the Anderson Galleries on May 17 raises enough money for a return trip to Europe.

Summer. Arrives in Paris in July for a short stay.

Winter. Arrives in Berlin in late November after having visited the American sculptor John Storrs in a château Storrs had rented near Orléans.

1922

Spring-Summer. Painterly still lifes of food, bowls and baskets, in brown tones (fig. 63; p. 72).

Fall. In September, begins making lithographs of still lifes which he finishes in 1923.

1923

Spring. Begins New Mexico Recollections series in April (fig. 64; p. 72).

Summer. In July, executes a group of pastel drawings of male and female nudes (fig. 65; p. 72), the first images to include figures since his 1908 drawings.

Winter. Travels to Italy where, after an eight-week stay in Florence, he goes to Rome to spend Christmas with Maurice Sterne.

1924

Winter. Sails for New York City in February to arrange the details of a syndicate which will finance his living expenses for the next four years.

Summer. Stops in London in June on the way back to France.

Arrives in Paris on July 25. Uses George Biddle's studio.

Continues the New Mexico Recollections (fig. 67; p. 73); begins fish still lifes and Paysage series, based on recollections of Maine (figs. 66, 68; p. 73) — both series continue into the following spring.

1925

Summer. Moves to Vence, France, in August; lives there for a year.

Landscapes of the Italian Alps (fig. 69; p. 74), and a series of modified Cubist still lifes (fig. 74; p. 75) which he works on into the following summer.

Portrait of Marsden Hartley by Arnold Rönnebeck, 1923 Plaster, 54.6 cm (21 ½") high. Present whereabouts unknown

Marsden Hartley, Ezra Pound, and Ferdinand Léger (from left to right), Café du Dôme, Paris, 1924.

Marsden Hartley on the beach at Cannes, 1925

Marsden Hartley, Georgetown, Maine, 1928. Photograph by Paul Strand; copyright 1971 by the Estate of Paul Strand

Marsden Hartley and Alfred Stieglitz at An American Place, ca. 1931. Snapshot by Dorothy Norman

1926

Fall. Moves in October to Aix-en-Provence, where he rents a room in the château "Canto Grihet."

House is sold and in December he moves into "Maison Maria" in the Château Noir forest, Aix-en-Provence.

1927

Winter-Spring. Travels to Paris, Berlin and Hamburg.

Summer. Returns to Aix-en-Provence in May.

Begins Mont Sainte-Victoire paintings (pl. 39; p. 89), and silverpoint landscapes in the style of Cézanne (fig. 71; p. 74).

Winter. Returns to Paris in December.

1928

Winter. Returns to New York City in January. Visits Chicago in March to see his exhibition at The Arts Club of Chicago. Continues on to Denver to see Arnold Rönnebeck, who had moved there.

Summer. Visits the Bullitts in June and July in Conway, New Hampshire.

Spends two weeks in August in Georgetown, Maine, with Paul and Rebecca Strand and Gaston and Mme. Lachaise.

Returns to Paris on August 20.

Winter. By December, begins a series of seashell still lifes with monochromatic backgrounds (fig. 75; p. 78), the first work he has done in over a year.

1929

Winter. The Mont Sainte-Victoire landscapes and Parisian still lifes are shown by Stieglitz at The Intimate Gallery, New York City, in January. They meet with critical rejection.

Spring. Leaves Paris in April for Aix-en-Provence. Stays again at Maison Maria.

Winter. Leaves on November 21 for a trip to Paris, Hamburg, Berlin and Dresden.

1930

Spring. Sails for New York City on March 5. Lives in Brooklyn with the family of Alice Miriam, once Rönnebeck's fiancée.

Summer. Settles for the summer in Sugar Hill near Franconia, New Hampshire.

Works on landscape paintings of New Hampshire (figs. 76, 77; p. 81).

Fall. Returns to New York City in November and lives in Brooklyn in the Pierrepont Hotel.

Does not paint for the next eight months.

1931

Winter. Ill with bronchitis.

Spring. Receives a Guggenheim grant in March to paint for a year. It stipulates that he work outside the country and he decides to go to Mexico the following spring.

Summer. Arrives in Gloucester, Massachusetts, in July for the summer.

Begins first of three series of paintings of Dogtown, a moraine on Cape Ann near Gloucester (fig. 78; p. 82).

Winter. Returns to New York City in December, then goes to Cleveland to spend Christmas with his family.

Haus Schober, Garmisch-Partenkirchen

1932

Spring. Leaves in March for Mexico City.

Travels in May to Cuernavaca, Mexico.

Summer. Paints a series of high-keyed, fanciful landscapes with esoteric symbols (fig. 82; p. 94).

Fall. Returns to Mexico City in November.

1933

Spring – Summer. Leaves from Vera Cruz, Mexico, in April for Germany.

Arrives in Hamburg in May and remains there through the summer.

Fall. Moves to Garmisch-Partenkirchen in the Bavarian Alps in September; lives in a chalet, "Haus Schober."

Begins a series of landscape paintings and lithographs of the Alps around the Garmisch-Partenkirchen area (fig. 84; p. 95).

1934

Winter. Sails for New York City in mid-February.

Spring. Employed by the Federal Government on the Public Works of Art Project in the easel division, March 29 – April 29, but does few paintings.

Summer. Returns to Gloucester, Massachusetts, in late July for the summer.

Begins work on the second Dogtown series (fig. 85; p. 96).

Fall. Returns to New York City.

1935

Winter. On January 4, destroys one hundred paintings and drawings stored in the Lincoln Warehouse, New York City, in order to accommodate all stored paintings in a single vault.

Summer. Travels in June to Bermuda for the summer.

Finishes paintings from the second Dogtown series.

Paints Bermuda landscapes and brightly colored gouaches and pastels based on fish and flower themes (fig. 87; p. 97).

Fall. Travels to Blue Rocks, Nova Scotia, in September. Moves in November to Eastern Points, a small island off the mainland, to live with the Francis Mason family.

Winter. Returns to New York City in December.

1936

Winter. Employed by the Works Progress Administration, January 29 – May 14.

Continues painting Bermuda Fantasies (fig. 88; p. 99).

Summer. Returns in July to Eastern Points, Nova Scotia, to stay with the Mason family.

Begins third Dogtown series from memory (fig. 90; p. 100), as well as monochromatic still lifes of fishing-related objects (fig. 89; p. 100).

On September 19, the two Mason family sons, of whom he is immensely fond, and a cousin drown at sea.

Paints dark seascapes reminiscent of Ryder (fig. 92; p. 101).

Winter. Returns to New York City in December.

1937

Winter. Health is bad.

Finishes paintings from the previous summer.

Spring. On April 20, opens last exhibition with Stieglitz at An American Place.

The Mason house, Eastern Points, Nova Scotia

Forest and Katie Young, Corea, Maine

Marsden Hartley's studio in Corea, Maine

Summer. In June, goes to Georgetown, Maine, for the summer. Paints landscapes of the area (fig. 95; p. 111).

Fall. Moves to Portland, Maine.

1938

Spring. First exhibition at the Hudson D. Walker Gallery, New York City.

Summer. Moves from Portland to Vinalhaven, an island off the Maine coast.

Continues Georgetown landscapes and begins a series based on Vinalhaven (Pl. 101 ; p. 176). Also begins a series of portraits of the Mason family done from memory (figs. 97, 99, 100; pp. 115, 116).

Fall. Moves to Boston in mid-November.

1939

Winter. Returns to New York City in February.

Continues working on portraits of the Masons.

Summer. Returns to Portland, Maine, in June.

In July, stays with John and Clair Evans in West Brookville, Maine.

Fall. Moves to Bangor, Maine, in September, where he teaches painting at the Bangor Society of Art.

In October, takes eight-day trip to Mt. Katahdin in northern Maine.

Applies for a Guggenheim grant for writing but is rejected.

Begins a series of paintings of Mt. Katahdin, on which he continues to work for the next three years (fig. 103; p. 118).

1940

Spring. Returns to New York City. On March 11, opens third and last exhibition at the Hudson D. Walker Gallery. The gallery closes permanently later the same year.

Summer. Moves to Corea, Maine, in August and lives with Katie and Forest Young.

Begins a series of figure paintings based on sunbathers and lobstermen (figs. 107, 108; p. 123), a series of religious subjects, and Maine landscapes (figs. 105, 106; p. 122), all of which he continues into the following spring.

Bust of Marsden Hartley by Jacques Lipchitz, 1942. Bronze, 36.8 cm (14½") high. University Gallery, University of Minnesota, Minneapolis; bequest of Hudson Walker from the Ione and Hudson Walker Collection

1941

Winter. Moves to Bangor, Maine, in January.

Spring. Returns to New York City in March and lives in Hotel Winslow, where he stays when in New York during the next three years. Begins to be represented by the Macbeth Gallery.

Hudson Walker purchases twenty-three paintings from Hartley for $5,000.

Painting very little; works mostly on poems and essays.

Summer. Returns to Corea, Maine. Suffers from high blood pressure and an enlarged heart.

Paints still lifes with monochromatic or seascape backgrounds (fig. 109; p. 124), and atmospheric landscapes (fig. 110; p. 124).

Winter. Travels to Cincinnati for a large joint exhibition with Stuart Davis at the Cincinnati Art Museum, then continues on to Cleveland to see his family for Christmas.

1942

Winter. Lectures on January 6 at the Cincinnati Art Museum: "Is Art Necessary — What is its Social Significance?" Returns to New York City shortly thereafter.

Summer-Fall. Returns to Corea, Maine, in mid-July.

In August, Paul Rosenberg & Co., New York, becomes his dealer.

Begins a series of flower still lifes, many with landscape backgrounds (fig. 111 p. 125) and a new group of landscapes, among them another series depicting Mt. Katahdin.

Winter. In December, he receives the Fourth Painting Purchase Prize of $2,000 in the exhibition "Artists for Victory" at The Metropolitan Museum of Art, New York.

1943

Winter. Returns to New York City in January.

Paints in George Platt Lynes' photographic studio.

Summer. In late July, returns to Corea, Maine, for the summer; is very ill.

September 2. Dies of heart failure in Ellsworth, Maine.

Marsden Hartley, Corea, Maine, 1943

Complete Bibliography and List of Exhibitions

Compiled by Peter Freeman

Because so much of the Hartley literature takes the form of exhibition catalogues and exhibition reviews, the list of exhibitions and the bibliography have been integrated. The exhibitions appear in italics; an asterisk denotes a one-man exhibition. Exhibition reviews follow the exhibition and are indented. The works included in each exhibition are listed individually if fewer than ten. Information enclosed in square brackets represents corrections of or additions to earlier literature.

1906

[Unsigned]. "Edmund Marsden Hartley of Lewiston, A Student and Painter of Nature." *Lewiston Saturday Journal,* December 29, 1906, p. 9.

1907

Home of Mrs. Ole Bull. Eliot, Maine. No checklist exists.

1908

Rowlands Gallery. Boston. Group Exhibition. One landscape painting by Hartley. No checklist exists.

1909

[Hartmann, Sadakichi]. "Unphotographic Paint: — The Texture of Impressionism." *Camera Work,* no. 28 (October 1909), pp. 20–23.

Photo-Secession Galleries. New York City. "Exhibition of Paintings in Oil by Mr. Marsden Hartley of Maine." May 8–18. 33 landscape paintings: Segantini-inspired landscapes, blizzard landscapes, and oil sketches. Catalogue: 4 pp.

> [Unsigned]. "Paintings by Marsden Hartley." *Camera Work,* no. 28 (October 1909), p. 51.

1910

Photo-Secession Galleries. New York City. "Younger American Painters." March 21–April 15. Exhibition also included works by: Putnam Brinley, Arthur B. Carles, Arthur Dove, Lawrence Fellows, John Marin, Alfred Maurer, Edward Steichen, Max Weber. No checklist exists.

> Newspaper reviews by Elizabeth L. Carey, Guy Dubois [*sic*], Mr. Harrington, Sadakichi Hartmann, James Huneker, B. P. Stephenson, James B. Townsend, and Israel White reprinted in *Camera Work,* no. 31 (July 1910), pp. 43–49; little mention of Hartley.

1911

Gallery of the Society of Beaux Arts Architects. New York City. "An Independent Exhibition." March 26–April 21. 174 works by 12 artists. 15 works by Hartley: 9 paintings (Dark Landscapes, 1909, Autumn Landscapes, 1910, and one still life), and 6 landscape drawings. Exhibition also included works by: Homer Boss, Glenn O. Coleman, Arthur B. Davies, Guy Pène Du Bois, Julius Golz, Rockwell Kent, George Luks, John Marin, Alfred Maurer, John McPherson, Maurice Prendergast. Catalogue: 4 pp.

1912

* Photo-Secession Galleries. New York City. "Recent Paintings and Drawings by Marsden Hartley." February 7–26. Cézanne-inspired still lifes. No checklist exists.

> Carey, Elizabeth L. "Delectable Fruits." *The New York Times Magazine,* February 11, 1912, p. 15; reprinted in *Camera Work,* no. 38 (April 1912), pp. 42–43.

> Chamberlin, Joseph Edgar. "A Return to Primitive Art: Marsden Hartley." *The Evening Mail,* February 17, 1912, p. 8; reprinted in *Camera Work,* no. 38 (April 1912), p. 42.

> Hapgood, Hutchins. "Hospitality in Art." *The Globe and Commercial Advertizer,* February 19, 1912, p. 8; reprinted in *Camera Work,* no. 38 (April 1912), pp. 43–44.

> [Huneker, James]. "Things Seen in the World of Art." *The Sun,* February 18, 1912, section 2, p. 10; reprinted in *Camera Work,* no. 38 (April 1912), p. 42

> Lloyd, David. "Art Notes: Retrospective Exhibitions by Renoir and Childe Hassam—Paintings by Otto Walter Beck, Max Weber, Marsden Hartley, Hamilton Field." *The Evening Post,* February 17, 1912, p. 7; reprinted in *Camera Work,* no. 38 (April 1912), p. 42.

1913

Caffin, Charles H. "New and Important Things in Art: As Hartley Sees and Feels it." *New York American,* December 22, 1913, p. 7.

69th Infantry Regiment Armory. New York City. "International Exhibition of Modern Art" (The Armory Show). February 17–March 15. Exhibition traveled: The Art Institute of Chicago, March 24–April 15; Copley Hall, Copley Society of Boston, April 28–May 18. Hartley in New York showing only. Exhibition included more than 1300 works by approximately 300 artists. 8 works by Hartley (2 paintings and 6 semi-abstract drawings, all executed in Paris in 1912): Still Life, No. 1 (unidentified); Still Life, No. 2 (unidentified); Drawings, No. 1 (unidentified); Drawings, No. 2 (unidentified); Drawings, No. 3 (unidentified); Drawings, No. 4 (unidentified); Drawings, No. 5 (unidentified); Drawings, No. 6 (unidentified). Catalogue: preface by Frederick James Gregg; 102 pp., Supplement: 32 pp.

Cox, Kenyon. "The 'Modern' Spirit in Art." Harper's Weekly, Marsh 15, 1913, p. 10.

Neue Kunst Salon of Max Dietzel. Munich. Group show. July. Exhibition included several abstractions by Hartley executed in Paris, 1912–13. No checklist exists.

Der Sturm. Berlin. "Erster deutscher Herbstsalon" ("First German Autumn Salon"). September 20–December 1. 352 works by 59 artists. 5 paintings by Hartley: 1912–13 Intuitive Abstractions (unidentified). Catalogue.

1914

*Photo-Secession Galleries. New York City. "Paintings by Marsden Hartley." January 12–February 12. Intuitive Abstractions executed in Paris, 1912–13, and first Berlin paintings, 1913. Brochure: texts by Mabel Dodge, Marsden Hartley and Gertrude Stein; 4 pp. No checklist exists.

Brochure texts reprinted in Camera Work, no. 45 (dated January 1914, published June 1914), pp. 16–18.

Caffin, Charles H. "New and Important Things in Art: Emotional 'Experiences' Shown by Hartley Paintings." New York American, January 19, 1914, p. 6; reprinted in Camera Work, no. 45 (January 1914), p. 22.

Chamberlin, J. Edgar. "Futurist Art of Mr. Hartley." The Evening Mail, January 20,

1914, p. 9; reprinted in Camera Work, no. 45 (January 1914), pp. 21–22.

[McBride, Henry]. "What is Happening in the World of Art." The Sun, January 18, 1914, section 6, p. 2; reprinted in Camera Work, no. 45 (January 1914), pp. 19–21.

Wolff, Adolph. From a review in the International, reprinted in Camera Work, no. 45 (January 1914), p. 23.

*Home of Nina Bull. Buffalo, New York. February. Selection of works from the Photo-Secession Galleries exhibition. No checklist exists.

*Home of Florence Bradley. Chicago, Illinois. Early March. Same works as shown in Buffalo. No checklist exists.

1915

*Daniel Gallery. New York City. "Paintings by Marsden Hartley; 'The Mountain Series.'" January–February 9. 17 paintings: Dark Landscapes, 1909; still lifes, 1911. Catalogue: 4 pp., ill.

[Unsigned]. "Art Notes: Second Modern French Group—Thirty Americans—The Work of Marsden Hartley, Marion Beckett, Katherine Rhoades, and Others—Notices." The Evening Post, January 30, 1915, section 1, p. 7, 9.

D[u Bois], G[uy] P[ène]. "Exhibitions in the Galleries. Marsden Hartley, A Modernist Who Looks Backward." Arts and Decoration 5(March 1915), pp. 192–93.

[Unsigned]. "Paintings by Marsden Hartley." The New York Times, January 31, 1915, section 3, p. 2.

Daniel Gallery. New York City. Group Exhibition. May. 15 artists. No checklist exists.

*Schames Galerie. Frankfurt, Germany. September. 45 drawings executed in Maine in 1908, none previously exhibited. No checklist exists.

*Münchener Graphik-Verlag. Berlin. October. 45 paintings and several drawings, executed in Europe after October 1912, and the 45 drawings shown in Frankfurt. Catalogue: Foreword by Hartley.

[Unsigned]. "American Artist Astounds Germans." The New York Times, December 19, 1915, p. 4.

1916

The Anderson Galleries. New York City. "The Forum Exhibition of Modern American Painters." March 13–25. 193 works by 19 artists. 9 works by Hartley: A Nice Time [1916]; Handsome Drinks [1916]; Movement [Movements, 1913]; One Portrait of One Woman [1916]; Portrait Movement (unidentified); Portrait of a Young Man [Portrait of a German Officer, 1914]; and 3 unidentified drawings. Catalogue: texts by Christian Brinton, Robert Henri, W. H. de B. Nelson, Alfred Stieglitz, John Weichsel, Willard Huntington Wright, and Explanatory Notes by 16 of the artists, including Hartley; 86 pp., bibl., ill.

Wright, Willard Huntington. "The Forum Exhibition." The Forum 55(April 1916), pp. 457–71.

*Photo-Secession Galleries. New York City. "Paintings by Marsden Hartley." April 4–22. German military series, 1914–15. Leaflet: Foreword by Hartley. No checklist exists.

Caffin, Charles H. "New and Important Things in Art: Latest Work by Marsden Hartley." New York American, April 17, 1916, p. 8; reprinted in Camera Work, no. 48(October 1916), pp. 59–60.

Cole, Robert J. "Studio and Gallery: Chinese and Russian Collections; Marsden Hartley's Heraldic Devices." New York Evening Sun, April 25, p. 13; reprinted in Camera Work, no. 48(October 1916), p. 60.

[Unsigned]. "The Martial Spirit of Hartley." American Art News 14(April 8, 1916), p. 9.

[McBride, Henry]. "Current News of Art and the Exhibitions." The Sun, April 9, 1916, section 6, p. 8; reprinted in Camera Work, no. 48(October 1916), pp. 58–59.

Wright, Willard Huntington. Revised excerpt from The Forum, cited above. Camera Work, no. 48(October 1916), p. 60.

1917

*Photo-Secession Galleries, New York City. "Marsden Hartley's Recent Work." January 22–February 7. Provincetown abstractions, 1916, and a selection of earlier paintings. No checklist exists.

[Unsigned]. "Art at Home and Abroad; Exhibitions of Modern Painting." The New York Times Magazine, January 28, 1917, p. 13.

Grand Central Palace. New York City. "First Annual Exhibition of The Society of Independent Artists." April 10–May 6. 2081 works by 1131 artists. 2 paintings by Hartley: Movement No. 7 [1914–15]; Movement No. 18 [unidentified, probably 1914–15]. Catalogue: 414 pp., ill. [There is also an unillustrated 108-page catalogue.]

Coady, R. J. "The Indeps." The Soil, no. 5 (July 1917), pp. 202–10.

*Ogunquit School of Painting and Sculpture. Ogunquit, Maine. Late August–September. 10 paintings on glass and 5 on canvas, all of 1917. No checklist exists.

1919

University of Oklahoma. Norman, Oklahoma. Group show. November. Approximately 10 works by 6 artists. 2 paintings by Hartley: Cochiti Window, New Mexico, 1919 [A New Mexican Window]; New Mexican Hills with Arroyo 1919 (unidentified). Exhibition also included works by: B. J. O. Nordfeldt, Albert Olson, Sheldon Parsons, Henry V. Poor, Birger Sandzen. No checklist exists.

1920

*Daniel Gallery. New York City. "Recent Paintings by Marsden Hartley." January 2–21. 24 works: 1 Intuitive Abstraction, 1912–13; Provincetown abstractions, 1916; glass paintings, 1917; New Mexico landscapes, 1918–19. Catalogue: 4 pp.

Carnegie Library, Bethany College. Lindsborg, Kansas. "Annual Professional Art Exhibit." March 28–April 4. Exhibition included 2 paintings by Hartley: Cochiti Window, New Mexico,

1919 [A New Mexican Window]; New Mexican Hills with Arroyo, 1919 (unidentified). No checklist exists.

Montross Gallery. New York City. "Special Exhibition: Early Works by Arthur B. Davies, William J. Glackens, Robert Henri, Maurice Prendergast." April. Exhibition of 29 works also included works by Charles Prendergast and Hartley. 5 works by Hartley: New Mexico pastels. Catalogue: 4 pp.

Société Anonyme, Inc. New York City. Group show. November 1–December 15. 14 works by 10 artists. No checklist exists.

McBride, Henry. "Modern Art." The Dial 70(February 1921), p. 235.

1921

[Unsigned]. "The Importance of Being 'Dada.'" International Studio 74(November 1921), p. LXIII.

McBride, Henry. "Modern Art." The Dial 70(January 1921), pp. 113–14.

[Unsigned]. "Pug Debs Make Society Bow." New York Dada, April 1921, p. [3].

Seligmann, Herbert J. "The Elegance of Marsden Hartley—Craftsman." International Studio 74(October 1921), pp. L-LIII.

Waldorf-Astoria. New York City. "Fifth Annual Exhibition of The Society of Independent Artists." February 26–March 24. 1879 works by 1052 artists. 1 painting by Hartley: Black Leaves (Still Life) [1920]. Catalogue: 164 pp. [There is also a 112-page catalogue.]

The Anderson Galleries. New York City. "Seventy-Five Pictures by James N. Rosenberg and 117 Pictures by Marsden Hartley." May 10–17. Exhibition and auction (May 17). Works by Hartley from all periods. Catalogue: texts by James N. Rosenberg and Alfred Stieglitz; 16 pp., ill.

[Unsigned]. "James N. Rosenberg and Marsden Hartley." The New York Times, May 15, 1921, section 6, p. 8.

McBride, Henry. "Art News and Reviews—Museum Purchases a Breughel;

Notes and Activities in the World of Art." The New York Herald, May 22, 1921, section 2, p. 4.

——————. "News and Reviews of Art—Portrait Painters' Annual Exhibition —Whitney Studio Show; The Hartley-Rosenberg Sale a Precedent." The New York Herald, May 8, 1921, section 3, p. 11.

[Unsigned]. "Two 'Modern' Artists Hold Auction Sale; James N. Rosenberg's Pictures Bring $1,026 and Marsden Hartley's $4,913—Many Artists Are Spectators." The New York Herald, May 18, 1921, p. 8.

1922

Rosenfeld, Paul. "The Paintings of Marsden Hartley." Vanity Fair 18(August 1922), pp. 47, 84, 94, 96.

Seligmann, Herbert J. "Hartley Discovers American Civilization." Manuscripts, no. 1(February 1922), pp. 14–15.

1924

Rosenfeld, Paul. Port of New York (New York: Harcourt, Brace and Company), "Marsden Hartley," pp. 83–101; reprinted, with an introduction by Sherman Paul (Urbana: University of Illinois Press, 1961).

1925

Rosenfeld, Paul. Men Seen (New York: The Dial Press), "Marsden Hartley," pp. 177–88.

Galerie Briant-Robert. Paris. "Six American Painters and Two American Sculptors." Janaury 19–February 19. Exhibition also included works by: John Barber, George Biddle, Paul Burlin, Hunt Diederich, Jules Pascin, Maurice Sterne, John Storrs. Brochure: text by Léonce Rosenberg; 8 pp. No checklist exists.

The Anderson Galleries. New York City. "Alfred Stieglitz Presents Seven Americans." March 9–28. 159 works. 25 works by Hartley: landscapes and still lifes, 1921–24. Exhibition also included works by: Charles Demuth, Arthur Dove, John Marin, Georgia O'Keeffe, Alfred Stieglitz, Paul Strand, plus a bust of Hartley by

Arnold Rönnebeck. *Catalogue: texts by Sherwood Anderson, Arthur Dove, Arnold Rönnebeck, Alfred Stieglitz; 16 pp., ill.*

Fulton, Deogh. "Cabbages and Kings." *International Studio* 81(May 1925), pp. 144–47.

1928

Debrol, Mme. M. "Marsden Hartley—Painter of Mountains." *Creative Art* 2(June 1928), pp. xxxv–vi.

J[ewell], A. E[dward]. "What is Imagination?—Doubts Surge Forward as Marsden Hartley Frames New Credo—Six Artists' Work." *The New York Times*, June 17, 1928, p. 19.

Ronnebeck (sic), Arnold. "Hartley Gives Talk on the 'Original Research of Cézanne.'" *The Rocky Mountain News* (Denver), March 25, 1928, p. 4.

The Arts Club of Chicago. "Modern American Paintings; Assembled by The Daniel Gallery, New York." February 10–24. 36 works by 17 artists. 2 paintings by Hartley: Abstraction No. 1 [unidentified, probably 1916], Abstraction No. 2 [unidentified, probably 1916]. Catalogue: 4 pp.

The Arts Club of Chicago. "Paintings and Water Colors by Marsden Hartley." February 28–March 13. 16 landscape and still-life paintings and a group of drawings, silverpoints, watercolors and lithographs, done in France and Germany, 1923–27. Catalogue: poem by Hartley, "The MOUNTAIN and the RECONSTRUCTION"; 6 pp.

1929

Pemberton, Murdock. "Soul Exposures." *Creative Art* 4(January 1929), pp. xlvii–xlix.

The Intimate Gallery. New York City. "Hartley Exhibition." January. 100 works: paintings, watercolors, silverpoints and pencil drawings, 1924–27. Brochure: Foreword by Lee Simonson; 8 pp.

[McBride, Henry]. "Attractions in the Galleries." *The New York Sun*, January 5, 1929, p. 12.

M[oore], D[orothy] L[efferts]. "Exhibitions Coming and Going." *The Arts* 15(February 1929), pp. 121–22.

[Unsigned]. "Mont Ste. Victoire's New Hermit." *The New York Times*, January 13, 1929, section 8, p. 12.

1930

Kootz, Samuel M. *Modern American Painters* (New York: Brewer & Warren), "Marsden Hartley," pp. 40–42.

An American Place. New York City. "Marsden Hartley—New Paintings." December 15–January 18, 1931. New Hampshire landscapes, 1930, and still lifes done in France, 1921–27. No checklist exists.

[Unsigned]. "Exhibitions in New York: Marsden Hartley; An American Place." *The Art News* 29(December 20, 1930), p. 56.

Jewell, Edward Alden. "Metamorphoses." *The New York Times*, December 21, 1930, section 8, p. 15.

[McBride, Henry]. "Marsden Hartley's 'Comeback'; A Repatriated American Artist Shows in an American Place." *The New York Sun*, December 20, 1930, p. 9.

Schnakenberg, H. E. "Exhibitions: Marsden Hartley." *The Arts* 27(January 1931), p. 274.

The Museum of Modern Art. New York City. "Painting and Sculpture by Living Americans." December 2–January 20, 1931. 134 works by 37 artists. 3 paintings by Hartley: Portrait of My Friend, 1914 [Portrait of a German Officer]; Rubber Plant, 1922 [1920]; Grapes, 1927. Catalogue: Foreword by A[lfred] H. B[arr], Jr.; 64 pp., ill.

1932

The Downtown Gallery. New York City. "Pictures of New England by a New Englander; Exhibition of Recent Paintings of Dogtown, Cape Ann, Massachusetts." April 26–May 15 [misprinted in catalogue as April 19–May 1]. 20 landscape paintings, all of 1931. Catalogue: poem by Hartley, "Return of the Native"; 4 pp., ill.

Jewell, Edward Alden. "Art in Review: Pictures of New England by Marsden Hartley on View at the Downtown Gallery." *The New York Times*, April 26, 1932, p. 24.

Shelley, Melvin Geer. "Around the Galleries: Downtown Gallery." *Creative Art* 10(June 1932), pp. 474–75.

Whitney Museum of American Art. New York City. "First Biennial Exhibition of Contemporary American Painting." November 22–January 5, 1933. 157 works by 157 artists. 1 painting by Hartley: Still Life, [New England Still Life, c. 1924]. Catalogue: Foreword by Juliana Force; 80 pp., ill.

1933

Galeria de la Escuela Central de Artes Plasticas. Mexico City. "Exposicion Marsden Hartley." February 28–March. 20 paintings done in Mexico, 1932-33. Catalogue: Foreword by the Director; 8 pp.

1934

Whitney Museum of American Art. New York City. "Second Biennial Exhibition of Contemporary American Painting." November 27–January 10, 1935. 153 works by 153 artists. 1 painting by Hartley: Alpine Vista [1933–34; unidentified]. Catalogue: 24 pp.

1935

Whitney Museum of American Art. New York City. "Abstract Painting in America." February 12–March 22. 134 works by 65 artists. 3 paintings by Hartley: A Nice Time, 1915 [1916]; Portrait of My Friend, 1914 [Portrait of a German Officer]; Provincetown, 1917 [1916; unidentified]. Catalogue: Introduction by Stuart Davis; 20 pp.

1936

Whitney Museum of American Art. New York City. "Second Biennial Exhibition; Part Two, Watercolors and Pastels." February 18–March 18. 208 works by 105 artists. 2 gouaches by Hartley: Sea Flora [1935]; Sea Ghosts [1935]. Catalogue: 16 pp.

*An American Place. New York City. "Marsden Hartley." March 22–April 14. 29 paintings: Bermuda Fantasies, 1935; Bavarian landscapes, 1933–34; second Dogtown landscape series, 1934. Catalogue: "An Outline in Portraiture of Self: From Letters Never Sent," and "This Portrait of a Seadove – Dead" (poem) by Hartley; 8 pp.

 Benson, E. M. "Exhibition Reviews: Marsden Hartley Returns to An American Place." The American Magazine of Art 29(May 1936), pp. 331–32.

 McB[ride], H[enry]. "Marsden Hartley Reappears; New England Artist Again at the American Place." The New York Sun, March 28, 1936, p. 32.

The Museum of Modern Art. New York City. "New Horizons in American Art." September 14–October 12. 435 works by 171 W. P. A. artists. 1 painting by Hartley: Tropic Fantasy [1936]. Catalogue: text by Holger Cahill; 176 pp.

An American Place. New York City. "Exhibition of Paintings." November 27–December 31. Exhibition also included works by: Charles Demuth, Arthur Dove, John Marin, Georgia O'Keeffe, Rebecca S. Strand. No checklist exists.

1937

University Gallery, University of Minnesota. Minneapolis. "5 painters." January 27–February 14. Exhibition also included works by: Charles Demuth, Arthur Dove, John Marin, Georgia O'Keeffe. 45 works. 10 works by Hartley: A Nice Time, 1915 [1916]; Provincetown, 1917 [1916]; Rio Grande River, 1918; Arroyo Hondo, 1918; Landscape – New Mexico, 1918; Still Life with Fish, 1921; Still Life, 1923 (unidentified); Alpspitz – Mettenwald Road, 1935 [Alpspitz – Mittenwald Road, 1933–34]; Flowers, 1935–36; Thursday Afternoons and – Summer, 1935–36 [Thursday Afternoon, and Summer]. Catalogue: text by Ruth Lawrence; 16 pp.

*An American Place. New York City. "Marsden Hartley; Exhibition of Recent Paintings, 1936." April 20–May 17. 21 works: third Dogtown landscape series; Nova Scotia landscapes; seashell still lifes; all of 1936. Catalogue: "On the Subject of Nativeness – a Tribute to Maine," and "Signing Family Papers" (poem) by Hartley; 8 pp.

 Breuning, Margaret. "Seeing the Shows: Marsden Hartley." Magazine of Art 30(June 1937), pp. 386, 388.

 D[avidson], M[artha]. "New Exhibitions of the Week: Marsden Hartley, Paintings of the North" Art News 35(May 8, 1937), pp. 16–17.

 J[ewell], E[dward] A. "A Quartet of Solo Flights." The New York Times, April 25, 1937, section 10, p. 10.

An American Place. New York City. "Beginnings and Landmarks: '291' 1905–1917." October 27–December 27. 72 works by 39 artists plus related documents. 2 paintings by Hartley: The Dark Mountain, Maine, 1909 [The Dark Mountain]; Autumn Landscape, Maine, 1909 (unidentified). Catalogue: text by Dorothy Norman, 8 pp.

Whitney Museum of American Art. New York City. "1937 Annual Exhibition of Contemporary American Painting." November 10–December 12. 115 works by 115 artists. 1 painting by Hartley: Jotham's Island (Now Fox) Off Indian Point. Georgetown, Maine. Mouth of Kennebec River. Sequin Light at Left [Fox Island, Georgetown, Maine, 1937]. Catalogue: 20 pp.

1938

Stieglitz, Alfred. "From a Letter to a Painter: Lake George. October – 1923"; published in Dorothy Norman, "From the Writings and Conversations of Alfred Stieglitz." Twice a Year, no. 1(Fall–Winter 1938), pp. 99–102.

*Hudson D. Walker Gallery. New York City. "Marsden Hartley; Recent Paintings of Maine." February 28–April 2. 23 paintings executed in Maine, 1937–38, and a group of drawings from the same period. Catalogue: 4 pp., ill.

 Devree, Howard. "A Reviewer's Notebook." The New York Times, March 6, 1938, section 11, p. 8.

 D[avidson], M[artha]. "New Exhibitions of the Week: The Climax of Hartley's Painting in Powerful Coastal Scenes." Art News 36(March 26, 1938), p. 21.

 [Unsigned]. "Not to 'Dilate Over the Wrong Emotion.'" The Art Digest 12(March 15, 1938), p. 9.

Whitney Museum of American Art. New York City. "1938 Annual Exhibition of Contemporary American Painting." November 2–December 11. 109 works by 109 artists. 1 painting by Hartley: Nova Scotia Fishermen [1938]. Catalogue: 20 pp.

1939

M[usick], J. B. "Smelt Brook Falls by Marsden Hartley (1877–   )." Bulletin of the City Art Museum of St. Louis 24(April 1939), pp. 21–22.

*Hudson D. Walker Gallery. New York City. "Marsden Hartley; 25th One Man Show." March 6–April 8. 20 paintings: portraits and Maine landscapes, all of 1938–39. Brochure: 4 pp., ill.

 B[rian], D[oris]. "New Exhibitions of the Week: Forceful Painting in a Twenty-fifth Show by Marsden Hartley." Art News 37(March 25, 1939), p. 14.

 [Unsigned]. "Hartley's Figures." Time, March 20, 1939, pp. 24–26.

 Jewell, Edward Alden. "Our Annual Non-Objective Field-Day: Paintings." The New York Times, March 12, 1939, section 11, p. 9.

 Klein, Jerome. "Native Artists Are Featured in Shows of Week; Marsden Hartley Exhibits." New York Post, March 11, 1939, p. 5.

 McCausland, Elizabeth. "Marsden Hartley, Max Beckmann and Others." The Springfield Sunday Union and Republican, March 5, 1939.

*Symphony Hall. Boston. "Marsden Hartley." December–January 6, 1940. Exhibition traveled: Louisiana State University, Baton Rouge, January 28–February 10; Witte Memorial Museum, San Antonio, Texas, March–April 15; Portland Art Museum, Portland, Oregon,

May 1–19; *California Palace of the Legion of Honor, San Francisco, July 5–August 6; Sheldon Memorial Art Galleries, University of Nebraska, Lincoln, September 15–October 15; Walker Art Center, Minneapolis, November. No checklist of the exhibition exists.*

Adlow, Dorothy. "Hartley Art at Symphony Hall." *The Christian Science Monitor*, December 21, 1939, p. 16.

Price, Lucien. "New England Art vs a Puritan Hangover." *Boston Sunday Globe*, January 7, 1940.

Whitney, Irma. "Marsden Hartley's Mystic Canvases at Symphony Hall." *The Boston Herald*, December 31, 1939.

The Institute of Modern Art. Boston, Massachusetts. "Art in New England; Contemporary New England Oil Paintings." May 18–September 4. 48 works by 48 artists. 1 painting by Hartley: Kennebec River at West Georgetown, *1938. Catalogue: Foreword by Nathaniel Saltonstall; 20 pp.*

1940

Whitney Museum of American Art. New York City. "1940 Annual Exhibition of Contemporary American Art." January 10–February 18: Wood Lot, Maine Woods *[1938]. Catalogue: 28 pp.*

The Pennsylvania Academy of the Fine Arts. Philadelphia. "The One Hundred and Thirty-Fifth Annual Exhibition of Painting and Sculpture." January 28–March 3. 435 works by 400 artists. 1 work by Hartley: End of Hurricane; Lanes Island, Maine *[End of Hurricane, 1938]. Received the J. Henry Scheidt Memorial Prize ($300) for an Oil Painting of Special Importance in the Exhibition. Catalogue: 104 pp., ill.*

*Hudson D. Walker Gallery. New York City. "Recent Paintings of Maine, Marsden Hartley." March 11–30. 22 paintings: Lincoln portraits, 1940; Wrestlers, *1940; Mt. Katahdin landscapes, 1939–40. Brochure: 4 pp., ill.*

L[ane], J[ames] W. "New Exhibitions of the Week: The Virile Paintings by Marsden Hartley." *Art News* 38(March 16, 1940), p. 15.

[Unsigned]. "The 'New' Hartley Emerges from Down East." *The Art Digest* 14(March 15, 1940), p. 8.

Whitney Museum of American Art. New York City. "1940–41 Annual Exhibition of Contemporary American Painting." November 27–January 8, 1941. 164 works by 164 artists. 1 work by Hartley: Maine Seacoast Still Life *[1940]. Catalogue: 16 pp.*

1941

The Metropolitan Museum of Art. New York City. "Contemporary Painting in the United States." April 19–27. 267 works by 113 artists. 3 works by Hartley: Ghosts of the Forest *[1937–38];* The Old Bars, Dogtown *[1936];* The Spent Wave *[The Spent Wave, Indian Point, Georgetown, 1937–38]. Exhibition traveled after New York showing; divided into three sections, each circulated along a different route through South America. Catalogue: Preface by Francis Henry Taylor; 24 pp.*

Cincinnati Art Museum. Cincinnati, Ohio. "Expressionism." April 20–May 20. 44 works by 34 artists. 1 work by Hartley: Granite by the Sea, ca. 1939 *[1937–38]. Catalogue: Foreword by Peggy Frank, Introduction by Ralph Flint; 16 pp.*

Cincinnati Art Museum. Cincinnati, Ohio. "Marsden Hartley/Stuart Davis." October 24–November 24. Exhibition organized by the Cincinnati Modern Art Society. 42 works. 21 works by Hartley from all periods. Catalogue: texts by Stuart Davis, Peggy Frank, Marsden Hartley; 32 pp., bio., bibl., ill.

1942

Mellquist, Jerome. *The Emergence of an American Art* (New York: Charles Scribner's Sons), pp. 199, 210, 356–61.

*Macbeth Gallery. New York City. "Marsden Hartley." March 9–28. 20 paintings: figures and landscapes, 1937–42. Brochure: 4 pp.

B[rian], D[oris]. "The Passing Shows: Hartley." *Art News* 41(March 15–31, 1942), p. 27.

Devree, Howard, "A Reviewer's Notebook: In Galleries; Brief Comment on Some Recently Opened Shows—Paintings by Marsden Hartley—Karl Mattern's Debut—Other Attractions." *The New York Times*, March 15, 1942, section 8, p. 5.

[Unsigned]. "Marsden Hartley." *Pictures on Exhibit* 5(March 1942), pp. 10–11.

[Unsigned]. "Marsden Hartley in Successful Solo Show." *Art Digest* 16(March 15, 1942), p. 15.

*Knoedler Galleries. New York City. "Early Drawings by Marsden Hartley." October 12–31.

Devree, Howard. "A Reviewer's Notebook: Brief Comment on Some Recently Opened Group and One-Man Shows in Galleries: Hartley Drawings." *The New York Times*, October 18, 1942, section 8, p. 9.

[Unsigned]. "Early Hartley Drawings on View." *Art Digest* 17 (October 15, 1942), p. 11.

Paul Rosenberg & Co. New York City. "Paintings by Hartley, Rattner, Weber." November 3–28. 11 works. 4 paintings by Hartley: Mt. Katahdin, *1939 [Mt. Katahdin, Autumn No. 2, 1939–40];* The Hunter, *21939 [Young Hunter Hearing Call to Arms];* Summer Sea Window, *1939 [Summer Sea Window No. 1];* Lobster Fishermen, *1940 [1940–41]. Catalogue: 4 pp.*

Whitney Museum of American Art. New York City. "1942–43 Annual Exhibition of Contemporary American Art." November 24–January 6, 1943. 230 works by 117 artists. 1 painting by Hartley: Granite by the Sea *[1937–38]. Catalogue: text by Juliana R. Force; 24 pp.*

The Metropolitan Museum of Art. New York City. "Artists for Victory." December 7–February 22, 1943. 1418 works by about 1000 artists, of which 532 were paintings by 287 artists. 1 painting by Hartley: Lobster Fishermen *[1940–41]. Received Fourth Painting Purchase Prize of $2,000. The 19 prize-winning paintings, including Hartley's, traveled to The Institute of Modern Art, Boston, May 26–June 18, 1943. Catalogue: Foreword by Francis Henry Taylor; 64 pp., ill.*

1943

*Paul Rosenberg & Co. New York City. "Recent Paintings by Marsden Hartley." February 2–27. 17 paintings: figures, seascapes, and still lifes, all 1942. Catalogue: 4 pp. [misdated 1942].

A. M. B. "Attractions in the Galleries." The New York Sun, February 5, 1943. p. 27.

B[oswell], H[elen]. "Marsden Hartley Shows Rugged Paintings." Art Digest 17(February 15, 1943), p. 8.

Cortissoz, Royal. "Caricature at the Morgan Library; Diverse Painters." New York Herald Tribune, February 7, 1943, section 6, p. 5.

Genauer, Emily. "Two Americans Give Solo Shows; Hartley and Davis Developed Since Exhibit of 30 Years Ago." New York World-Telegram, February 6, 1943, p. 7.

Jewell, Edward Alden. "All Sorts and Conditions; The Uncompromising Hartley: A Rock-Ribbed Idiom." The New York Times, February 7, 1943, section 2, p. 8.

[Unsigned]. "The Passing Shows." Art News 42(February 15–28, 1943), p. 24.

Carnegie Institute. Pittsburgh. "Painting in the United States." October 14–December 12. 304 works by 304 artists. 1 painting by Hartley: Young Hunter Hearing Call to Arms [1939]. Catalogue: 152 pp., ill.

*Phillips Memorial Gallery. Washington, D.C. "Marsden Hartley." October 24–November 23. No checklist exists.

Obituaries:

K[ent], N[orman]. "Marsden Hartley (1877–1943)." American Artist 7(October 1943), p. 3.

[Unsigned]. "Marsden Hartley, Noted Artist, Dies." The New York Times, September 3, 1943, p. 19.

Mellquist, Jerome. "Marsden Hartley, Visionary Painter." The Commonweal 39(December 31, 1943), pp. 276–78.

R[iley], M[aude]. "Death Takes Hartley." Art Digest 18(October 1, 1943), p. 9, 29.

Rosenberg, Paul. "Marsden Hartley." The Nation 157(September 18, 1943), p. 326.

1944

Phillips, Duncan. "Marsden Hartley." Magazine of Art 37(March 1944), pp. 82–87.

*Columbus Gallery of Fine Arts. Columbus, Ohio. "Marsden Hartley Memorial Exhibition." January 8–February 7. 38 paintings from all periods. Typescript checklist.

A[dams], P[hilip] R. "Marsden Hartley Memorial." Columbus Gallery of Fine Arts Monthly Bulletin 14(January 1944), pp. 1–2.

*The Museum of Modern Art. New York City. "Marsden Hartley." October 24–Janaury 14, 1945. 106 works from all periods. Catalogue, Feininger/Hartley (joint catalogue for contemporaneous retrospectives): Foreword by Monroe Wheeler, many excerpts from Hartley's essays and letters; 96 pp., chron., bibl., ill.

Burrows, Carlyle. "Art of the Week." New York Herald Tribune, October 29, 1944, section 4, p. 7.

Coates, Robert M. "Two Pairs." The New Yorker, November 4, 1944, pp. 50–51.

Greenberg, Clement. "Art." The Nation 159(December 30, 1944), pp. 810–11.

Jewell, Edward Alden. "Diverse Art Shows." The New York Times, October 29, 1944, p. 8.

————. "2 Art Exhibitions Open at Museum." The New York Times, October 25, 1944, p. 27.

L[ouchheim], A[line] B. "Expressionist and Cubist: America's Version; Hartley and Feininger Dual Retrospective." Art News 43(November 1–14, 1944), pp. 18–19, 32.

[Unsigned]. "Maine Man." Time, November 20, 1944, p. 50.

McCausland, Elizabeth. "Marsden Hartley's Work In Retrospective Show." The Springfield Sunday Union and Republican, November 5, 1944, p. 4C.

Riley, Maude. "The Modern Shows Hartley & Feininger." Art Digest 19(November 1, 1944), pp. 6–7.

Tselos, Demitri. "Lionel Feininger and Marsden Hartley." Gazette des Beaux-Arts 32(November 1947), pp. 190–91.

*M. Knoedler & Co. and Paul Rosenberg & Co. New York City. "Drawings and Paintings by Marsden Hartley." December 11–30. 28 drawings at Knoedler, 20 paintings at Rosenberg, all from the period 1929–43. Catalogue: 4 pp.

Devree, Howard. "Among the New Exhibitions." The New York Times, December 17, 1944, section 2, p. 4.

Upton, Melville. "Marsden Hartley Again; Two Galleries Present His Work—Other Exhibitions." The Sun. December 16, 1944, p. 9.

1945

Wells, Henry W. "The Pictures and Poems of Marsden Hartley." Magazine of Art 38(January 1945), pp. 26–30, 32.

The Institute of Modern Art. Boston. "Four Modern American Painters." March 2–April 1. Exhibition also included works by Peter Blume, Stuart Davis, Jacob Lawrence. 52 works. 14 works by Hartley: 10 paintings, 1908–42, 3 drawings, 1934–40, and 1 pastel, 1940. Catalogue: 8 pp., bio.

Paul Rosenberg & Co. New York City. "Still Life Paintings by Avery, Hartley, Knaths, Rattner, Weber." October 1–27. 15 works. 3 paintings by Hartley: Fruit Bowl, 1928; Rope and Wishbone, 1936; Flowers, 1941. Catalogue: 4 pp.

*Macbeth Gallery. New York City. "Marsden Hartley, Paintings and Drawings." November 26–December 15. 19 landscape and still-life paintings and a group of drawings executed in: Vence, 1925–28; New Hampshire, 1930; Dogtown, 1931, 1934; Mexico, 1933; Maine, 1938. Catalogue: 4 pp., ill.

Breuning, Margaret. "The Rugged Intensity of Marsden Hartley." Art Digest 20(December 1, 1945), p. 17.

*The Arts Club of Chicago. "Marsden Hartley; Memorial Exhibition." December 7–31. 61 works from all periods: 50 works from the 1944 Museum of Modern Art retrospective, 11 works from other sources, and 2 portraits of Hartley by other artists. Catalogue: 4 pp.

1946

Museum of Art, Rhode Island School of Design. Providence. "Museums' Choice Exhibition." February 6–28. 51 works. 5 works by Hartley: Summer, Sea, Window, Red Curtain [Summer Sea Window, Red Curtain, 1942]; The Log Jam [Log Jam, Penobscot Bay, 1940]; Boots [1941]; Hurricane Island, Vinal haven [Hurricane Island, Vinalhaven, Maine, 1942]; The Wave [1940]. 17 museums were asked to lend their finest post-1929 American paintings. Hartley was represented by more works than any other artist. Checklist.

Allen Memorial Art Museum, Oberlin College. Oberlin, Ohio. "Five Expressionists." April. 35 works. 9 works by Hartley: Shells, 1928 [Two Shells]; Autumn Landscape, Hills and Trees, N. H., 1930; Landscape (unidentified); Cynical Blue and Jovial Brown, Dogtown, 1931; Jetty Seen Through Window, 1935–36 [1936]; Lobster Pots and Buoys [1940–41]; Alps [Alpspitz, 1934 (lithograph)]; Dish of Grapes [Grapes in Bowl, 1923 (lithograph)]; Flowers [unidentified, 1923 (lithograph)]. Exhibition also included works by: Karl Hofer, Oskar Kokoschka, Edvard Munch, Karl Schmidt-Rottluff. Catalogue: texts by Lester Pross, Carrie Yoffe; 24 pp., bio.

*Columbus Gallery of Fine Arts. Columbus, Ohio. "Marsden Hartley Drawings." April 8–30. No checklist exists.

Whitney Museum of American Art. New York City. "Pioneers of Modern Art in America." April 9–May 19. 192 works by 34 artists. 8 paintings by Hartley: Carnival of Autumn, 1909 [1908–9]; The Dark Mountain, 1909; Still Life, 1912; Brass Band with Numbers, 1913 [Military, 1913]; Himmel, 1915 [1914]; The Red Cross, ca. 1915 [The Iron Cross, 1914–15]; Abstraction, Provincetown, 1916; Movement No. 6, 1916 [Movement No. 6, Provincetown]. Catalogue: Foreword by Hermon More, Introduction by Lloyd Goodrich; 48 pp., ill.

*Los Angeles County Museum of Art. Los Angeles. "Marsden Hartley." May 12–June 13. 17 paintings dating from 1927 to 1942, from the Estate of Marsden Hartley. Brochure: 4 pp.

1947

F[oster], J[ames], W. Jr. "Two New Purchases." Baltimore Museum of Art News 10(December 1947), pp. 4–6.

H[artt], F[rederick]. "A Marsden Hartley." Smith College Museum of Art Bulletin, nos. 25–28(June 1947), p. 41.

Larkin, Oliver. "Alfred Stieglitz and 291." Magazine of Art 40(May 1947), pp. 178–83.

1948

Gallup, Donald. "The Weaving of a Pattern: Marsden Hartley and Gertrude Stein." Magazine of Art 41(November 1948), pp. 256–61.

*Bertha Schaefer Gallery. New York City. "Exhibition of Paintings by Marsden Hartley Before 1932." April 5–17. 14 paintings, 1906–31. Catalogue: excerpt from "Art—And the Personal Life," (1928) by Hartley; 8 pp., ill.

A[rb], R[enée]. "Spotlight On: Hartley." Art News 47(April 1948), p. 33.

Wolf, Ben. "The Early Hartley." Art Digest 22(April 15, 1948), p. 29.

*Rosenberg Galleries. New York City. "Paintings by Marsden Hartley." October 18–November 12. 20 works: landscapes of Dogtown and Maine, figures, still lifes, all dating from the period 1934–42. Catalogue: 4 pp.

Breuning, Margaret. "Marsden Hartley Seen in Late, Great Works." Art Digest 23(November 1, 1948), p. 12.

Burrows, Carlyle. "Art in Review: Three Modern Painters; Related Expressions by Marsden Hartley, John Minton, and Jankel Adler." New York Herald Tribune, October 24, 1948, section 5, p. 8.

Coates, Robert M. "Marsden Hartley's Maine." The New Yorker, October 30, 1948, pp. 85–86.

Devree, Howard. "Expressionist Veins; Work by Hartley, Kollwitz and Others In a Main Current of Modernism." The New York Times, October 24, 1948, section 2, p. 9.

1949

Institute of Contemporary Art. Boston. "American Painting in Our Century." February. Exhibition traveled: Colorado Springs Fine Arts Center; Art Association of Montreal; M. H. de Young Memorial Museum, San Francisco; Cleveland Museum of Art; Los Angeles County Museum. 50 works by 50 artists. 1 painting by Hartley. Fox Island, Maine 1937–38 [Fox Island, Georgetown, Maine, 1937]. Catalogue: text by Frederick S. Wight; 136 pp., ill.

Dame, Lawrence. "Boston Institute Surveys American Painting." Art Digest 23(February 1, 1949), pp. 12, 31.

1950

Slusser, Jean Paul. "Three Modern Paintings." Bulletin, (University of Michigan Museum of Art) 1(May 1950), pp. 4–8.

*Rosenberg Galleries. New York City. "Paintings by Marsden Hartley." January 9–28. 23 paintings: still lifes, Maine and Nova Scotia landscapes, and bird paintings, all from the period 1927–43. Catalogue: 4 pp.

Breuning, Margaret. "The Hard Core of Hartley's Native Genius." Art Digest 24(January 15, 1950), p. 45.

L[a] F[arge], H[enry]. "Reviews and Previews: Marsden Hartley." Art News 48(January 1950), p. 45.

Bertha Schaefer Gallery. New York City. "Hartley/Maurer; Contemporaneous Paintings." November 13–December 2. 14 works. 7 paintings by Hartley: Garmisch-Partenkirchen, 1933–34; Viaduct in Provence, 1927; Still Life with Pears, 1925–26; Still Life with Blue Bowl, 1922–23; Still Life with Artichoke, 1925–26; The Embittered Afternoon of November, 1931; Still Life with Bottle and Pitchers, 1922–23. Brochure: note by Clement Greenberg; 6 pp., ill.

Breuning, Margaret. "Moderns Vis-à-Vis." *Art Digest* 25(November 15, 1950), p. 19.

_____. "Paintings by Marsden Hartley and Alfred Maurer." *Arts* 30(April 1950), p. 47.

G[oodnough]. R[obert]. "Reviews and Previews: Hartley—Maurer." *Art News* 49(November 1950), p. 48.

1951

Baur, John I. H. *Revolution and Tradition in Modern American Art* (Cambridge: Harvard University Press), pp. 39–40, 53, 54, 74.

McCausland, Elizabeth. "The Daniel Gallery and Modern American Art." *Magazine of Art* 44(November 1951), pp. 280–85.

Richardson, E. P. "Painting in America: The Historian's Problem." *Art Quarterly* 14(Winter 1951), pp. 326–40.

The Museum of Modern Art. New York City. "Abstract Painting and Sculpture in America." January 23–March 25. 108 works by 79 artists. 2 paintings by Hartley: E, 1915 [1914–15]; Abstraction, ca. 1916 [1911]. Catalogue: text by Andrew Carnduff Ritchie; 160 pp., bio., bibl., ill.

   Krasne, Belle. "The Modern Presents 37 Years of Abstraction in America." *Art Digest* 25(February 1, 1951), pp. 11, 21.

Yale University Art Gallery. New Haven. "Pictures for a Picture of Gertrude Stein as a Collector and Writer on Art and Artists." February 11–March 11. 38 works by 19 artists. 1 painting by Hartley: The Lost Felice, 1939–40 [1939]. Exhibition traveled to the Baltimore Museum of Art, March 21–April 21. Catalogue: Preface and Foreword by Lamont Moore, excerpts from the writings of Gertrude Stein; 54 pp., ill.

Rosenberg Galleries. New York City. "Paintings by Marsden Hartley." April 16–May 12. 22 works dating from 1914 to 1942. Catalogue: 4 pp.

   C[ampbell], L[arry]. "Reviews and Previews: Marsden Hartley." *Art News* 50(May 1951), p. 42.

Cole, Mary. "Marsden Hartley's Poetry of Paint." *Art Digest* 25(May 1, 1951), p. 17.

1952

McCausland, Elizabeth. *Marsden Hartley* (Minneapolis: University of Minnesota Press).

_____. "The Return of the Native: Marsden Hartley." *Art in America* 40(Spring 1952), pp. 55–79.

Wildenstein and Co. New York City. "Loan Exhibition of Seventy XX Century American Paintings." February 21–March 22. Exhibition chosen by the art critics of seven publications, proceeds to benefit a special purchase fund for contemporary art at the Whitney Museum of American Art. 70 works by 51 artists. 3 paintings by Hartley: The Wave [1940]; Portrait of Albert Pinkham Ryder, 1938 [1938–39]; Mt. Katahdin, Autumn No. 1, 1939–40. Catalogue: Foreword by Hermon More; 20 pp., ill.

University Gallery, University of Minnesota. Minneapolis. "Marsden Hartley Retrospective." May 5–June 13. Smaller version of the exhibition traveled to 14 museums around the country, July 20, 1952–June 28, 1954. 158 works from the Ione and Hudson Walker Collection.

   [Unsigned]. "Marsden Hartley; Fame Finally Catches Up to Poet-Painter of Maine." *Life*, June 16, 1952, pp. 84–89.

1953

Burlingame, Robert Northcutt. *Marsden Hartley: A Study of His Life and Creative Achievement* (Dissertation: Brown University, Providence, Rhode Island).

Mellquist, Jerome. "Marsden Hartley." *Perspectives USA*, no. 4(Summer 1953), pp. 62–77.

1954

Kramer, Hilton. "Hartley's Lonely Vigil." *Art Digest* 28(June 1, 1954), p. 8, 23, 27.

Bertha Schaefer Gallery. New York City. "Marsden Hartley–A. H. Maurer; Landscapes

1907–1931." February 15–March 13. Brochure. No checklist exists.

   C[ampbell], L[awrence]. "Reviews and Previews: Maurer and Hartley." *Art News* 53(March 1954), p. 53.

   [Unsigned]. "Works of Hartley and Maurer." *The New York Times*, February 17, 1954, p. 26.

1955

Brown, Milton W. *American Painting from the Armory Show to the Depression* (Princeton: Princeton University Press), pp. 144–47.

Martha Jackson Gallery. New York City. "The Berlin Period 1913–1915." January 3–29. 12 paintings and 6 drawings. Checklist.

   Devree, Howard. "Abstract Variety." *The New York Times*, January 9, 1955, section 2, p. 15.

   Kramer, Hilton. "Abstract Interlude." *Arts Digest* 29(January 1, 1955), p. 9.

Paul Rosenberg & Co. New York City. "Paintings by Marsden Hartley." April 4–30. 21 works dating from 1927 to 1943. Catalogue: 4 pp.

   C[ampbell], L[awrence]. "Reviews and Previews: Marsden Hartley." *Art News* 54(May 1955), p. 48.

   Coates, Robert M. "Sea and Sand." *The New Yorker*, April 16, 1955, pp. 109–11.

1956

[Unsigned]. "The Age of Experiment." *Time*, February 13, 1956. pp. 62–67.

Geist, Sidney. "Prelude: The 1930's." *Arts* 30(September 1956), pp. 49–55.

Seligmann, Herbert J. "Marsden Hartley of Maine." *Down East* 3(November–January, 1956–57), pp. 26–29, 40–41.

Bertha Schaefer Gallery. New York City. "Marsden Hartley–A. H. Maurer; American Pioneers: 1868–1943." April 16–May 5. 19 works. 10 paintings by Hartley: Blue Mountain

[The Summer Camp, *1908–9*]; Small Landscape [*1910*]; New Mexico Landscape[*1923*]; Still Life with Pears [*1925–26*]; Roses [*c. 1935–36*]; Rock Doxology—Dogtown [*1931*]; Altar Boulder—Dogtown [*1931*]; Lobster Buoys and Nets [*1936*]; Camden Hills from Baker's Island [Camden Hills from Baker's Island, Penobscot Bay, *1938*]; Still Life (*unidentified*). Flyer: checklist, ill.

T[aylor], P[arker]. "Reviews and Previews: Marsden Hartley, A. H. Maurer." *Art News* 55(April 1956), pp. 84–85.

1957

Williams, William Carlos. "Beginnings: Marsden Hartley." *The Black Mountain Review*, no. 7(Autumn 1957), pp. 164–66.

The Downtown Gallery. New York City. "New Mexico; As Painted by Stuart Davis, Marsden Hartley, Yasuo Kuniyoshi, John Marin, Georgia O'Keeffe, John Sloan." March 2–30. 31 works. 4 works by Hartley: Landscape, New Mexico, *1919*; Landscape, New Mexico, *1919*; Indian Jug, *1919*; Landscape, *1919* (pastel). Catalogue: *10 pp., ill.*

Babcock Galleries. New York City. "Marsden Hartley." April 2 – May 4. No checklist exists.

Martha Jackson Gallery. New York City. "Hartley; Landscape and Still-Life in Oil." May 14–June 14. No checklist exists.

P[orter], F[airfield]. "Reviews and Previews: Marsden Hartley." *Art News* 56(Summer 1957), p. 70.

Y[oung], V[ernon]. "In the Galleries: Marsden Hartley." *Arts* 31(June 1957), p. 48.

1958

Burlingame, Robert. "Marsden Hartley's *Androscoggin*: Return to Place." *The New England Quarterly* 31(December 1958), pp. 447–62.

Museum of New Mexico Art Gallery. Santa Fe. "Marsden Hartley." February. 21 works, 1908–20, from the Ione and Hudson Walker

Collection. Catalogue: text by Frederick Black; 8 pp., chron., ill.

Pomona College Galleries. Claremont, California. "Stieglitz Circle." October 11–November 15. 66 works by 7 artists. 9 works by Hartley: Abstraction: Blue, Yellow, *1911* or *1916* [Abstraction—Blue, Yellow and Green, *1913*]; Musical Theme No. 1, *1913* [Musical Theme No. 1 (Bach Preludes), *1912*]; Painting No. 5, *1914–15*; Grand Canyon, *1918* (*unidentified*); Portrait of Albert Pinkham Ryder, *1938* [*1938–39*]; Knotting Rope, *1939* [Hands Knotting Rope, *1938–39*]; Boots, *1941*; Evening Storm, Schoodic, Maine, Number 2, *1942*; Atlantic Window [Atlantic Window in the New England Character, *1917*]. *Exhibition also included works by: Ansel Adams, Charles Demuth, Arthur Dove, John Marin, Georgia O'Keeffe, Max Weber. Catalogue: Foreword by Peter Selz; texts by the artists; 32 pp., chron., ill.*

Seldis, Henry J. "The Stieglitz Circle Show at Pomona College." *Art in America* 46 (Winter 1958–59), pp. 62–65.

Babcock Galleries. New York City. "Marsden Hartley." December 8–January 3, 1959. 24 paintings, 1908–43, and a group of drawings and lithographs. Catalogue: 12 pp., ill.

Breuning, Margaret. "Marsden Hartley as Antaeus." *Arts* 33(December 1958), p. 50.

C[ampbell], L[awrence]. "Reviews and Previews: Marsden Hartley." *Art News* 57(December 1958), p. 13.

Coates, Robert M. "Hartley and Maurer." *The New Yorker*, December 20, 1958, pp. 83–85.

1959

[Buckley, Charles E.]. "A Landscape by Marsden Hartley." *The Currier Gallery of Art Bulletin* (May 1959), pp. 1–3.

Babcock Galleries. New York City. "Marsden Hartley; Drawings and Lithographs." January 5–24. 21 drawings from all periods and a group of lithographs. Typescript checklist.

Ashton, Dore. "Art: Hartley Lithographs." *The New York Times*, January 8, 1959), pp. 26.

C[ampbell], L[awrence]. "Reviews and Previews: Marsden Hartley." *Art News* 57(January 1959), pp. 10–11.

M[ellow], J[ames] R. "In the Galleries: Marsden Hartley." *Arts* 33(January 1959), p. 58.

1960

H[arris], P[aul] S[tewart]. "A Post-Impressionist Landscape by Hartley." *The J. B. Speed Art Museum Bulletin* 21(April 1960), pp. 1–5.

Babcock Galleries. New York City. "Hartley 1877–1943." January 4–30. 20 paintings and 3 pastels dating from 1908 to 1942. Catalogue: 8 pp., ill.

Breuning, Margaret. "Marsden Hartley." *Arts* 34(January 1960), p. 46.

Coates, Robert M. "Marsden Hartley." *The New Yorker*, January 30, 1960, pp. 69–73.

C[rehan], H[ubert]. "Reviews and Previews: Marsden Hartley." *Art News* 58(January 1960), p. 15.

Paul Rosenberg & Co. New York City. "Drawings by Marsden Hartley." February 16–March 12. Drawings dating from 1927 to 1941. No checklist exists.

T[illim], S[idney]. "In the Galleries: Marsden Hartley." *Arts* 34(April 1960), pp. 61–62.

Alfredo Valente Gallery. New York City. "Marsden Hartley." September 28–November 5. 20 paintings and 1 drawing dating from 1923 to 1943. Catalogue: 4 pp., ill.

S[chafran], L[ynn] H. "Reviews and Previews: Marsden Hartley." *Art News* 59(November 1960), pp. 13–14.

T[illim], S[idney]. "In the Galleries: Marsden Hartley." *Arts* 35(November 1960), pp. 56–57.

American Federation of Arts Traveling Exhibition. "Marsden Hartley." Itinerary: Marion Koogler McNay Art Institute, San Antonio, Texas, December 6–31, 1960; Stedelijk

Museum, Amsterdam, February 3–March 6, 1961; Amerika Haus, Berlin, March 15–April 6; Städt und Lenbachgalerie, Munich, April 16–May 7; Amerika Haus, Stuttgart, May 10–June 1; American Embassy, London, June 15–July 15; Portland Museum of Art, Portland, Maine, August 12–September 2; Walker Art Center, Minneapolis, September 25–October 31; City Art Museum, St. Louis, November 15–December 15; Cincinnati Art Museum, January 1–31, 1962; Whitney Museum of American Art, New York City, March 7–April 8. 52 paintings, 14 drawings, and 7 lithographs dating from 1906–7 to 1943. Catalogue: Introduction by William Sandberg, text by Elizabeth McCausland; 40 pp., ill.

Canaday, John. "Marsden Hartley; Whitney's Retrospective Summarizes The Difficulties of a Gap-Closer." The New York Times, March 11, 1962, p. 27.

Coates, Robert M. "Hartley and de Kooning." The New Yorker, March 24, 1962, pp. 131–34.

Genauer, Emily. "Art Is Marching Back to the 'New'." New York Herald Tribune, March 11, 1962, section 4, p. 8.

————. "Marsden Hartley's Art on Exhibit at Whitney." New York Herald Tribune, March 7, 1962, p. 18.

Lynes, Russell. "Down-Easterner Off to Europe." Harper's Magazine, January 1961. pp. 26, 28.

R[aynor], V[ivien]. "In the Galleries: Marsden Hartley." Arts Magazine 36(May–June 1962), pp. 92–93.

1961

Kramer, Hilton. "Hartley and Modern Painting." Arts 35(February 1961), pp. 42–45.

Lord, Alice Frost. "Marsden Hartley, Lewiston Born Painter, Too Long Unsung Here." Lewiston Journal Magazine Section, August 5, 1961, pp. 1, 6, 7.

Munson, Gorham. "Homage to Marsden Hartley; The Painter from Maine." Arts 35(February 1961), pp. 33–41.

*Babcock Galleries. New York City. "Marsden Hartley, Drawings and Pastels." April 18–May 6. 25 works. Brochure: 4 pp., ill. No checklist exists.

P[eterson], V[alerie]. "Reviews and Previews: Marsden Hartley." Art News 60(April 1961), p. 12.

R[aynor], V[ivien]. "In the Galleries: Marsden Hartley." Arts 35 (April 1961), pp. 50–51.

*David Anderson Gallery. New York City. "Marsden Hartley; Paintings and Drawings." April 22–May 20. No checklist exists.

S[andler], I[rving] H. "Reviews and Previews: Marsden Hartley." Art News 60(Summer 1961), p. 54.

1962

McCausland, Elizabeth. "The Lithographs of Marsden Hartley." Artist's Proof 2(Spring 1962), pp. 30–32.

————. "Tradition and Marsden Hartley." The Texas Quarterly 5(Winter 1962), pp. 193–99.

*Alfredo Valente Gallery. New York City. "Marsden Hartley." March 5–30. 21 paintings and 6 drawings dating from 1909 to 1943. Catalogue: 4 pp., ill.

Bertha Schaefer Gallery. New York City. "Paintings by Five Americans." March 5–31. Exhibition also included works by: Will Barnet, Oscar Bleumner, Morris Kantor, Alfred Maurer. No checklist exists.

C[ampbell], L[awrence]. "Reviews and Previews: Paintings by Five Americans." Art News 61(March 1962), p. 50, 52.

*Shore Galleries. Boston. "Marsden Hartley 1877–1943." March 7–24. 28 paintings, 6 drawings and 1 gouache dating from 1908 to 1942; on loan for the benefit of The Heart Fund. Catalogue: text by R. R. Campbell; 12 pp., ill.

Adlow, Dorothy. "The Vivid Gusto of a Maine Artist; Hartley Retrospective at the Shore Galleries." The Christian Science Monitor, March 9, 1962, p. 5.

*Babcock Galleries. New York City. "Marsden Hartley." March 27–April 14. No checklist exists.

L[a] F[arge], H[enry]. "Reviews and Previews: Marsden Hartley." Art News 61(May 1962), p. 12.

R[aynor], V[ivien]. "In the Galleries: Marsden Hartley." Arts Magazine 36(May-June 1962), pp. 92–93.

1963

The Amon Carter Museum of Western Art. Fort Worth, Texas. "Taos and Santa Fe; The Artist's Environment 1882–1942." April 5–May 26. Exhibition traveled to the Art Gallery, University of New Mexico, Albuquerque, October 10–November 3. 109 works by 61 artists. 2 paintings by Hartley: El Santo, c. 1919 [1918]; Landscape, New Mexico, 1920. Catalogue: text by Van Deren Coke; chron., bio., bibl., ill.

Coke, Van Deren. "Taos and Santa Fe." Art in America 51(October 1963), pp. 44–47.

Munson-Williams-Proctor Institute. Utica, New York. "1913 Armory Show 50th Anniversary Exhibition 1963." February 17–March 31. Exhibition traveled to the Armory of the Sixtyninth Regiment, New York City, April 6–28. 331 works by 133 artists. 2 paintings by Hartley: Still Life No. 1, 1913 [1912]; Still Life No. 2, 1913 [1911?]. [Note: of these two paintings only Still Life No. 1 could have been in the 1913 Armory Show.] Catalogue: texts by Alexander Archipenko, Maurice Becker, Milton Brown, Paul Burlin, Randall Davey, Stuart Davis, Nathan Dolinsky, Marcel Duchamp, Leon Kroll, Victor Salvatore, Charles Sheeler, Carl Sprinchorn, William Zorach and reprints of contemporary documents and reviews; 212 pp., ill.

Whitney Museum of American Art. New York City. "The Decade of the Armory Show." February 27–April 14. Exhibition traveled: City Art Museum of St. Louis, June 1–July 14; The Cleveland Museum of Art, August 6–September 15; Pennsylvania Academy of the Fine Arts, Philadelphia, September 30–October 30; The Art Institute of Chicago, November 15–December 29; Albright–Knox Art Gallery, Buffalo, Janaury 20–February 23, 1964. 115 works by 47 artists. 3 paintings by Hartley: Snow

Landscape, *1908* [The Blast of Winter]; Painting No. 5, *1914–15*; Movement No. 2, *1916*. *Catalogue: text by Lloyd Goodrich; 84 pp., ill.*

1964

Hopkins, Henry T. "Marsden Hartley's 'The Lost Felice'." *Los Angeles County Museum of Art Bulletin* 16, no. 3(1964), pp. 3–11.

Babcock Galleries. New York City. "Hartley–Maurer–Still Life." January 7–February 15. 23 paintings. 12 paintings by Hartley dating from 1910 to 1938. Catalogue: 6 pp., ill.

F[aunce], S[arah] C. "Reviews and Previews: Marsden Hartley and Alfred Maurer." *Art News* 62(January 1964), p. 12.

*Alfredo Valente Gallery. New York City. "Marsden Hartley; Oils, Drawings, Pastels 1909–1964"[sic]. March 24–April 30. 17 paintings, 4 drawings and 2 pastels dating from 1909 to 1943. Catalogue: 4 pp., ill.

N[eumann], T[homas]. "Reviews and Previews: Marsden Hartley." *Art News* 63(April 1964), p. 16.

The Baltimore Museum of Art. "1914; An Exhibition of Paintings, Drawings and Sculpture Created in 1914." October 6–November 15. 240 works by 115 artists. 4 works by Hartley: Painting Number 5, 1914–15; Painting Number 47, 1914–15; Indian Composition, 1914–15 [1914]; Military Symbols II [1914]. Catalogue: texts by George Boas, Lincoln F. Johnson, Jr., Charles Parkhurst, Henri Peyre, Gertrude Rosenthal; 96 pp., ill.

1965

Geldzahler, Henry. *American Painting in the Twentieth Century* (New York: The Metropolitan Museum of Art), pp. 57–62.

National Collection of Fine Arts. Washington, D.C. "Roots of Abstract Art in America, 1910–1930." December 2–January 6, 1966. 200 works by 41 artists. 10 paintings and 1 drawing by Hartley dating from 1908 to 1916. Catalogue: texts by Adelyn D. Breeskin, Duncan Phillips, David W. Scott and reprinted texts from the 1916 Forum Exhibition catalogue by John Marin and Alfred Stieglitz; 94 pp., bio., ill.

Stevens, Elizabeth. "Washington: A Half-Century of Abstraction." *Arts Magazine* 40(March 1966), pp. 46–47.

1966

Davidson, Abraham A. "Cubism and the Early American Modernist." *Art Journal* 26(Winter 1966–67), pp. 122–29.

La Jolla Museum of Art. La Jolla, California. "Marsden Hartley/John Marin." February 12–March 27. 75 works. 33 paintings from all periods. Catalogue: texts by Donald Brewer, Sheldon Reich; 48 pp., ill.

ACA Heritage Gallery. New York City. "Commemorating the 50th Anniversary of 'The Forum Exhibition of Modern American Painters' March 1916." March 14–April 9. 42 works by 17 artists. 3 paintings by Hartley: Movement No. 2 [1916]; Military [1913]; Painting No. 1 [1913]. [Note: none of these paintings were in the Forum Exhibition.] Catalogue: Foreword by John Weichsel; reprints the five Forewords from the Forum Exhibition catalogue (see above) and excerpts from the 16 Explanatory Notes by the artists; 28 pp., ill.

*American Federation of Arts Traveling Exhibition. "Late Works of Marsden Hartley." Itinerary: Birmingham Museum of Art, Birmingham, Alabama, October 2–23; University of Minnesota, Minneapolis, November 6–27; Oklahoma Art Center, Oklahoma City, January 15–February 5, 1967; Portland Art Museum, Portland, Oregon, February 19–March 12; University of Iowa, Iowa City, March 26–April 16; Colby College, Waterville, Maine, May 14–June 11; Charles and Emma Frye Art Museum, Seattle, July 29–August 20; Wichita Art Museum, Wichita, Kansas, September 6–27; Munson-Williams-Proctor Institute, Utica, New York, October 11–November 1. 41 paintings and 21 drawings and prints from the period 1930–43.

1967

Harithas, James. "Marsden Hartley's German Period Abstractions." *The Corcoran Gallery of Art Bulletin* 16(November 1967), pp. 22–26.

Gropper Art Gallery. Cambridge, Massachusetts. "Marsden Hartley and Carl Sprinchorn." June 7–30. 28 works by Hartley. Catalogue: excerpts from Hartley's writings; 8 pp., ill. No

checklist exists.

Wilson, Patricia Boyd. *The Christian Science Monitor,* June 20, 1967, p. 8.

*Martha Jackson Gallery. New York City. "Still Life Compositions; Lithographs, 1923–24." October 28–November 18. No checklist exists.

1968

Agee, William. "New York Dada, 1910–1930." *Art News Annual XXXIV* (October 1968), pp. 104–13.

"Marsden Hartley" (a transcript of a taped interview with Hudson Walker, conducted by Elizabeth McCausland and Mary Bartlett Cowdrey). *Journal of the Archives of American Art* 8(January 1968), pp. 9–21.

*The Knoedler Galleries. New York City. "Marsden Hartley; A Selection of Paintings and Drawings of the Twenties and Thirties." January 9–27. 30 paintings and 9 drawings. Catalogue: 8 pp., chron., ill.

Kramer, Hilton. "Marsden Hartley, American Yet Cosmopolitan." *The New York Times,* June 20, 1968, p. 25.

S[imon], R[ita]. "In the Galleries: Marsden Hartley." *Arts Magazine* 42(February 1968), p. 66.

*University Galleries, University of Southern California. Los Angeles. "Marsden Hartley; Painter/Poet 1877–1943." November 20–December 20. Exhibition traveled: Tucson Art Center, Tucson, Arizona, January 10–February 16, 1969; University Art Museum, University of Texas at Austin, March 10–April 27. 108 works from all periods. Catalogue: 28 pp., chron., ill.

[Unsigned]. "Marsden Hartley." *Connisseur* 171(August 1969), pp. 282–83.

1969

Dijkstra, Bram. *The Hieroglyphics of a New Speach* (Princeton: Princeton University Press), pp. 113–22.

Plagens, Peter. "Marsden Hartley Revisited; Or, Were We Really Ever There?" *Artforum* 7(May 1969), pp. 40–43.

*Bernard Danenberg Galleries. New York City. "Marsden Hartley; A Retrospective Exhibition." September 16 – October 4. 36 paintings and a group of watercolors, pastels, drawings and lithographs from all periods. Catalogue: text by Frederick S. Wight; reprint of Hartley's "Art – And the Personal Life"; 32 pp., chron., ill.

A[llen], W[illiam] D. "In the Galleries: Marsden Hartley." Arts Magazine 44(September – October 1969), p. 64.

[Unsigned]. "Hartley's Heros." Apollo 90(December 1969), p. 535.

K[line], K[atherine]. "Reviews and Previews: Marsden Hartley." Art News 68(November 1969), p. 19c.

Kramer, Hilton. "Marsden Hartley: The Return of the Native." The New York Times, September 21, 1969, section 2, p. 29.

1970

Jaffe, Irma B. "Cubist Elements in the Painting of Marsden Hartley." Art International 14(April 1970), pp. 33 – 38.

Wildenstein Galleries. New York City. "The Ferdinand Howald Collection." May 19 – July 3. 180 works by 36 artists. 16 paintings by Hartley dating from 1909 to 1923.

Linville, Kasha. "Critique; The Howald Collection at Wildenstein." Arts Magazine 44(Summer 1970), pp. 16, 18.

*Smithsonian Institution Traveling Exhibition Service. "Ninety-Nine Drawings by Marsden Hartley." Exhibition traveled to 18 museums around the country, November 2, 1970 – February 24, 1974. 99 drawings, 1913 – 43, from the Marsden Hartley Memorial Collection, Bates College, Lewiston, Maine. Catalogue: text by William J. Mitchell; 136 pp., bibl., ill.

1971

Szekely, Gillian M. Hill. The Beginnings of Abstraction in America: Art and Theory in Alfred Stieglitz's New York Circle (Dissertation: University of Edinburgh), pp. 29 – 30, 101 – 119, 137 – 147.

Fine Arts Gallery of San Diego. San Diego, California. "Color & Form 1909 – 1914." November 20 – January 2, 1972. Exhibition traveled: The Oakland Museum, Oakland, California, January 25 – March 5, 1972; Seattle Art Museum, March 24 – May 7. 80 works by 32 artists. 3 paintings by Hartley: Composition, 1913; Composition, 1914; Abstraction – Blue, Yellow and Green, 1916 [1913]. Catalogue: texts by William C. Agee, Herschel B. Chipp, Henry G. Gardiner, Lilli Lonngren, Peter Selz, Joshua Taylor; 104 pp., chron., bibl., ill.

1972

*Babcock Galleries. New York City. "Marsden Hartley." January 8 – 29. 17 paintings. No checklist exists.

M[unson], G[retchen] T. "Reviews and Previews: Marsden Hartley." Art News 70(January 1972), p. 16.

*The University of Kansas Museum of Art. Lawrence. "Marsden Hartley; Lithographs and Related Works." March 19 – April 16. 17 prints and 16 drawings and paintings, 1921 – 34. Catalogue: text by Charles C. Eldredge; 40 pp., ill.

[Unsigned]. "Dear Old Maine." Apollo 96(August 1972), p. 157.

1973

Eldredge, Charles C. "Marsden Hartley, Lithographer." American Art Journal 5(May 1973), pp. 46 – 53.

Homer, William Innes. "Stieglitz and 291." Art In America 61(July – August 1973), pp. 50 – 57.

Washburn Gallery. New York City. "291." February 7 – March 3. 27 works by 15 artists, 2 paintings by Hartley: Landscape, Maine, ca. 1909 [1909]; Movement, Sails, 1916. Brochure: 8 pp., ill; typescript checklist.

Schwartz, Sanford. "New York Letter." Art International 17(May 1973), pp. 42 – 43.

Cape Ann Historical Association. Gloucester, Massachusetts. "Portrait of a Place; Some American Landscape Painters in Gloucester." July 25 – September 5. 31 works by 11 artists. 3 works

by Hartley: Summer Outward Bound, Dogtown, 1931; Rock Doxology, 1931; Whale's Jaw, Dogtown (pastel), 1934 or 1936 [1934]. Catalogue: text by John Wilmerding; 96 pp., ill.

1974

Gillespie, H. Gary. A Collateral Study of Selected Paintings and Poems from Marsden Hartley's Maine Period (Dissertation: Ohio University, Athens).

Homer, William Innes. "Alfred Stieglitz and an American Aesthetic." Arts Magazine 49(September 1974), pp. 25 – 28.

Washburn Gallery. New York City. "Seven Americans." February 6 – March 2. 25 works by 7 artists. 3 works by Hartley: Landscape, New Mexico, No. 7, ca. 1918 – 20 [ca. 1918 – 19] (pastel); Landscape, New Mexico, ca. 1918 – 20 [1919 – 20]; Still Life with Bowl of Fruit on Table, ca. 1922 – 23. Brochure: texts by Arthur Dove, Alfred Stieglitz; 12 pp.; ill.; typescript checklist.

*Gallery. Bangor, Maine. "Marsden Hartley." August 16 – September 14. 15 works from all periods. Brochure: note by John W. Pierce; 4 pp., ill.

1975

Rose, Barbara. American Art Since 1900 (New York: Praeger, 1967; revised edition, 1975), pp. 53 – 58, 89 – 90.

———. Readings in American Art Since 1900 (New York: Praeger, 1968; revised edition, 1975), pp. 6 – 7, 12, 57 – 59.

Zilczer, Judith Katy. The Aesthetic Struggle in America, 1913 – 1918: Abstract Art and Theory in the Stieglitz Circle (Dissertation: University of Delaware, Newark).

Delaware Art Museum;. Wilmington, Delaware. "Avant-Garde Painting & Sculpture in America 1910 – 25." April 4 – May 18. 131 works by 56 artists. 5 paintings by Hartley: Abstraction, 1911; Military, 1913; Abstract Forms, 1914 [Flower Abstraction]; Indian Fantasy, 1914 – 15 [1914]; Trixie, 1916. Catalogue: 67 essays by various authors, "Marsden Hartley" by Patrick L. Stewart, Jr.; 176 pp., chron., bibl., ill.

Kramer, Hilton. "Delaware Museum Show Updates the Avant-Garde." *The New York Times*, April 23, 1975, p. 31.

*Babcock Galleries. New York City. "Marsden Hartley." October 1–29. 15 works dating from 1908 to 1943. No checklist exists.

Kramer, Hilton. "Art: Works by Marsden Hartley." *The New York Times*, October 25, 1975, p. 23.

Zucker, Barbara. "New York Reviews: Marsden Hartley." *Art News* 74(December 1975), p. 122.

The Art Galleries, University of California. Santa Barbara. "O'Keeffe, Hartley and Marin in the Southwest." November 4–December 14. 10 works. 6 works by Hartley. Landscape, c. 1925; Arroyo Hondo, 1918 (pastel); Sagebrush, c. 1918 (pastel); New Mexico: Landscape, 1919; Santos, 1920 [1918]; New Mexico, 1918. Checklist.

1976

Levin, Sandra Gail. *Wassily Kandinsky and the American Avant-Garde* (Dissertation: Rutgers University, New Brunswick, New Jersey), pp. 79–140.

Lynch, Michael. "A Gay World After All; Marsden Hartley (1877–1943)." *Our Image: The Body Politic Review Supplement*, no. 6(December–January 1976–77), pp. 1–3.

Schwartz, Sanford. "A Northern Seascape." *Art in America* 64(January–February 1976), pp. 72–76.

————. "When New York Went to New Mexico." *Art in America* 64(July–August 1976), pp. 93–97.

Wilmerding, John. *American Art* (Harmondsworth: Penguin Books), pp. 178–79.

Solomon R. Guggenheim Museum. New York City. "Twentieth-Century American Drawing: Three Avant-Garde Generations." January 23–March 21. 223 works by 29 artists. 3 drawings by Hartley: Military Symbol I, c. 1913–14 [1914]; Military Symbol II, c. 1913–14 [1914]; Military Symbol III, c. 1913–14 [1914]. *Catalogue: text by Diane Waldman; 128 pp., bibl., ill.*

Kramer, Hilton. "What Is a Drawing? Where Can We Draw the Line?" *The New York Times*, February 1, 1976, section 2, p. 31.

Smith, Roberta. "Drawing Now (and Then)." *Artforum* 14(April 1976), pp. 52–59.

The Museum of Modern Art. New York City. "The Natural Paradise; Painting in America 1800–1950." September 29–November 30. 153 works by 67 artists. 4 paintings by Hartley: Landscape, New Mexico, c. 1918 [1919–20]; Off to the Banks, 1936; Northern Seascape—Off the Banks, 1936–37; Evening Storm, Schoodic, Maine, 1942. *Catalogue: texts by Barbara Novak, Robert Rosenblum, John Wilmerding; artists' writings edited by Kynaston McShine; 180 pp., chron., bibl., ill.*

1977

Homer, William Innes. *Alfred Stieglitz and The American Avant-Garde* (Boston: New York Graphic Society), pp. 147–63, 220–33.

Levin, Gail. "Marsden Hartley, Kandinsky, and Der Blaue Reiter." *Arts Magazine* 52(November 1977), pp. 156–60.

C. W. Post Art Gallery. Greenvale, New York. "Marsden Hartley 1877–1943." November 6–December 14. 47 works from all periods. Catalogue: text by H. Harvard Arnason; 36 pp., chron., bibl., ill.

Paris, Jeanne. "Art Review/Hartley's Evolution." *Newsday*, November 11, 1977.

Preston, Malcolm. "Art Review/Hartley's Fight to Find A Style." *Newsday*, November 11, 1977.

Shirey, David L. "The Poetry of Toughness." *The New York Times*, December 4, 1977, Long Island Supplement, p. 23.

Royal Scottish Academy, Edinburgh. "The Modern Spirit; American Painting 1908–1935." August 20–September 11. Exhibition traveled to the Hayward Gallery, London, September 28–November 20. 204 works by 93 artists. 6 paintings by Hartley: Hall of the Mountain King, 1908 [1908–9]; Mountain Lake, 1912 [Mountain Lake, Autumn, 1910]; Berlin Abstraction, 1914–15 [Painting No. 49, Berlin,

1914]; Movement No. 2, 1916; New Mexico Recollection, 1923; The New England Fishhouse, 1934 [New England Sea View—Fish House]. *Catalogue: texts by Milton W. Brown and Naomi Rosenblum; 96 pp., bibl., ill.*

1978

Haskell, Barbara. "Marsden Hartley: Two New Additions to the Permanent Collection." *Whitney Review* 1976/77 (1978), pp. 20–23.

Tashjian, Dickran. *William Carlos Williams and the American Scene* (Berkeley: University of California Press, and New York: Whitney Museum of American Art), pp. 24, 27, 50–54.

Whitney Museum of American Art. New York City. "Synchromism and American Color Abstraction 1910–1925." January 24–March 26. Exhibition traveled: The Museum of Fine Arts, Houston, Texas, April 20–June 18; Des Moines Art Center, Des Moines, Iowa, July 6–September 3; San Francisco Museum of Modern Art, September 22–November 19; Everson Museum of Art, Syracuse, New York, December 15–January 28, 1979; Columbus Gallery of Fine Arts, Columbus, Ohio, February 15–March 24. 204 works by 32 artists. 6 paintings by Hartley: Portrait Arrangement No. 2, 1912–13 [1913]; Painting No. 6, 1913 [1912]; Abstraction, c. 1913 [1913]; Abstraction Blue, Yellow and Green, c. 1913 [Abstraction—Blue, Yellow and Green, 1913]; Composition, 1914 [Pre-War Pageant]. *Catalogue: text by Gail Levin; 144 pp., bibl., ill.*

Treat Gallery, Bates College. Lewiston, Maine. "Marsden Hartley Memorial Collection." May 14–June 30. 97 works: 94 drawings and 3 paintings of figures, landscapes and religious themes, dating from 1910–43.

Washburn Gallery. New York City. "From The Intimate Gallery." October 4–28. 30 works by 10 artists. 3 works by Hartley: Woods, 1927 (drawing); Still Life with Fruit, ca. 1923; Landscape No. 2, France, 1925(?) [1925–26]. *Brochure: text by Dorothy Norman; 12 pp; ill; typescript checklist.*

1979

Barnett, Vivian Endicott. "Marsden Hartley's Return to Maine." *Arts Magazine* 54(October 1979), pp. 172–76.

Barry, Roxana. "The Age of Blood and Iron: Marsden Hartley in Berlin." *Arts Magazine* 54(October 1979), pp. 166–71.

Levin, Gail. "Marsden Hartley and the European Avant-Garde." *Arts Magazine* 54(September 1979), pp. 158–63.

——————. "Hidden Symbolism in Marsden Hartley's Military Pictures." *Arts Magazine* 54(October 1979), pp. 154–58.

Scott, Gail R. "Marsden Hartley at Dogtown Common." *Arts Magazine* 54(October 1979), pp. 159–65.

University Gallery, University of Minnesota. Minneapolis. "The Mountains of Marsden Hartley." March 26–April 29. 19 works dating from 1908 to 1941. Catalogue: text by Carol Rice; 16 pp., ill.

Städtische Kunsthalle Düsseldorf. "2 Jahrzehnte amerikanische Malerei 1920–1940" ("Two Decades of American Painting"). June 10–August 12. Exhibition traveled: Kunsthaus Zürich, August 23–October 28; Palais des Beaux-Arts, Brüssel, November 10–December 30. 164 works by 18 artists. 16 paintings by Hartley dating from 1913 to 1943. Catalogue: text by Peter Selz and Dore Ashton; 156 pp., ill.

Marsden Hartley, ca. 1942. Photograph by George Platt Lynes; collection of Mel Bochner, New York City

Marsden Hartley: Published Writings

Compiled by Peter Freeman

Most of Hartley's writings have remained unpublished and are now part of the Collection of American Literature in the Beinecke Library, Yale University. Hartley began writing poems as early as 1902. At first, he felt he needed to separate Hartley the writer and Hartley the painter; the distinction was taken to an extreme around 1908 when he briefly adopted the pen name "Benio Horbia," derived from two family names, Bennett and Horbury. He did not begin to write essays until about 1915, while living in Berlin. A conversational tone dominates these essays — informal, chatty communiqués about how he felt about particular artists or issues, or how he defined his own aesthetic position at a particular moment. The majority of his published work is concentrated in the years 1917 to 1923, during which time he was a frequent contributor to established magazines such as *The Dial*, *Poetry*, and the *Nation*, and to the important smaller magazines *Contact*, *Others*, *The Little Review*, and *New York Dada*. Many of the published essays were reprinted in his 1921 book, *Adventures in the Arts*. He began to publish less frequently after his return to Europe in 1921, but had renewed his commitment to writing by the early 1930s and, for the last ten years of his life, he tended to divide his days between painting and writing. His first book of verse was published in 1923, yet it was not until 1940 and 1941 that Hartley published books again. *Androscoggin* and *Sea Burial* consisted of verses from these late years, and were among the last things published during his lifetime. The most complete bibliography to date of the unpublished writings is found in Robert Burlingame's *Marsden Hartley*, 1953 (see Bibliography).

1914

"Foreword" to *Paintings by Marsden Hartley*, exhibition catalogue (New York: Photo-Secession Galleries); reprinted in *Camera Work*, no. 45(dated January 1914, published June 1914), p. 17.

1915

"What is 291?" *Camera Work*, no. 47(dated July 1914, published January 1915), pp. 35–36.

"Foreword" to the exhibition catalogue of his one-man show at the Münchener Graphik-Verlag, Berlin (October); reprinted in "American Artist Astounds Germans." *The New York Times*, December 19, 1915, p. 4.

1916

"Explanatory Note." *The Forum Exhibition of Modern American Painters*, exhibition catalogue (New York: Anderson Galleries), p. 53; facsimile reprint (New York: Arno Press, 1968).

"Foreword" to *Paintings by Marsden Hartley*, exhibition catalogue (New York: Photo-Secession Galleries); reprinted in *Camera Work*, no. 48(October 1916), p. 12.

"Epitaph for Alfred Stieglitz." *Camera Work*, no. 48(October 1916), p. 70.

1917

"The Twilight of the Acrobat." *Seven Arts* 1(January 1917), pp. 287–91.

"Odilon Redon." *The New Republic* 9(January 20, 1917), pp. 321–23.

"Albert P. Ryder." *Seven Arts* 2(May 1917), pp. 93–96.

"A Painter's Faith." *Seven Arts* 2(August 1917), pp. 502–6.

1918

"John Barrymore's Ibbetson." *The Dial* 64(March 14, 1918), pp. 227–29.

"Kaleidoscope" (4 poems: "In the Frail Wood," "Spinsters," "Her Daughter," "After Battle"). *Poetry* 12(July 1918), pp. 195–201.

"Emily Dickinson." *The Dial* 65(August 15, 1918), pp. 95–97.

"The Reader Critic; Divagations." *The Little Review* 5(September 1918), pp. 59–62.

"Breakfast Resume." *The Little Review* 5(November 1918), pp. 46–50.

"Tribal Esthetics." *The Dial* 65(November 16, 1918), pp. 399–401.

"Tribute to Joyce Kilmer: As Friend of an Earlier Time." *Poetry* 13(December 1918), pp. 149–54.

"Poetic Pieces" (2 poems: "The Ivory Woman," "Sunbather"). *The Little Review* 5(December 1918), pp. 26–28.

"Aesthetic Sincerity." *El Palacio* 5(December 9, 1918), pp. 332–33.

1919

"Local Boys and Girls Small Town Stuff," "Salutations to a Mouse," "Synthesized Perfumes and Essences," "Fishmonger," "The Flaterers," "Evening Quandary" (6 poems). *Others for 1919; An Anthology of the New Verse*, ed. Alfred Kreymborg (New York: Nicholas L. Brown), pp. 61–68.

"Two Lily Satires" (2 poems: "Pernicious Celebates," "The Very Wise Virgins"). *Playboy*, no. 3(1919), p. 11.

"The Dowager's Distress" (poem). *Playboy*, nos. 4–5(1919), p. 23.

"Scaramouche" (poem). *Others* 5(February 1919), p. 16.

"Swallows" (poem). *Others* 5(March 1919), p. 14.

"Rex Slinkard; Ranchman and Poet-Painter." *Memorial Exhibition; Rex Slinkard 1887–1918*, exhibition catalogue (Los Angeles: Museum of History, Science and Art), pp. 6–12; reprinted in *Rex Slinkard 1887–1918; Memorial Exhibition* (New York: M. Knoedler & Co., 1920), pp. 1–2, 7–8.

"The Beautiful Neglected Arts; Satire and Seriousness." *The Little Review* 6(June 1919), pp. 59–64.

"The Poet of Maine." *The Little Review* 6(July 1919), pp. 51–55.

"Art and Wallace Gould." *The Little Review* 6(October 1919), pp. 24–29.

"The Business of Poetry." *Poetry* 15(December 1919), pp. 152–58.

1920

"Red Man Ceremonials: An American Plea for American Esthetics." *Art and Archaeology* 9(January 1920), pp. 7–14.

"The Poetry of Arthur B. Davies' Art." *Touchstone* 6(February 1920), pp. 277–84.

"Vaudeville." *The Dial* 68(March 1920), pp. 335–42.

"Sunlight Persuasions" (7 poems: "The Festival of the Corn," "Español," "Girl with the Camelia Smile," "The Topaz of the Sixties," "The Asses' Out-House," "To C——," "Saturday"). *Poetry* 16(May 1920), pp. 59–70.("The Festival of the Corn" was reprinted in *The Turquoise Trail*, ed. Alice Corbin Henderson [Boston: Houghton Mifflin Co., 1928], pp. 44–51.)

"Aperatifs [sic]," "A Portrait" (2 prose poems). *Contact*, no. 1(December 1920), pp. 8–9.

"Concerning Fairy Tales." *Touchstone* 8(December 1920), pp. 172–79.

1921

Adventures in the Arts (New York: Boni and Liveright; facsimile reprint, New York: Hacker Art Books, 1972).

"Canticle for October" (poem). *Contact*, no. 3(1921), pp. 11–12.

"Dissertation on Modern Painting." *The Nation* 112(February 9, 1921), pp. 235–36.

"The Crucifixion of Noël" (poem). *The Dial* 70(April 1921), pp. 378–80; reprinted in *Lyric America,* ed. Alfred Kreymborg (New York: Coward-McCann, Inc., 1930), pp. 460–62.

"Yours with Devotion; Trumpets and Drums" (poem; unsigned). *New York Dada*, April 1921, p. [4].

1922

"The Scientific Esthetic of the Redman." Part I, "The Great Corn Ceremony at Santo Domingo," *Art and Archaeology* 13(March 1922), pp. 113–19; part II, "The Fiesta of San Geronimo at Taos," *Art and Archaeology* 14(September 1922), pp. 137–39.

"Marie Laurencin." *Der Querschnitt* 2(Summer 1922), p. 103. (An excerpt from "Some Women Artists in Modern Painting," *Adventures in the Arts*, 1921, pp. 114–16.)

"A Propos du Dome, etc." *Der Querschnitt* 2(Christmas 1922), pp. 235–38.

1923

Twenty-Five Poems (Paris: Contact Publishing Co.).

"Georgia O'Keeffe." *Alfred Stieglitz Presents One Hundred Pictures Oil, Water-Colors Pastels, Drawings by Georgia O'Keeffe American,* exhibition catalogue (New York: The Anderson Galleries), pp. [5–6]. (An excerpt from "Some Women Artists in Modern Painting," *Adventures in the Arts*, 1921, pp. 116–19.)

1924

"The Greatest Show on Earth: An Appreciation of the Circus from One of its Grown-up Admirers." *Vanity Fair* 22(August 1924), pp. 33, 88.

1925

"The Woman distorts, with hunger." *Contact Collection of Contemporary Writers*, ed. Robert McAlmon (Paris: Three Mountain Press), pp. 87–90.

1928

"Art—And the Personal Life." *Creative Art* 2(June 1928), pp. xxxi–xxxiv.

"The MOUNTAIN and the RECONSTRUCTION" (poem). *Paintings and Water colors by Marsden Hartley,* exhibition catalogue (Chicago: The Arts Club of Chicago), pp. [2–4].

1931

"Four Poems" ("1.—From a Paris Window—High," "2. [untitled]," "3. [untitled]," "4.—Corniche—Marseilles"). *American Caravan IV,* eds. Alfred Kreymborg, Lewis Mumford, Paul Rosenfeld (New York: The Macaulay Company), pp. 445–47.

"New England on the Trapeze." *Creative Art* 8(February 1931), pp. 57–58.

"The Paintings of Florine Stettheimer." *Creative Art* 9(July 1931), pp. 18–23.

1932

"Scenes" (2 poems: "Brautigam," "Window-Washer—Avenue C"). *Poetry* 40(April 1932), pp. 22–23.

"Return of the Native" (poem). *Contact* 1(May 1932), p. [28]. (Also printed in *Pictures of New England by a New Englander; Exhibition of Recent Paintings of Dogtown, Cape Ann, Massachusetts,* exhibition catalogue (New York: The Downtown Gallery), p. [2].)

1934

"291—And the Brass Bowl." *America & Alfred Stieglitz; A Collective Portrait,* eds. Waldo Frank, Lewis Mumford, Dorothy Norman, Paul Rosenfeld, and Harold Rugg (New York: Doubleday, Doran & Company, Inc.), pp. 236–42; reprinted (New York: Aperture, Inc., 1979), pp. 119–21.

1935

"George Grosz at An American Place." *George Grosz: Exhibition of Water Colors (1933–1934)*, exhibition catalogue (New York: An American Place), pp. 3–5.

1936

"As to John Marin, and His Ideas." *John Marin: Watercolors, Oil Paintings, Etchings*, exhibition catalogue (New York: The Museum of Modern Art), pp. 15–18.

"Albert Pinkham Ryder." *The New Caravan*, eds. Alfred Kreymborg, Lewis Mumford and Paul Rosenfeld (New York: W. W. Norton & Co.), pp. 540–51.

"Farewell Charles." *The New Caravan*, pp. 552–62.

"An Outline in Portraiture of Self: From Letters Never Sent," and "This Portrait of a Seadove—Dead" (poem). *Marsden Hartley*, exhibition catalogue (New York: An American Place), pp. 3–6; 8.

1937

"Concerning the Work of Richard G." *Exhibition of Paintings by Richard Guggenheimer*, exhibition catalogue (New York: Lilienfeld Galleries), pp. [2–3].

"Seeing the Shows: Paintings of Harry Watrous." *Magazine of Art* 30(March 1937), p. 176.

"Signing family papers" (poem), "On the Subject of Nativeness—A Tribute to Maine. *Marsden Hartley; Exhibition of Recent Paintings, 1936*, exhibition catalogue (New York: An American Place), inside front cover; pp. 1–5.

"The Six Greatest New England Painters." *Yankee* 3(August 1937), pp. 14-16.

1938

"The Berry House," "She Went Without Telling" (2 poems). *The Triad Anthology of New England Verse*, ed. Louise Hall Littlefield (Portland, Maine: Falmouth Book House), pp. 32–33; 48–50.

1939

"Three Notes" (essays: "Mary with the Child—of Leonardo, in the Pinakothek, Munich," "Memling Portraits," "Thinking of Gaston Lachaise"). *Twice a Year*, nos. 3–4(1939–40), pp. 253–63. (Excerpt from "Thinking of Gaston Lachaise" reprinted in *The Sculpture of Gaston Lachaise* [New York: The Eakins Press], pp. 27–29.)

1940

Androscoggin (Portland, Maine: Falmouth Publishing House).

1941

Sea Burial (Portland, Maine: Leon Tebbetts Editions).

"Spring, 1941." *Story* 19(September–October 1941), pp. 97–98.

"Pictures." *Marsden Hartley/Stuart Davis*, exhibition catalogue (Cincinnati: Cincinnati Modern Art Society), pp. 4–6.

"Commentary." *Paintings by John Blomshield*, exhibition catalogue (New York: James St. L. O'Toole Galleries), pp. 2–3.

1942

"Sprinchorn Today." *Exhibition by Carl Sprinchorn*, exhibition catalogue (Philadelphia: American Swedish Historical Museum).

1945

Selected Poems, ed. Henry W. Wells (New York: The Viking Press).

1948

"Letter to Jacques Lipchitz (1935)." *Lipchitz: Early Stone Carvings and Recent Bronzes*, exhibition catalogue (New York: Buchholz Gallery), pp. 1–5.

1954

"Excerpt . . ." *Carl Sprinchorn Drawings—Retrospective 1914–1951*, exhibition catalogue (New York: Passedoit Gallery), p. [2].

1976

Eight Poems and One Essay (Lewiston, Maine: Bates College).

1977

"The Drawings of Nijinsky." *Nijinsky, Pavlova, Duncan; Three Lives in Dance*, ed. Paul Magriel (New York: Da Capo Press), pp. 68–73.

Catalogue of the Exhibition

Dimensions are given first in centimeters, then in inches; height precedes width.

Except where noted, all of the works will be shown at each of the museums participating in the exhibition:

Whitney Museum of American Art, New York
The Art Institute of Chicago
Amon Carter Museum of Western Art, Fort Worth, Texas
University Art Museum, University of California, Berkeley

1 Storm Clouds, Maine 1906–7   Pl. 70
Oil on canvas, 77.5 × 64.8 (30½ × 25½)
Walker Art Center; gift of the T.B. Walker Foundation
Signed l.r.: EDMOnD MarSDEN Hartley

Provenance: the artist; auction at Anderson Galleries, New York City, May 17, no. 48b; Mr. and Mrs. Otto D. Steiner, New York City (purchased, 1921); Mrs. Otto D. Steiner, New York City (inherited, 1925); Bertha Schaefer Gallery, New York City (purchased, 1948, as *Approaching Storm*, before 1909); Ione and Hudson Walker, Forest Hills, New York (purchased, 1948); Walker Art Center, Minneapolis, (gift, 1954, through the T.B. Walker Foundation, there dated 1908), acc. no. 54.8.

2 Carnival of Autumn 1908–9   Pl. 1
Oil on canvas, 76.2 × 76.2 (30 × 30)
Museum of Fine Arts, Boston; Charles Henry Hayden Fund
Unsigned

Provenance: Alfred Stieglitz, New York City; Estate of Alfred Stieglitz; Ione and Hudson Walker, Forest Hills, New York (purchased, 1949); Museum of Fine Arts, Boston, (purchased, 1968, through Babcock Galleries, New York City), acc. no. 68.296.

3 Cosmos 1908–9   Pl. 71
Oil on canvas, 76.1 × 76.5 (30 × 30⅛)
Columbus Museum of Art, Ohio; gift of Ferdinand Howald
Signed l.r.: MARSDEN HARTLEY

Provenance: Alfred Stieglitz, New York City; Charles Daniel Gallery, New York; Ferdinand Howald, New York City and Columbus (purchased, 1917); Columbus Gallery of Fine Arts (now the Columbus Museum of Art), Columbus, Ohio (gift, 1931, as *The Mountains,* 1909), acc. no. 31.179.

4 The Summer Camp 1908–9   Pl. 2
Oil on canvas, 76.2 × 86.4 (30 × 34)
The Fine Arts Museums of San Francisco; gift of Mr. and Mrs. John D. Rockefeller 3rd
Unsigned

Provenance: Alfred Stieglitz, New York City; Charles Daniel Gallery, New York City; Bertha

Schaefer Gallery, New York City (purchased, 1952); Hirschl & Adler Galleries, New York City; Mr. and Mrs. John D. Rockefeller 3rd (purchased, as *The Summer Camp [Blue Mountain],* 1909); The Fine Arts Museums of San Francisco (gift, 1979), acc. no. 1979.7.47.
Berkeley only

5 The Dark Mountain 1909   Pl. 3
Oil on composition board, 49 × 59.1 (19¼ × 23¼)
The Art Institute of Chicago; The Alfred Stieglitz Collection
Unsigned

Provenance: Alfred Stieglitz, New York City; Estate of Alfred Stieglitz; The Art Institute of Chicago (gift, 1949), acc. no. 49.542.

6 Deserted Farm 1909   Pl. 4
Oil on composition board, 61 × 50.8 (24 × 20)
University Gallery, University of Minnesota, Minneapolis; gift of Ione and Hudson Walker
Signed l.l.: MARSDEN HARTLEY

Provenance: Charles Daniel Gallery, New York; Robert Laurent, Brooklyn, New York and Ogunquit, Maine; Paul Rosenfeld, New York City; Ione and Hudson Walker, Forest Hills, New York (purchased, 1945); University Gallery, University of Minnesota, Minneapolis (gift, 1962), acc. no. 62.1.

7 Birch Grove, Autumn 1910   Pl. 5
Oil on cardboard, 30.8 × 30.8 (12⅛ × 12⅛)
The Museum of Modern Art, New York; The Lee Simonson Bequest
Unsigned

Provenance: Alfred Stieglitz, New York City; Lee Simonson (purchased, 1920s); The Museum of Modern Art, New York City (bequest, 1967), acc. no. 335.67.
New York, Chicago, only

8 Landscape 1910   Pl. 72
Oil on board, 29.2 × 29.2 (11½ × 11½) (sight)
Fogg Art Museum, Harvard University, Cambridge, Massachusetts; gift of James N. Rosenberg
Unsigned

Provenance: the artist; auction at Anderson Galleries, New York, May 17, 1921; James N. Rosenberg, New York City (purchased, 1921); Fogg Art Museum, Harvard University, Cambridge, Massachusetts (gift, 1958), acc. no. 1958.304.

9   Maine Mountains, Autumn   1910   Pl. 6
Oil on cardboard, 30.8 × 30.8 (12⅛ × 12⅛)
The Museum of Modern Art, New York; The Lee Simonson Bequest
Signed l.r.: <u>MARSDEN HARTLEY</u>

Provenance: Alfred Stieglitz, New York City; Lee Simonson (purchased, 1920s); The Museum of Modern Art, New York City (bequest, 1967), acc. no. 448.67.
Fort Worth, Berkeley only

10   Red Tree   1910   Pl. 7
Oil on cardboard, 35.6 × 30.3 (14 × 11-15/16)
National Collection of Fine Arts, Smithsonian Institution, Washington, D.C.; gift of Flora E. H. Shawan
Signed l.l.: MARSDEN HARTLEY

Provenance: the artist; auction at Anderson Galleries, New York City, May 17, 1921; Ferdinand Howald, New York City and Columbus, (purchased, 1921); Flora E. H. Shawan (inherited, 1934); National Collection of Fine Arts, Smithsonian Institution, Washington, D.C. (gift, 1966, as *Untitled*, n.d.), acc. no. 1966.33.1.

11   Musical Theme No. 1 (Bach Preludes)   1912   Pl. 10
Oil on canvas, mounted on masonite, 66 × 53.3 (26 × 21)
Mr. and Mrs. Paul C. Schorr, III, Lincoln, Nebraska
Unsigned

Provenance: the artist; Carl Sprinchorn; The New Gallery, New York City (purchased, as *Bach Preludes et Fugues No. 4*, 1912–13); The Downtown Gallery, New York City; auction at Sotheby Parke Bernet, New York City, March 14, 1973, no. 40; Mr. and Mrs. Paul C. Schorr, III, Lincoln, Nebraska (purchased, 1973).

12   Still Life   1912   Pl. 8
Oil on composition board, 81.3 × 65.1 (32 × 25⅝)
University Gallery, University of Minnesota, Minneapolis; bequest of Hudson Walker from the Ione and Hudson Walker Collection
Unsigned

Provenance: the artist; Ione and Hudson Walker, Forest Hills, New York (purchased, 1940); University Gallery, University of Minnesota, Minneapolis (bequest, 1978), acc. no. 78.21.25.

13   Still Life No. 1   1912   Pl. 9
Oil on canvas, 80 × 65 (31½ × 25⅝)
Columbus Museum of Art, Ohio; gift of Ferdinand Howald
Signed l.l.: Marsden Hartley

Provenance: Alfred Stieglitz, New York City; Charles Daniel Gallery, New York City; Ferdinand Howald, New York City and Columbus (purchased, 1917); Columbus Gallery of Fine Arts (now the Columbus Museum of Art), Columbus, Ohio (gift, 1931), acc. no. 31.184.

14   Musical Theme (Oriental Symphony)   1912–13   Pl. 73
Oil on canvas, 100 × 80.6 (39⅜ × 31¾)
Brandeis University Art Collection, Rose Art Museum, Waltham, Massachusetts; gift of Samuel Lustgarten, Sherman Oaks, California.
Unsigned

Provenance: Alfred Stieglitz, New York City; John Quinn, New York City (purchased, 1916, as *Oriental Symphony*); auction at American Art Association, New York City, "The John Quinn Collection: Paintings and Sculpture of the Moderns," February 9–11, 1927, no. 122 (as *Elements*); Samuel Lustgarten, Chicago and Sherman Oaks, California (purchased, 1927); Brandeis University Art Collection, Rose Art Museum, Waltham, Massachusetts (gift, 1952), acc. no. 1267.

15   Abstraction with Flowers   1913   Pl. 11
Oil on canvas, 99.7 × 81.3 (39¼ × 32)
University Gallery, University of Minnesota, Minneapolis; bequest of Hudson Walker from the Ione and Hudson Walker Collection
Unsigned

Provenance: Charles Daniel, New York City; auction at Parke-Bernet Galleries, New York City, March 14, 1946, no. 98; Ione and Hudson Walker, Forest Hills, New York (purchased, 1946); University Gallery, University of Minnesota, Minneapolis (bequest, 1978), acc. no. 78.21.243.

16   Military   1913   Pl. 15
Oil on canvas, 99.7 × 99.7 (39¼ × 39¼)
Wadsworth Atheneum, Hartford, Connecticut; The Ella Gallup Sumner and Mary Catlin Sumner Collection
Unsigned

Provenance: Alfred Stieglitz, New York City (as *Brass Band with Numbers*); Estate of Alfred Stieglitz; Ione and Hudson Walker, Forest Hills, New York (purchased, 1949); Berta Walker, New York City; Babcock Galleries, New York (purchased, 1971); Wadsworth Atheneum, Hartford, Connecticut (purchased, 1973 through Peter H. Davidson and Co., Inc., New York City), acc. no. 73.2.

17   Movements   1913   Pl. 75
Oil on canvas, 120 × 120 (47¼ × 47¼)
The Art Institute of Chicago; The Alfred Stieglitz Collection
Unsigned

Provenance: Alfred Stieglitz, New York City; Estate of Alfred Stieglitz; The Art Institute of Chicago (gift, 1949, then dated 1915), acc. no. 49.544.

18   Painting No. 1   1913   Pl. 74
Oil on canvas, 101 × 81 (39¾ × 31⅞)
University of Nebraska, Lincoln Art Galleries; F.M. Hall Collection
Unsigned

Provenance: Alfred Stieglitz, New York City (as *Spot Movements*); Estate of Alfred Stieglitz; Ione and Hudson Walker, Forest Hills, New York (purchased, 1949); University of Nebraska, Lincoln Art Galleries, Lincoln (purchased, 1971, through Babcock Galleries, New York City), acc. no. H39.

19 Painting No. 48, Berlin 1913 Pl. 14
Oil on canvas, 119.9 × 119.7 (47-3/16 × 47⅛)
The Brooklyn Museum; The Dick S. Ramsay
Fund
Unsigned

Provenance: Estate of the artist, no. 141; Albright Art Gallery, Buffalo, New York (purchased, 1955, through Martha Jackson Gallery, New York City, acc. no. 55:5; Martha Jackson Gallery, New York City (traded, 1956, for *Painting No. 46, Berlin*); Zabriskie Gallery, New York (purchased, 1958); The Brooklyn Museum, Brooklyn, New York (purchased, 1958) acc. no. 58.158.

20 Portrait of Berlin 1913 Pl. 13
Oil on canvas, 99.7 × 100 (39¼ × 39⅜)
Collection of American Literature, Beinecke
Rare Book and Manuscript Library, Yale University, New Haven; gift of Mabel Dodge
Luhan
Unsigned

Provenance: Alfred Stieglitz, New York City; Mabel Dodge Luhan, New York (purchased, 1914); Collection of American Literature, Yale University, New Haven, Connecticut (gift, 1951), acc. no. U 1951.60.
New York only

21 The Warriors 1913 Pl. 12
Oil on canvas, 121.3 × 120.7 (47¾ × 47½)
Max Zurier, Palm Springs, California
Unsigned

Provenance: Estate of the artist, no. 250 (there dated 1914); Max Zurier, Palm Springs, California (purchased, 1959, through Paul Rosenberg & Co., New York City).

22 The Aero 1914 Pl. 80
Oil on canvas with painted frame,
106.7 × 87.6 (42 × 34½) overall
National Gallery of Art; Andrew W. Mellon
Fund, 1970
Unsigned

Provenance: the artist; auction at Anderson Galleries, New York City, May 17, 1921, probably no. 46 (as *Pre-War Pageant*); Hamilton Easter Field, Brooklyn, New York and Ogunquit, Maine (purchased, 1921); Robert Laurent, Brooklyn, New York and Ogunquit,

Maine; Mr. and Mrs. John Laurent, York, Maine; National Gallery of Art, Washington, D.C. (purchased, 1970), acc. no. 2534.

23 Berlin Ante-War 1914 Pl. 17
Oil on canvas with painted frame, 106 × 87.6
(41¾ × 34½) overall
Columbus Museum of Art, Ohio; gift of Ferdinand Howald
Unsigned

Provenance: the artist; Arthur B. Davies, New York City; auction at American Art Association, New York, April 17, 1929, no. 436 (as *Berlin Anti-War*, ca. 1914–15); Ferdinand Howald, New York City and Columbus (purchased, 1929); Columbus Gallery of Fine Arts (now the Columbus Museum of Art), Columbus, Ohio (gift, 1931), acc. no. 31.173.

24 Flower Abstraction 1914 Pl. 79
Oil on canvas with painted frame, 125.4 × 108
(49⅜ × 42½) overall
Mr. and Mrs. Meyer P. Potamkin
Unsigned

Provenance: the artist; Charles Daniel, New York City; M. Knoedler & Co., New York City; auction at Parke-Bernet Galleries, New York City, March 14, 1946, no. 102 (as *Abstraction*); Mr. and Mrs. Milton Lowenthal, New York City (purchased, 1946); Bernard Danenberg Galleries, New York City; Mr. and Mrs. Meyer P. Potamkin (purchased, 1973, as *Abstract Forms*).

25 Forms Abstracted, Berlin 1914 Pl. 18
Oil on canvas with painted frame, 107.3 × 88
(42¼ × 34⅝) overall
Whitney Museum of American Art, New York;
gift of Mr. and Mrs. Hudson Walker (and exchange), 1952
Unsigned

Provenance: Charles Daniel Gallery, New York City; Victor Emanuel, New York City (acquired, 1946, in lieu of back rent); M. Knoedler & Co., New York City, and Ralph N. Chate (purchased jointly, 1946); Ione and Hudson Walker, Forest Hills, New York (purchased, 1947); Whitney Museum of American Art, New York City (gift, 1952, through exchange for *Kinsman Falls, Profile Road, Franconia, New Hampshire*, 1930), acc. no. 52.37.

26 Himmel 1914 Pl. 19
Oil on canvas with painted frame,
125.4 × 125.7 (49⅜ × 49½) overall
William Rockhill Nelson Gallery and Atkins
Museum of Fine Arts; Friends of Art Collection
Unsigned

Provenance: Estate of the artist, no. 66 (there dated 1915–16); William Rockhill Nelson Gallery and Atkins Museum of Fine Arts, Kansas City, Missouri (purchased, 1956, through Paul Rosenberg & Co., New York City, then dated 1915), acc. no. 56.118.

27 Indian Composition 1914 Pl. 76
Oil on canvas, 121.3 × 121.3 (47¾ × 47¾)
Vassar College Art Gallery; gift of Edna Bryner
Unsigned

Provenance: Alfred Stieglitz, New York City; John Quinn, New York City (purchased, 1916, as *Indian Tents*); auction at American Art Association, New York City; "The John Quinn Collection: Paintings and Sculpture of the Moderns," February 9–11, 1927, no. 128; Paul Rosenfeld, New York City (purchased, 1927, as *Indian Encampment*); Edna Bryner; Vassar College Art Gallery, Poughkeepsie, New York (gift, 1950), acc. no. 50.1.5.

28 Indian Fantasy 1914 Pl. 16
Oil on canvas, 119.4 × 100.3 (47 × 39½)
North Carolina Museum of Art; Museum Purchase Fund
Unsigned

Provenance: Mr. and Mrs. Charles J. Liebman, New York City; auction at Parke-Bernet Galleries, New York City, December 7, 1955, no. 68; Martha Jackson Gallery, New York City (purchased, 1955); Nelson-Taylor Consultant Gallery, New York City (purchased, 1959); Dr. and Mrs. Norman Simon, New York City; North Carolina Museum of Art, Raleigh (purchased, 1975, through Hirschl & Adler Galleries, New York City), acc. no. 75.1.4.

29 Painting No. 4 (Black Horse) 1914
Pl. 78
Oil on canvas with painted frame,
106.7 × 88.3 (42 × 34¾) overall
Philadelphia Museum of Art; The Alfred Stieglitz Collection
Unsigned

Provenance: Alfred Stieglitz, New York City (as *Arrangement – Black Horse,* 1913); Estate of Alfred Stieglitz; Philadelphia Museum of Art, Philadelphia, Pennsylvania (gift, 1949, then dated 1915), acc. no. 49.18.8.
New York only

30 Painting No. 49, Berlin 1914 Pl. 81
Oil on canvas, 119.4 × 100.3 (47 × 39½)
Barney A. Ebsworth, St. Louis, Missouri
Unsigned

Provenance: Estate of the artist, no. 142 (there dated 1915–16); Babcock Galleries, New York City (as *Portrait of a German Officer,* 1914); Zabriskie Gallery, New York City; Felix Landau Gallery, Los Angeles; Arnold H. Maremont, Chicago; auction at Sotheby Parke Bernet, New York City, May 1, 1974, no. 12 (as *Berlin Abstraction*); Peter H. Davidson and Co., Inc., New York City (purchased, 1974); Barney A. Ebsworth, St. Louis, Missouri (purchased, 1977, through Babcock Galleries, New York City).

31 Portrait Arrangement 1914 Pl. 77
Oil on canvas with painted frame, 107.9 × 87.6 (42½ × 34½) overall
The McNay Art Institute, San Antonio, Texas
Unsigned

Provenance: Alfred Stieglitz, New York City; Estate of Alfred Stieglitz, E. Weyhe Gallery, New York City (purchased; 1949); The McNay Art Institute, San Antonio, Texas (purchased, 1959), acc. no. 1959.2.

32 Portrait of a German Officer 1914 Pl. 82
Oil on canvas, 173.4 × 105.1 (68¼ × 41⅜)
The Metropolitan Museum of Art; The Alfred Stieglitz Collection, 1949
Unsigned

Provenance: Alfred Stieglitz, New York City (as *Portrait of My Friend,* and *Portrait of a Young Man*); Estate of Alfred Stieglitz; The Metropolitan Museum of Art, New York City (gift, 1949), acc. no. 49.70.42.

33 Abstraction (Military Symbols)
1914–15 Pl. 20
Oil on canvas, 101.6 × 81.3 (40 × 32)
Washburn Gallery, New York City
Unsigned

Provenance: Alfred Stieglitz, New York City; K. W. Baasch, Baldwin, New York (purchased, c. 1917); Washburn Gallery, New York City.

34 The Iron Cross 1914–15 Pl. 83
Oil on canvas, 118.7 × 118.7 (46¾ × 46¾)
Washington University Gallery of Art, St. Louis, Missouri
Unsigned

Provenance: Estate of the artist, no. 163 (as *The Red Cross,* 1915); Washington University Gallery of Art, St. Louis, Missouri (purchased, 1952, through Paul Rosenberg & Co., New York City), acc. no. WU 3840.

35 Painting No. 5 1914–15 cover
Oil on canvas. 100.3 × 80.6 (39½ × 31¾)
Whitney Museum of American Art, New York; anonymous gift, 1958
Unsigned

Provenance: Alfred Stieglitz, New York; private collection; Whitney Museum of American Art, New York City (gift, 1958), acc. no. 58.65.

36 Painting No. 46, Berlin 1914–15
Pl. 21
Oil on canvas, 99.7 × 81.3 (39¼ × 32)
Albright Knox Art Gallery, Buffalo, New York; Philip Kirwen Fund
Unsigned

Provenance: Estate of the artist, no. 139 (there dated 1915); Martha Jackson Gallery, New York City; Albright Art Gallery (now the Albright-Knox Art Gallery), Buffalo, New York (acquired by exchange, 1956, for *Painting No. 48, Berlin*), acc. no. 56:5.

37 Painting No. 47, Berlin 1914–15
Pl. 22
Oil on canvas, 100.3 × 80.3 (39½ × 31⅝)
Hirshhorn Museum and Sculpture Garden, Smithsonian Institution
Signed on stretcher: Hartley, Berlin

Provenance: Estate of the artist, no. 140 (there dated 1915); Martha Jackson Gallery, New York City (purchased, 1958); Joseph H. Hirshhorn, Greenwich, Connecticut (purchased, 1968); Hirshhorn Museum and Sculpture Garden, Smithsonian Institution, Washington, D.C. (gift, 1972), acc. no. 72.148.
New York only

38 Abstraction, Provincetown 1916
Pl. 86
Oil on composition board, 61.3 × 50.9 (24⅛ × 20)
The Art Institute of Chicago; The Alfred Stieglitz Collection
Unsigned

Provenance: Alfred Stieglitz, New York City; Estate of Alfred Stieglitz; The Art Institute of Chicago (gift, 1949), acc. no. 49.545.

39 Elsa 1916 Pl. 25
Oil on composition board, 50.8 × 40.6 (20 × 16)
University Gallery, University of Minnesota, Minneapolis; bequest of Hudson Walker from the Ione and Hudson Walker Collection
Unsigned

Provenance: Alfred Stieglitz, New York City; Estate of Alfred Stieglitz; Ione and Hudson Walker, Forest Hills, New York (purchased, 1949); University Gallery, University of Minnesota, Minneapolis (bequest, 1978, then dated 1917), acc. no. 78.21.46.

40 Handsome Drinks 1916 Pl. 84
Oil on composition board, 61 × 50.8 (24 × 20)
The Brooklyn Museum; gift of Mr. and Mrs. Milton Lowenthal
Unsigned

Provenance: Charles Daniel, New York City (then dated 1915); auction at Parke-Bernet Galleries, New York City, March 14, 1946, no. 79 (then dated 1910); Mr. and Mrs. Milton Lowenthal, New York (purchased, 1946); The Brooklyn Museum, Brooklyn, New York (gift, 1972; then dated ca. 1912), acc. no. 72.3.
New York only

41 **Movement No. 8, Provincetown** 1916
Pl. 26
Oil on composition board, 59 × 48.8
(23¼ × 19¼) (sight)
Wadsworth Atheneum, Hartford, Connecticut; gift of Mrs. Robert E. Darling
Unsigned

Provenance: Alfred Stieglitz, New York City;
Estate of Alfred Stieglitz; E. Weyhe Gallery,
New York City (purchased, 1949); Wadsworth
Atheneum, Hartford, Connecticut (purchased,
1959, as *Movement No. 2,* through funds given
by Mrs. Robert E. Darling), acc. no. 59.5.

42 **Movement No. 9** 1916 Pl. 85
Oil on composition board, 61.3 × 51.1
(24⅛ × 20⅛)
Walker Art Center; gift of the T.B. Walker
Foundation
Unsigned

Provenance: Alfred Stieglitz, New York City;
Estate of Alfred Stieglitz; Ione and Hudson
Walker, Forest Hills, New York (purchased,
1949); Bertha H. Walker, Forest Hills, New
York; Walker Art Center, Minneapolis, Minnesota (gift, 1971, through the T.B. Walker
Foundation), acc. no. 71.45.

43 **One Portrait of One Woman** 1916
Pl. 23
Oil on composition board, 76.2 × 63.5
(30 × 25)
University Gallery, University of Minnesota,
Minneapolis; bequest of Hudson Walker from
the Ione and Hudson Walker Collection
Unsigned

Provenance: Alfred Stieglitz, New York City;
Estate of Alfred Stieglitz; Ione and Hudson
Walker, Forest Hills (purchased, 1949); University Gallery, University of Minnesota, Minneapolis (bequest, 1978), acc. no. 78.21.64.

44 **A Bermuda Window in a Semi-Tropic
Character** 1917 Pl. 27
Oil on composition board, 80.6 × 66
(31¾ × 26)
The Fine Arts Museums of San Francisco; Dr.
T. Edward and Tulla Hanley Memorial Collection
Unsigned

Provenance: Alfred Stieglitz, New York City;
Estate of Alfred Stieglitz; E. Weyhe Gallery,
New York City (purchased, 1949); Ione and
Hudson Walker, Forest Hills, New York (purchased, 1951); Dr. and Mrs. T. Edward Hanley,
Bradford, Pennsylvania (purchased through
Babcock Galleries, New York City); The Fine
Arts Museums of San Francisco (gift, 1969),
acc. no. 69.30.94.
Chicago, Fort Worth, Berkeley only

45 **Red Calla in Blue Vase** 1917 Pl. 29
Oil on glass, 53.3 × 26 (21 × 10¼)
Mr. and Mrs. John Laurent, York, Maine
Unsigned

Provenance: the artist; Robert Laurent, Brooklyn, New York and Ogunquit, Maine; Mr. and
Mrs. John Laurent, York, Maine.

46 **Still Life** 1917 Pl. 31
Oil on glass, mounted on board, 41.9 × 40.6
(16½ × 16)
Private collection
Signed on verso: Marsden/Hartley

Provenance: the artist; auction at Anderson
Galleries, New York City, May 17, 1921, no. 87
(as *Painting on Glass*); Albert Roothbert, New
York City (as *Flowers in Basket*); The Topstone
Trust, New York City; auction at Parke-Bernet
Galleries, New York City, May 21, 1970, no. 84
(as *Still Life: Painting on Glass*); auction at
Parke-Bernet Galleries, October 14, 1970, no.
88 (as *Still Life: Painting on Glass*); Mr. and
Mrs. Seymour Hecht, Harrison, New York
(purchased, 1970).

47 **Blessing the Melon. The Indians Bring the
Harvest to Christian Mary for Her Blessing** 1918 Pl. 87
Oil on composition board, 82.6 × 60.6
(32½ × 23⅞)
Philadelphia Museum of Art; The Alfred Stieglitz Collection
Unsigned

Provenance: Alfred Stieglitz, New York City;
Estate of Alfred Stieglitz; Philadelphia
Museum of Art (gift, 1949), acc. no. 49.18.13.
New York only

48 **El Santo** 1918 Pl. 32
Oil on canvas, 91.4 × 81.3 (36 × 32)
Museum of New Mexico, Santa Fe; anonymous gift
Unsigned

Provenance: the artist; Museum of New
Mexico, Santa Fe (purchased, 1919, through
funds given by an anonymous donor), acc. no.
532/23P.

49 **Landscape, New Mexico** 1919–20
Pl. 89
Oil on canvas, 71.1 × 91.4 (28 × 36)
Whitney Museum of American Art, New York;
gift of Frances and Sydney Lewis, 1977
Unsigned

Provenance: Paul Kantor Gallery, Beverly
Hills, California; Esther Robles Gallery, Los
Angeles; Montgomery Family, California;
California private collection; auction at
Parke-Bernet Galleries, New York City, April
15, 1959, no. 75; New York City private collection; Washburn Gallery, New York City;
Whitney Museum of American Art, New York
(purchased, 1977, through funds given by
Frances and Sydney Lewis), acc. no. 77.23.

50 **Landscape No. 3, Cash Entry Mines, New
Mexico** 1920 Pl. 88
Oil on canvas, 70.6 × 90.8 (27¾ × 35¾)
The Art Institute of Chicago; The Alfred Stieglitz Colleciton
Signed l.r.: Marsden Hartley/1920

Provenance: Alfred Stieglitz, New York City
(also called *Cash Entry Mine, New Mexico*);
Estate of Alfred Stieglitz; The Art Institute of
Chicago (gift, 1949), acc. no. 49.549.

51 **Still Life with Pears** 1921 Pl. 90
Oil on canvas, 27.3 × 45.7 (10¾ × 18)
Helen and George Ratkai, New York City
Unsigned

Provenance: Estate of the artist, no. 191; Babcock Galleries, New York (purchased, 1954);
Helen and George Ratkai, New York (purchased, 1957).

52 **Still Life** ca. 1922–23 Pl. 34
Oil on canvas, 50.2 × 73 (19¾ × 28¾)
Mrs. Hazel B. Strand; courtesy of The Currier
Gallery of Art, Manchester, New Hampshire
Unsigned

Provenance: the artist, or Alfred Stieglitz, New
York City; Paul Strand, New York City; Mrs.
Hazel B. Strand (inherited, 1973); The Currier
Gallery of Art, Manchester, New Hampshire
(on long-term loan).

53 **Landscape, New Mexico** 1923 Pl. 35
Oil on canvas, 55.2 × 90.8 (21¾ × 35¾)
Babcock Galleries, New York City
Unsigned

Provenance: the artist; Carl Sprinchorn (also
called *Mountains with Clouds No. 2,* 1922);
Babcock Galleries, New York City.

54 **New Mexico Recollections** 1923
Pl. 91
Oil on canvas, 73.7 × 104.8 (29 × 41¼)
William H. Lane Foundation, Leominster,
Massachusetts
Unsigned

Provenance: Estate of the artist, no. 135 (there
dated 1922–23); William H. Lane Foundation,
Leominster, Massachusetts (purchased, 1958,
through Babcock Galleries, New York City;
also called *Recollection of New Mexico –
Storm*).

55 **New Mexico Recollections No. 10**
1923 Pl. 36
Oil on canvas, 76.2 × 101.6 (30 × 40)
Private collection, Great Neck, New York
Unsigned

Provenance: Estate of the artist, no. 119 (as
Mountain Landscape, 1922–23); Babcock Galleries, New York City (purchased, 1959); Private collection, Great Neck, New York (purchased, 1966).

56 **Landscape, Vence** 1925–26 Pl. 37
Oil on canvas, 64.8 × 80.6 (25½ × 31¾)
University Gallery, University of Minnesota,
Minneapolis; bequest of Hudson Walker from
the Ione and Hudson Walker Collection
Unsigned

Provenance: the artist; Adelaide Kuntz, New
York City; Ione and Hudson Walker, Forest
Hills, New York (acquired, 1945, in exchange
for another Hartley painting); University Gallery, University of Minnesota, Minneapolis
(bequest, 1978), acc. no. 78.21.256.

57 **Purple Mountains** 1925–26 Pl. 38
Oil on canvas, 64.6 × 81.3 (25¾ × 32)
Phoenix Art Museum; gift of Mr. and Mrs.
Orme Lewis
Unsigned

Provenance: Estate of the artist, no. 159 (there
dated 1924–26); Dr. Ronald Lawrence, Los
Angeles (purchased, 1960, through Paul
Rosenberg & Co., New York City); auction at
Parke-Bernet Galleries, New York City,
January 29, 1964, no. 84; Terry de Lapp Gal-
lery, Los Angeles (purchased, 1964); Mr. and
Mrs. Orme Lewis (purchased, 1965, as *Vence,*
ca. 1928); Phoenix Art Museum, Phoenix,
Arizona (gift, 1977), acc. no. 77/147.
Chicago, Fort Worth, Berkeley only

58 **Mont Sainte-Victoire** 1927 Pl. 92
Oil on canvas, 80.6 × 99.7 (31¾ × 39¼)
Mr. and Mrs. Harry W. Anderson, Atherton,
California
Unsigned

Provenance: Estate of the artist, no. 103 (as
Mont Ste Victoire, 1928); Babcock Galleries,
New York City (purchased, 1960, through Paul
Rosenberg & Co., New York City); Mr. and
Mrs. Harry W. Anderson, Atherton, California
(purchased, 1968).

59 **Mont Sainte-Victoire** 1927 Pl. 39
Oil on canvas, 80.6 × 99.7 (31¾ × 39¼)
Des Moines Art Center; gift of Mr. and Mrs.
Fred Bohen
Unsigned

Provenance: Estate of the artist, no. 101 (as
*Mont Ste Victoire #*3, 1928); Babcock Galleries, New York City (purchased, 1958); Des
Moines Art Center, Des Moines, Iowa (purchased, 1958, as *Mont Ste Victoire,* 1928,
through funds given by Mr. and Mrs. Fred Bohen), acc. no. 58.63.

60 **Mont Sainte-Victoire, Aix-en-Provence**
1927 Pl. 40
Oil on canvas, 64.8 × 81 (25½ × 31⅞)
Mr. and Mrs. Carl D. Lobell, New York
Unsigned

Provenance: Estate of the artist, no Estate
number (there dated 1928); Mrs. Herbert C.
Morris, Philadelphia (purchased, 1945,
through Paul Rosenberg & Co., New York
City; Edward Knox Morris, Gladwyne,
Pennsylvania (gift); Mr. and Mrs. Carl D.
Lobell, New York City (purchased, 1979,
through Joshua Strychalski, New York City).

61 **Mountains No. 19** 1930 Pl. 41
Oil on board, 91.4 × 83.8 (36 × 33)
Private collection
Unsigned

Provenance: Estate of the artist, no. 110 (as
Mountains #19); Martha Jackson Gallery,
New York City (purchased, 1958); Nelson-
Taylor Consultant Gallery, New York City
(purchased, 1959); private collection (pur-
chased, 1961, as *Mont Sainte-Victoire,* through
Martha Jackson Gallery, New York City).

62 **Flaming Pool, Dogtown** 1931 Pl. 42
Oil on academy board, 45.7 × 61 (18 × 24)
Collection of American Literature, Beinecke
Rare Book and Manuscript Library, Yale University, New Haven; gift of Adelaide Kuntz
Signed on verso: Flaming Pool/Dogtown
1931/Marsden Hartley
Inscribed on verso: Beethoven (in Dogtown)/
Deep chested trills arise —/from organ pipes of
juniper/Oboe's throat expands — mezzo
cries/of blueberry & sage and ferns prefer/to
die among the rocks, nobly perish/mire of tor-
rid green —/Summer's strident blades of
damascene/hot tone or here is garish/the vox
humain swells and dwells/Persistently mid
nuances of lapis grey/So much more wonderful
this way/than summer in a trance/of
chlorophyll or other circumstances

Provenance: The Downtown Gallery, New
York City; Adelaide Kuntz (purchased from
The Downtown Gallery or the artist); Collec-
tion of American Literature, Yale University,
New Haven (gift, 1952), acc. no. U 1952.27.1.
New York only

63   Rock Doxology, Dogtown   1931   Pl. 94
Oil on board, 45.7 × 61 (18 × 24)
Private collection
Unsigned

Provenance: the artist: Adelaide Kuntz, New York City; Bertha Schaefer Gallery, New York City; Kraushaar Galleries, New York City; private collection (purchased, 1972).

64   Summer Outward Bound, Dogtown
1931   Pl. 93
Oil on board, 45.7 × 61 (18 × 24)
Private collection
Signed on verso: Summer Outward Bound./ Dogtown 1931. Marsden Hartley.

Provenance: the artist; Adelaide Kuntz, New York City; Eli Diamond; Bernard Danenberg Galleries, New York City; private collection (purchased, 1972).

65   Earth Cooling, Mexico   1932   Pl. 95
Oil on cardboard, mounted on masonite, 62.2 × 86 (24½ × 33⅞)
Amon Carter Museum, Fort Worth, Texas
Signed on verso: EARTH — COOLING/
MARSDEN/HARTLEY/^{MEXICO} 1932

Provenance: Estate of the artist, no. 34; The Downtown Gallery, New York City (purchased, 1958); Dr. and Mrs. Michael Watter, Philadelphia; auction at Parke-Bernet Galleries, New York City, October 19, 1967, no. 27; Amon Carter Museum (purchased, 1967), acc. no. 191.67.

66   The Mountain of the North (After Design of Cosmas the Monk, 900 A.D.)   1932
Pl. 43
Oil on cardboard, 62.2 × 85.1 (24½ × 33½)
Mr. and Mrs. Alan Schwartz, New York City; lent in memory of Robert L. Livingston
Signed on verso: The Mountain of the North/ after design of Cosmas the monk (900 A.D.)/Marsden Hartley/Mexico 1932.

Provenance: Estate of the artist, no. 122; Babcock Galleries, New York City (purchased, 1959); Robert L. Livingston, New York (purchased, 1970).; Mr. and Mrs. Alan Schwartz, New York City (inherited, 1979).

67   Bavarian Alps, Garmisch-Partenkirchen
1933   Pl. 46
Oil on composition board, 76.2 × 45.7 (30 × 18)
Private collection
Unsigned

Provenance: the artist; Adelaide Kuntz, New York City; Frances Malek, New York City; Babcock Galleries, New York City; Private collection (purchased, 1973).

68   Eight Bells' Folly, Memorial for Hart Crane   1933   Pl. 96
Oil on canvas, 80.3 × 100.3 (31⅝ × 39½)
University Gallery, University of Minnesota, Minneapolis; gift of Ione and Hudson Walker
Signed on verso: Eight Bells'/Folly. Memorial/ for Hart/Crane Marsden/Hartley Mexico/ 1933

Provenance: the artist; Adelaide Kuntz, New York City; Bertha Schaefer Gallery, New York City; Ione and Hudson Walker, Forest Hills, New York; University Gallery, University of Minnesota, Minneapolis (gift, 1961), acc. no. 61.4.

69   Garmisch-Partenkirchen   1933   Pl. 97
Oil on composition board, 75.1 × 56.6 (29¾ × 22¼)
Mr. and Mrs. William J. Poplack, Birmingham, Michigan
Unsigned

Provenance: the artist; Ione and Hudson Walker, Forest Hills, New York; Babcock Galleries, New York City (purchased, 1963); Mr. and Mrs. William J. Poplack, Birmingham, Michigan (purchased, 1963).

70   Garmisch-Partenkirchen   1933   Pl. 45
Oil on canvas, 44.9 × 75.2 (17-11/16 × 29⅝)
Milwaukee Art Center Collection; bequest of Max E. Friedman
Unsigned

Provenance: Hudson D. Walker Gallery, New York City; Max E. Friedman, Milwaukee, Wisconsin; Milwaukee Art Center (bequest, 1954), acc. no. M1954.3.

71   Dogtown, The Last of the Stone Wall
1934   Pl. 48
Oil on academy board, 45.7 × 61 (18× 24)
University Gallery, University of Minnesota, Minneapolis; bequest of Hudson Walker from the Ione and Hudson Walker Collection
Signed l.r.: M•H; inscribed on verso: Dogtown/The Last of the Stone Wall/Marsden Hartley

Provenance: the artist; Louis Schapiro, Pigeon Cove, Massachusetts (acquired, 1943); Childs Gallery, Boston; Ione and Hudson Walker; Forest Hills, New York (purchased, 1951); University Gallery, University of Minnesota, Minneapolis (bequest, 1978), acc. no. 78. 21.246.

72   New England Sea View — Fish House
1934   Pl. 49
Oil on board, 45.7 × 61 (18 × 24)
Mrs. Hudson D. Walker, Forest Hills, New York
Unsigned

Provenance: Estate of the artist, no Estate number (as *New England Fish House*); Mr. and Mrs. Arthur B. Lathrup, Indianapolis (purchased, 1946, through Paul Rosenberg & Co., New York City); auction at Parke-Bernet Galleries, New York City, December 10, 1970, no. 39; Babcock Galleries, New York City (purchased, 1970); Hudson and Ione Walker, Forest Hills, New York (purchased, 1971); Mrs. Hudson D. Walker (inherited, 1976)

73   Whale's Jaw, Dogtown Common   1934
Oil on board, 45.7 × 60.8 (18 × 23-15/16)
Henry Art Gallery, University of Washington, Seattle
Inscribed on verso: Whales Jaw/Dogtown Common/Cape Ann/Mass/1934

Provenance: Estate of the artist, no Estate number; United States Department of State, Washington, D.C., War Assets Collection (purchased, 1946, through Paul Rosenberg & Co., New York City); auction at War Assets Administration, New York City, June 19, 1948, no. 38 (as *Whale's Jaw, Dogtown*); University of Washington, Seattle (purchased, 1948), acc. no. 48.3.
Fort Worth, Berkeley only

74 Whale's Jaw, Dogtown Common, Cape Ann 1934 Pl. 47
Oil on canvas, 44.5 × 59.7 (17½ × 23½)
Yale University Art Gallery; gift of Walter Bareiss, B.A. 1940
Signed on verso

Provenance: Estate of the artist, no Estate number (as *Whale's Jaw #2, Dogtown Common*); Walter Bareiss, Greenwich, Connecticut (purchased, 1944, through Paul Rosenberg & Co., New York City); Yale University Art Gallery, New Haven, Connecticut (gift, 1951), acc. no. 1951.1.1.
Chicago, Fort Worth, Berkeley only

75 The Last Stone Walls, Dogtown 1936 Pl. 51
Oil on canvas, 44.5 × 59.7 (17½ × 23½)
Yale University Art Gallery; gift of Walter Bareiss, B.A. 1940
Unsigned

Provenance: Estate of the artist, no Estate number; Walter Bareiss, Greenwich, Connecticut (purchased, before 1951, through Clifton Newell, the original administrator of the Estate); Yale University Art Gallery, New Haven, Connecticut (gift, 1951), acc. no. 1951.1.2
Chicago, Fort Worth, Berkeley only

76 The Old Bars, Dogtown 1936 Pl. 50
Oil on composition board, 45.7 × 61 (18 × 24)
Whitney Museum of American Art, New York; purchase, 1937
Unsigned

Provenance: An American Place, New York City; Whitney Museum of American Art, New York City (purchased, 1937), acc. no. 37.26.

77 Northern Seascape, Off the Banks 1936–37 Pl. 98
Oil on cardboard, 46.2 × 61 (18-3/16 × 24)
Milwaukee Art Center Collection; bequest of Max E. Friedman
Unsigned

Provenance: Hudson D. Walker Gallery, New York City; Max E. Friedman, Milwaukee, Wisconsin (purchased, 1939); Milwaukee Art Center (bequest, 1954), acc. no. M1954.4.

78 Smelt Brook Falls 1937 Pl. 99
Oil on board, 71.1 × 55.9 (28 × 22)
The St. Louis Art Museum; purchase: Eliza McMillan Fund
Unsigned

Provenance: Hudson D. Walker Gallery, New York City; The City Art Museum of St. Louis (now The St. Louis Art Museum), St. Louis, Missouri (purchased, 1939), acc. no. 9:39.

79 Granite by the Sea 1937
Oil on composition board, 50.8 × 71.1 (20 × 28)
Whitney Museum of American Art, New York City; purchase, 1942
Unsigned

Provenance: Macbeth Gallery, New York City; Whitney Museum of American Art (purchased, 1942), acc. no. 42.31.

80 Rising Wave, Indian Point, Georgetown, Maine 1937–38 Pl. 100
Oil on academy board, 55.9 × 71.1 (22 × 28)
The Baltimore Museum of Art; The Edward Joseph Gallagher III Memorial Collection
Signed l.r.: M.H.

Provenance: Estate of the artist, no. 165; Edward J. Gallagher, Jr. (purchased, 1952, through Paul Rosenberg & Co., New York City); The Baltimore Museum of Art (gift, 1958), acc. no. 58.41.

81 Camden Hills From Baker's Island, Penobscot Bay 1938 Pl. 101
Oil on academy board, 71.1 × 55.9 (28 × 22)
Stedelijk Museum, Amsterdam
Unsigned

Provenance: the artist; Ione and Hudson Walker, Forest Hills, New York (purchased, 1941); Stedelijk Museum, Amsterdam (gift, 1961), acc. no. A 20357.

82 Fishermen's Last Supper. 1938 Pl. 54
Oil on academy board, 55.9 × 71.1 (22 × 28)
Mrs. Hudson D. Walker, Forest Hills, New York
Unsigned

Provenance: the artist; Ione and Hudson Walker, Forest Hills, New York (purchased, 1941); Mrs. Hudson D. Walker, Forest Hills, New York (inherited, 1978).

83 Adelard the Drowned, Master of the Phantom 1938–39 Pl. 102
Oil on academy board, 71.1 × 55.9 (28 × 22)
University Gallery, University of Minnesota, Minneapolis; bequest of Hudson Walker from the Ione and Hudson Walker Collection
Signed on verso: Adelard—The Drowned—/Master of the "Phantom"—/Marsden Hartley/1938-9

Provenance: the artist; Ione and Hudson Walker, Forest Hills, New York (purchased, 1941); University Gallery, University of Minnesota, Minneapolis (bequest, 1978), acc. no. 78.21.236.

84 Portrait of Albert Pinkham Ryder 1938–39 Pl. 103
Oil on academy board, 72.4 × 56.5 (28½ × 22¼)
Mr. and Mrs. Milton Lowenthal, New York City
Unsigned

Provenance: Estate of the artist, No Estate number; Mr. and Mrs. Milton Lowenthal, New York City (purchased, 1946, through Paul Rosenberg & Co., New York City).

85 Robin Hood Cove, Georgetown, Maine 1938–39 Pl. 53
Oil on board, 55.9 × 66 (22 × 26)
Mrs. Hudson D. Walker, Forest Hills, New York
Unsigned

Provenance: the artist; Mrs. Hudson D. Walker, Forest Hills, New York.

86 The Lost Felice 1939 Pl. 104
Oil on canvas, 101.6 × 76.2 (40 × 30)
Los Angeles County Museum of Art; Mr. and Mrs. William Preston Harrison Collection
Unsigned

Provenance: Estate of the artist, no Estate number (there dated 1939–40); Mr. and Mrs. Walter Bareiss, Greenwich, Connecticut (purchased, 1946, through Paul Rosenberg & Co., New York City); Paul Kantor Galleries, Los Angeles; Los Angeles County Museum of Art (purchased, 1963), acc. no. 1963.5.

87   Sustained Comedy—Portrait of an Object   1939   Pl. 57
Oil on board, 71.4 × 55.9 (28⅛ × 22)
Museum of Art, Carnegie Institute, Pittsburgh, Pennsylvania; gift of Mervin Jules
Signed on verso: Sustained/Comedy—/Portrait of an object/"O Big Earth"—/or—the sustained travesty/Marsden Hartley/1939

Provenance: the artist; Hudson Walker, Forest Hills, New York; Mervin Jules, Northampton, Massachusetts (gift); Museum of Art, Carnegie Institute, Pittsburgh, Pennsylvania (gift, 1976), acc. no. 76.64.

88   Mount Katahdin, Autumn No. 1
1939–40   Pl. 105

Oil on canvas, 76.5 × 101.6 (30⅛ × 40)
University of Nebraska, Lincoln Art Galleries; F.M. Hall Collection
Unsigned

Provenance: Paul Rosenberg & Co., New York City; University of Nebraska, Lincoln Art Galleries, Lincoln (purchased, 1943), acc. no. H232.

89   Madawaska—Acadian Light-Heavy (2nd Arrangement)   1940   Pl. 56
Oil on masonite, 101.6 × 76.2 (40 × 30)
A. James Speyer, Chicago
Signed on verso: Madawaska—Acadian/Light-Heavy/Marsden Hartley/1940

Provenance: Estate of the artist, no. 94; Eva Lee Gallery, Great Neck, New York (purchased, 1960); Alan Gallery, New York City; A. James Speyer, Chicago (purchased, 1962).

90   Young Worshipper of the Truth   1940
Pl. 58
Oil on academy board, 71.1 × 55.9 (28 × 22)
Nebraska Art Association, Nelle Cochrane Woods Collection; courtesy of the Sheldon Memorial Gallery, Lincoln
Signed on verso: Young Worshipper/of the truth/Marsden Hartley/1940

Provenance: the artist; Ione and Hudson Walker, Forest Hills, New York (purchased, 1941); Babcock Galleries, New York City; Nebraska Art Association, Lincoln (purchased, 1976), acc. no. N348.

91   Fishermen's Last Supper   1940–41
Pl. 55
Oil on board, 77.9 × 104.1 (29⅞ × 41)
Roy R. Neuberger, New York City
Signed l.r.: M•H/40–41

Provenance: Paul Rosenberg & Co., New York City; Roy R. Neuberger, New York City (purchased, 1943).

92   The Lighthouse   1940–41   Pl. 61
Oil on composition board, 76.2 × 101.9 (30 × 40⅛)
Mr. and Mrs. William A. M. Burden, New York City
Signed l.r.: M•H• / 40–41

Provenance: Macbeth Gallery, New York City; Mr. and Mrs. William A. M. Burden, New York City (purchased, 1943).
New York only

93   Log Jam, Penobscot Bay   1940–41
Pl. 59
Oil on masonite, 76.4 × 104 (30-1/16 × 40-15/16)
The Detroit Institute of Arts; gift of Robert H. Tannahill
Signed l.r.: M•H/40–41

Provenance: Paul Rosenberg & Co., New York City; The Detroit Institute of Arts (purchased, 1944, through funds given by Robert H. Tannahill), acc. no. 44.5.

94   On the Beach   1940–41   Pl. 60
Oil on masonite, 55.8 × 71.1 (22 × 28)
Suzanne Vanderwoude, New York
Unsigned

Provenance: Estate of the artist, no Estate number; Wright Ludington, Santa Barbara, California (purchased, 1946, through Paul Rosenberg & Co., New York City); auction at Sotheby Parke Bernet, New York City, April 29, 1976, no. 183; Suzanne Vanderwoude, Great Neck, New York (purchased, 1976).

95   Black Duck No. 1   1941   Pl. 68
Oil on masonite, 70.8 × 55.9 (27⅞ × 22)
The Detroit Institute of Arts; gift of Robert H. Tannahill
Signed l.r.: M•H/'41

Provenance: Paul Rosenberg & Co., New York City; Robert H. Tannahill, Detroit (purchased, 1944); The Detroit Institute of Arts (gift, 1949), acc. no. 1949.512.

96   Mount Katahdin   1941   Pl. 67
Oil on masonite, 55.6 × 70.8 (21⅞ × 27⅞)
Hirshhorn Museum and Sculpture Garden, Smithsonian Institution
Signed l.r.: M•H/41

Provenance: Estate of the artist, no Estate number; Joseph H. Hirshhorn, Greenwich, Connecticut (purchased, through Paul Rosenberg & Co., New York City); Hirshhorn Museum and Sculpture Garden, Smithsonian Institution, Washington, D.C. (gift, 1966), acc. no. 66.2369.

97   Evening Storm, Schoodic, Maine   1942
Pl. 106
Oil on composition board, 76.2 × 101.6 (30 × 40)
The Museum of Modern Art, New York; acquired through the Lillie P. Bliss Bequest, 1943
Signed l.r.: M•H/42

Provenance: Paul Rosenberg & Co., New York City; The Museum of Modern Art, New York City (purchased, 1943), acc. no. 66.43.
New York only

98   Hurricane Island, Vinalhaven, Maine
1942   Pl. 109
Oil on masonite, 76.2 × 102.2 (30 × 40¼)
Philadelphia Museum of Art; gift of Mrs. Herbert Cameron Morris
Signed c.r.: M H/42

Provenance: Paul Rosenberg & Co., New York City; Mrs. Herbert Cameron Morris, Philadelphia; Philadelphia Museum of Art (gift, 1943), acc. no. 43.5.1.
New York only

99   **Mount Katahdin**   1942   Pl. 107
Oil on masonite, 76.2 × 101.9 (30 × 40⅛)
National Gallery of Art; gift of Mrs. Mellon Byers, 1970
Signed l.r.: M•H•/42.

Provenance: Estate of the artist, no. 74 (as *Katahdin, Autumn Rain*); Ione and Hudson Walker, Forest Hills, New York (purchased, 1951); Babcock Galleries, New York City; National Gallery of Art, Washington, D.C. (purchased, 1970, through funds given by Mrs. Mellon Byers), acc. no. 2543.

100   **Off to the Banks at Night**   1942   Pl. 63
Oil on masonite, 76.2 × 101.6 (30 × 40)
The Phillips Collection, Washington
Signed l.r.: M•H/42

Provenance: Paul Rosenberg & Co., New York City; The Phillips Gallery (now the Phillips Collection), Washington, D.C. (purchased, 1943).

101   **Sea Window, Tinker Mackerel**   1942
Pl. 65
Oil on masonite, 101.6 × 76.2 (40 × 30)
Smith College Museum of Art, Northampton, Massachusetts; purchased, 1947
Signed l.r.: $^{M}_{•H}$/42

Provenance: Estate of the artist, no Estate number (as *Sea Window—Tinker Mackerel*); Smith College Museum of Art, Northampton, Massachusetts (purchased, 1947, through Paul Rosenberg & Co., New York City), acc. no. 1947.8.

102   **Summer Clouds and Flowers**   1942
Pl. 108
Oil on masonite, 55.9 × 71.1 (22 × 28)
Mr. and Mrs. Milton Lowenthal, New York City
Signed l.r.: M•H/42

Provenance: Paul Rosenberg & Co., New York City; Mrs. Herbert Cameron Morris, Philadelphia; Paul Rosenberg & Co.; Mr. and Mrs. Milton Lowenthal, New York (purchased, 1944).

103   **Summer Sea Window, Red Curtain**
1942   Pl. 64
Oil on canvas, 101.6 × 76.2 (40 × 30)
Addison Gallery of American Art, Phillips Academy, Andover, Massachusetts
Signed l.r.: $^{M}_{H}$/42

Provenance: Paul Rosenberg & Co., New York City (as *Sea Windows, Red Curtain*); Addison Gallery of American Art, Phillips Academy, Andover, Massachusetts (purchased, 1944), acc. no. 1944.81.
New York only

104   **White Cod**   1942   Pl. 66
Oil on composition board, 55.9 × 71.1 (22 × 28)
Mr. and Mrs. Milton Lowenthal, New York City
Signed l.r.: $^{M}_{H}$/42

Provenance: Estate of the artist, no Estate number; Mr. and Mrs. Milton Lowenthal, New York City (purchased, 1948, through Paul Rosenberg & Co., New York City).

105   **Gull**   1942–43   Pl. 69
Oil on composition board, 71.1 × 55.9 (28 × 22)
Mr. and Mrs. Milton Lowenthal, New York City
Unsigned

Provenance: Estate of the artist, no Estate number; Mr. and Mrs. Milton Lowenthal, New York City (purchased, 1948, through Paul Rosenberg & Co., New York City).

The following additions to the catalogue should be noted:

The Blast of Winter   1908   Fig. 10
Oil on canvas, 76.2 × 76.2 (30 × 30)
Mr. and Mrs. Everett Birch, St. Thomas

Berlin Abstraction   1914–15
Oil on canvas, 81.3 × 66 (32 × 26)
Corcoran Gallery of Art, Washington, D.C.
New York and Chicago only

Elsa Kobenhavn   1916
Oil on composition board, 61 × 50.8 (24 × 20)
University Gallery, University of Minnesota, Minneapolis; bequest of Hudson Walker from the Ione and Hudson Walker Collection

Movement, Sails   1916
Oil on board, 59.7 × 49.5 (23½ × 19½)
Loretta and Robert K. Lifton, New York City

Santos, New Mexico   1918
Oil on composition board, 80.3 × 60 (31⅝ × 23⅝)
University Gallery, University of Minnesota, Minneapolis; bequest of Hudson Walker from the Ione and Hudson Walker Collection

Still Life with Pears   1925–26   Fig. 74
Oil on canvas, 49.5 × 61 (19½ × 24)
Whitney Museum of American Art, New York; gift of Dr. Meyer A. Pearlman, 1964

End of Storm, Vinalhaven, Maine   1937–38   Fig. 112
Oil on masonite, 76.2 × 101.6 (30 × 40)
The Benton Collection; courtesy of The William Benton Museum of Art, Storrs, Conn.

Give Us This Day   1938–39   Fig. 102
Oil on canvas, 76.2 × 101.6 (30 × 40)
Fine Arts Work Center, Provincetown, Mass.

Windy Day, Maine Coast   1941   Fig. 109
Oil on canvas, 51.4 × 41 (20¼ × 16⅛)
Munson-Williams-Proctor Institute, Utica, New York; anonymous gift
Chicago, Fort Worth, Berkeley only

Storm Down Pine Point Way, Old Orchard Beach, Maine, ca. 1941–43
Oil on masonite, 55.9 × 71.1 (22 × 28)
Babcock Galleries, New York City
Chicago, Fort Worth, Berkeley only

Acknowledgments

The success of a project as large as this one depends on a great many people, and I am deeply grateful to the many individuals who took time to show me the paintings in their collections and to share with me their recollections of Hartley. In particular, I would like to thank Monroe Wheeler, Glenway Wescott, Joseph Young, John and Nancy Laurent, Dorothy Norman, Herbert J. Seligmann, Alan Chidsey, John Driscoll, Anne d'Harnoncourt, Ida Balboul, Jim McLaughlin, Mrs. Hudson D. Walker and Berta Walker, Charles Helsell, Nancy Carlisle, Catherine Glasgow, and Diane Lenox. In addition, Michael St. Claire of the Babcock Galleries made available his files and supplied much needed information about the present ownership of many of Hartley's paintings. I am indebted to Norma Berger for her kind permission to reproduce photographs and to quote from the Hartley letters and manuscripts in her custodianship. Donald Gallup, Curator of the Collection of American Literature at the Beinecke Rare Book and Manuscript Library, and William Woolfenden of the Archives of American Art, have both been helpful and gracious. Georgia O'Keeffe assisted in securing loans and allowed me to quote from the Stieglitz Papers at Yale.

The generosity of spirit shown by my colleagues in the field was a great source of encouragement. Gail Levin and Sanford Schwartz were especially helpful and supportive, as were Alvord Eisman, Hans Roethel, Jeff Spaulding, Dickran Tashjian, Peter Selz, Michael Lynch, and Doris Bry.

I have had an especially high level of assistance from the staff that worked with me. The contribution of Peter Freeman in particular has been invaluable: he was responsible for assembling much of our working catalogue raisonné and took an active role in gathering primary research data, as well as preparing the bibliography and catalogue list. I am also extremely grateful to Lisa Maddox, Kristie Jayne, Roxanna Robinson, Antoinette LaFarge, Margaret Civetta, Karl Willers, and Mary Anne Staniszewski, whose thoroughness, sense of responsibility, and willingness to work late hours contributed greatly to the success of the project. Louise Thompson, Kay Larson, and April Bernard read early drafts of the manuscript and made valuable suggestions. My thanks go to them as well as to Nathan Garland, the designer of this book, for his sensitivity and his willingness to accommodate divergent preferences.

My colleagues at the Whitney Museum are to be thanked for their patience and support. Tom Armstrong has my deep gratitude for his commitment to the project and for his sensitive intervention at crucial moments. The same is true of Palmer Wald and Patterson Sims: their insights and spirited enthusiasm were both helpful and encouraging. Jim Leggio and Anita Duquette are also to be thanked, as is Sheila Schwartz, whose immensely valuable editorial skill is greatly appreciated. Finally, my deep appreciation goes to Doris Palca, not only for her sustaining support but for her high level of professionalism in connection with the catalogue preparation.

Most of all, I would like to thank the collectors and institutions who believed in the significance of this project, and generously agreed to share their important paintings with the public for such a long tour.

B.H.

Marsden Hartley, 1942. Photograph by Alfredo Valente

Photographic Credits

Photographs of the works of art reproduced have been supplied, in the majority of cases, by the owners or custodians of the works, as cited in the captions. The following list applies to photographs for which additional acknowledgment is due.

Andover Art Studio: Fig. 37
Archives of American Art, Elizabeth McCausland Papers: pp. 185 bottom, 191, 192 bottom. Rockwell Kent Papers: p. 187 bottom
Cradoc Bagshaw: Fig. 56
Oliver Baker: Pl. 56
Bates College, Marsden Hartley Memorial Collection: Figs. 1, 2, 62; pp. 185 top, 186 top, 186 bottom, 187 top, 189 top, 189 middle, 189 bottom, 193 right
Beinecke Rare Book and Manuscript Library, Yale University: Figs. 96, 98
E. Irving Blomstrann: Pls. 15, 26
Brenwasser: Figs. 65, 70, 82, 111; Pls. 35, 36, 43, 46
Will Brown: Pls. 79, 87
Barney Burstein: Fig. 27
Geoffrey Clements: Figs. 16, 42, 64, 74, 75, 77, 87, 90, 95, 106; Pls. 18, 31, 49, 55, 89
Jerome Drown: Fig. 78
Roy M. Elkind: Figs. 3, 50, 110, 113; Pls. 41, 53, 54
eeva-inkeri photographers Fig. 18
Robert L. French: Fig. 79
Frick Art Reference Library: Fig. 102
Greenberg, Wrazen & May: Pl. 21
Helga Photo Studios, Inc.: Figs. 11, 88, 101, 103; Pls. 2, 62, 66, 69, 103, 108
Thomas Ives: Fig. 69
Tom Jones Photography: Fig. 4
Max Klekstobel: p. 192 top
Paulus Leeser: Pl. 81
Robert E. Mates: Figs. 24, 44, 51; Pl. 30
Maxwell Galleries: Fig. 114
Gary Mortensen: Pls. 4, 8, 11, 23, 25, 48, 96; p. 193 left
O. E. Nelson: Fig. 10
The New York Public Library, General Research and Humanities Division; Astor, Lenox, and Tilden Foundations: Fig. 9
Eric Pollitzer: Fig. 26
David Stansbury: Pl. 65
Soichi Sunami: Fig. 89
Taylor & Dull, Inc.: Fig. 112
Herbert P. Vose: Fig. 8
Joseph Young: p. 192 middle